The Migration of
Musical Film

The Migration of Musical Film

From Ethnic Margins to American Mainstream

DESIRÉE J. GARCIA

RUTGERS UNIVERSITY PRESS

NEW BRUNSWICK, NEW JERSEY, AND LONDON

LIBRARY OF CONGRESS CATALOGING-IN-PUBLICATION DATA

Garcia, Desirée J., 1977–
The migration of musical film : from ethnic margins to American mainstream
/ Desirée J. Garcia.
    pages cm
Includes bibliographical references and index.
ISBN 978–0–8135–6865–2 (hardback)—ISBN 978–0–8135–6864–5 (pbk.)—ISBN
978–0–8135–6866–9 (e-book)
    1. Musical films—United States—History and criticism. I. Title.
PN1995.9.M86G37 2014
791.43'6—dc23

                                                                2013040626

A British Cataloging-in-Publication record for this
book is available from the British Library.

Visit our website: http://rutgerspress.rutgers.edu

Manufactured in the United States of America

For my family

CONTENTS

ACKNOWLEDGMENTS

This book was made possible by the support of the following individuals and institutions. First, I wish to thank my mentors. Marilyn Halter and Roy Grundmann have shepherded this project from its earliest conception to the present. They have provided vital criticism and guidance and have expanded my thinking about the musical film, contexts of migration, and American culture. Vicki Ruiz has given generously of her time by reading chapters and offering professional advice. Robin Blaetz saw the merits of my work early in my career and has continued to serve as a source of inspiration and guidance.

Drawing from no single archive, this project has necessitated a great deal of travel and financial sponsorship. For their support, I wish to thank the Mellon Mays University Fellowship, the Ford Foundation Diversity Dissertation Fellowship, the Consortium for Faculty Diversity in Liberal Arts Colleges, Mount Holyoke College, the Center for the Study of Race and Ethnicity in America at Brown University, and the Institute for Humanities Research at Arizona State University. My gratitude also goes to archivists Bob Dickson, Barbara Hall, Jenny Romero, and Faye Thompson at the Margaret Herrick Library of the Academy of Motion Picture Arts and Sciences, Beverly Hills, and to Edward Comstock at the Cinematic Arts Library at the University of Southern California, Los Angeles.

In my travels, I have encountered colleagues at various institutions who have provided an invigorating intellectual community. At Ursinus College, I wish to thank Carol Dole and Patricia Schroeder for their liberal offering of mentorship. I am indebted to Deborah Barkun, Meredith Goldsmith, and Elizabeth Ho for creating an environment that was at once professionally stimulating and spiritually reviving. For their constant support and encouragement, I am grateful to my colleagues at Arizona State University: Aaron Baker, Ed Escobar, Paul Espinosa, Gayle Gullett, Bambi Haggins, Marta Sanchez, Kevin Sandler, and Carlos Velez-Ibañez. At the University of Texas, Austin, I extend my appreciation to Charles Ramirez-Berg, who was an advocate for this project in its incipient phases. And thank you to Frances Gateward at California State University, Northridge, who was an early reader of the book proposal.

To Rutgers University Press, and especially Leslie Mitchner, I am much obliged for steering the manuscript through the murky waters of academic publishing. I also extend my heartfelt appreciation to Sean Griffin, who has offered points of critique that have transformed the book for the better.

Chapter 3 is a revised version of an article published in the *Journal of American Ethnic History*, copyright © 2010 by the Board of Trustees of the University of Illinois. It is used with the kind permission of the University of Illinois Press.

I am fortunate to have a family of people who have given their loyalty, guidance, and love over the years. I could not have asked for a better cohort while in graduate school at Boston University. Thank you to Laura D'Amore, John S. Gordon, Aaron Lecklider, Carney Maley, and Ginger Myhaver. I am indebted to Deborah and Preston Heller, Joe and Diane Steinberg, and Danielle Pinet and Jeff Keil for their friendship and generosity as I completed my degree. Deborah, I am especially thankful for the thoughtful read you gave the manuscript.

The members of my new family, Jan and Dave Garcia and Mauricio and Timotea Garcia-Mendez, have welcomed me with open arms and have made my cares and worries theirs. For their love and acceptance, I am deeply grateful. I extend special appreciation to Cheva Garcia and José D. Garcia, who contributed their unique perspective to this book. To my parents, Noé and Charmi, and my brother, Saul, who have fostered and often participated in my obsession with musicals, I give my sincere devotion.

And finally, I dedicate this book to two people: to Sarah Heller, my kindred spirit and the strongest person I know; and to Matt, my husband, whose love inspires my every day.

The Migration of
Musical Film

Introduction

There's No Place Like Home

On the surface, there would appear to be little in common between *The Wizard of Oz* (1939) and *Cabin in the Sky* (1943), two musical productions by MGM. The first film is based on a classic work of American children's literature that charts a young girl's journey from Kansas to the fantastical world of Oz. *Cabin in the Sky*, by contrast, has its origins in a popular Broadway show and features an all-black cast in a parable of sin and salvation.

In spite of their differences, the films' final scenes bear a striking resemblance. In both, the lead characters, Dorothy Gale (Judy Garland) and Little Joe (Eddie "Rochester" Anderson), respectively, have sustained an injury that has caused them to fall into a delirious sleep. They are disoriented and weary as they recount their dreams to the friends and family who gather at their bedsides. Earlier in the films, Dorothy and Little Joe express a desire for experiences beyond what their everyday lives can offer. Dorothy longs for a world away from the struggles of farm life, a place "beyond the rainbow" where "troubles melt like lemon drops." In journeying to that other land, she leaves behind the farm and its inhabitants and replaces them with people and places both frightening and beautiful. Little Joe also expresses dissatisfaction with his circumstances. He seeks the excitement of nightclubs where gambling, jazz, and loose women abound. Despite the best efforts of his wife, Petunia (Ethel Waters), to keep him wedded to home, family, and community, Little Joe strays. Once Dorothy and Little Joe encounter trouble in their new worlds, however, they realize the error of their ways and return home, waking in their own beds.

The same MGM tornado footage that explicates Dorothy's migration to the land of Oz also prompts Little Joe's return home.[1]

As friends and family listen to each character's dream, they communicate sympathetic amusement. Dorothy tightly embraces her dog Toto and glances about, declaring, "I'm not going to leave here ever, ever again because I love you all." She looks at her Auntie Em, who has been a stern, but loving mother figure, and states emphatically, "There's no place like home."

Little Joe expresses a similar sentiment to Petunia upon waking from his dream. Like Auntie Em, Petunia has been an affectionate guardian over Little Joe, who has always needed tough love. Little Joe gives her credit: "Petunia, you was right all the time about me gamblin' and the bad company I was keepin'. . . . I had a narrow escape, I'll tell ya that." Petunia's response is one of relief. Her loved one has returned to her and is contrite about his past indiscretions. Singing the last refrain of "Takin' a Chance on Love," she is joyful about the contented life they will lead from now on: "Things are mending now / we'll have a happy ending now / takin' a chance on love."

In both scenes, the camera frames a picture of domestic bliss. With the bed in the extreme foreground (facing to the right of the frame in *The Wizard of Oz* and to the left in *Cabin in the Sky*), the friends and family in the middle, and the home, with its window onto the countryside, in the background, the shots reveal a unity of place for the characters and their environment. As M. M. Bakhtin has established, the "unity of place" is a literary device that roots "the life of generations to a single place, from which this life, in all its events, is inseparable."[2] The foregrounding of place, and the characters' interconnectedness with it, is central to both of these musical films. The final sequences display a home that is decorated simply, but warmly. This place also provides a visual reprieve to the characters' dream spaces, bewildering locales that offer dangerous excitement rather than the comfort of that which is familiar. Safely ensconced within their beds and surrounded by that which is known, Dorothy and Little Joe are where they belong.

The unity of place between characters and home indicates a broader and more fundamental issue that is explored in these musical films. Once Dorothy and Little Joe choose home and family over the pursuit of personal gain, they indicate a preference for one value-laden form of social organization over another. Dorothy and Little Joe support and are a part

1. *The Wizard of Oz* copyright 1939 by MGM.

2. *Cabin in the Sky* copyright 1943 by MGM.

of a collective. Their adventures have made apparent the many gifts to be enjoyed among kin, including love, comfort, support, and a sense of belonging, values that are absent in a society of separate individuals. These film musicals suggest that the happiest and most contented people are those who appreciate and dedicate themselves to home, family, and community. Such messages provide a buffer against the unsettling forces of change brought about by modernity and the self-interest promoted by capitalist society. As a generic product that has endured since the beginnings of sound cinema, the musical film mediates social tensions in American life.

The Wizard of Oz and Cabin in the Sky belong to a Hollywood subgenre identified by Rick Altman as the "folk musical." This particular generic pattern features stories about resilient families and cohesive communities that express themselves in an organic fashion with folk (or folk-like) song and dance. Often, Altman observes, the folk musical "projects the audience into a mythicized version of the cultural past" by setting its narratives in idyllic rural communities or small-town Main Streets of the late nineteenth and early twentieth century. There, the subgenre suggests, an authentic way of being can be found, one that privileges the family (as a referent of the larger community), a deep connection to the land, and the shared, cyclical celebration of life's everyday events.[3]

What is less obvious and little understood, however, is where the folk musical comes from and how it evolved over time. In his study of the genre, Altman identifies European operetta and Broadway as sources of the folk musical. Among Hollywood creators, he champions King Vidor (Hallelujah!, 1929) and Rouben Mamoulian (High, Wide and Handsome, 1937) for developing a folk musical syntax that uses integrated musical numbers to communicate the identity of a group.[4] Although these figures and entertainment forms contributed to the folk musical's development, they do not include some of the most important influences on this generic pattern. By limiting our attention to Hollywood, the Broadway stage, and Europe, we miss the significant contributions made by other cinemas, both inside and outside of the United States, each with its own pre-filmic influences and sociohistorical contexts. This book seeks to fill that void with a comparative analysis of the musical films produced by ethnic cinemas for racialized audiences in the United States, namely, the independent cinemas of

African Americans and Jewish immigrants and the commercial cinema of
Mexico. These cinemas complicate the evolution of the musical genre as
one developed primarily by the Hollywood studio system for a mainstream
audience. Rather, this study argues, peoples who have occupied and contested the margins of culture and society played an important role in the
evolution of the musical film, one of the most enduring of American cultural forms.

When the Hollywood studios began making folk musicals regularly
in the 1940s, neither industry personnel nor critics referred to the films
as such.[5] The common usage of "musical comedy," "musical picture," and
"screen musical" was often elaborated upon to indicate this folk pattern
within the genre, with descriptors such as "rustic," "nostalgic," "colorful," "gay," "light," "charming," and "Americana." In the 1950s and 1960s,
the noun "musical" appears more often in the trade press in reference to
what we now recognize as folk musicals, with occasional references to the
"period musical" by producers like Arthur Freed or to the "musical folk
comedy" by film critics like Bosley Crowther.[6]

Although the description "folk musical" is useful for the purposes
of categorization, it is nevertheless an anachronistic term that belies the
historical process by which this particular pattern of the musical genre
took shape. Within what we understand as the "folk musical" is a complexity that stems from its diverse creators, both inside and outside of Hollywood, and profound transformations in American society. *The Migration
of Musical Film* provides a historical reassessment of this generic pattern
and demonstrates its relevance to the genre's evolution over the twentieth and twenty-first centuries. I do not wish to jettison the concept of the
folk musical, for the usage of folk idioms, song, and dance is central to
the films' narrative structure and the ways in which they make meaning.
An alternative rubric for the analysis of the folk musical, however, one
that traces the history of its "meaning-bearing structures" across time and
space, usefully foregrounds the ways in which various producers of the folk
musical have wielded its syntax to attenuate modernity.[7]

For the purposes of this study, the "folk" in folk musicals refers to a
form of social ordering. It is a collective rooted in mythic space and time
before the dislocation and alienation of the modern era fundamentally
altered relationships to people and to homeland. Over the course of the

folk musical's history, the folk has been in service to a diverse group of makers and audiences. In the hands of ethnic cinema producers, it projected social belonging for outsiders to American society. Hollywood audiences of the 1960s, by contrast, embraced the folk musical as indicative of traditional American values that resisted the intrusion of outsiders into the mainstream. As a generic pattern, the folk musical is not exceptional in this regard. As Thomas Schatz reminds us, genres have the capacity to "play it both ways, to both criticize and reinforce the values, beliefs, and ideals of our culture within the same narrative context."[8]

If setting the parameters of social belonging is foundational to the folk musical's syntax, then the characters and settings that make up its semantics are equally engaged in this project. Home and its antithesis, the city, are two places to which the folk musical returns again and again. Tracing the subgenre's semantics over time and space necessitates a chronotopic analysis rather than a categorical one. Bakhtin advanced the concept of the "chronotope" ("time space") in order to reflect the "intrinsic connectedness of temporal and spatial relationships that are artistically expressed in literature."[9] Of particular note is his study of "folkloric time" and the "idyll": "Here was first constituted that feeling for time that had at its heart a taking-apart and putting-together of social everyday time." Events experienced collectively were connected to the cycles of nature. "Time here is sunk deeply in the earth," he describes, "implanted in it and ripening in it." Such representations altered dramatically as society became stratified along class lines. This transformation, which cultural theorist Raymond Williams has located at various points in human history with his metaphor of the "escalator" moving through time and space, had profound consequences for artistic expression. Such works, Williams argues, constitute a "structure of feeling" that recalls a utopian moment in the past, a pastoral existence before the mass migrations from country to city.[10]

Bakhtin locates the restoration of this utopian and mythicized past in the "idyll." Multiple forms of the idyll—love/pastoral, agricultural, craftwork, and familial—all have in common that same relationship to place. Time connects to space in the idyll with "an organic fastening-down, a grafting of life and its events to a place, to a familiar territory with all its nooks and crannies, its familiar mountains, valleys, fields, rivers and forests, and one's own home." Entrenched in an agricultural, pastoral moment, the idyll structures time cyclically, mirroring the rhythms of nature and life's events (birth, marriage, death). These rhythms do not move in linear fashion, but rather in ritualistic cycles.[11]

Bakhtin's chronotope has been usefully applied to the study of cinema and, specifically, to film genres.[12] In the American folk musical, the concepts of folkloric time and the idyll, especially the agricultural and familial idylls, exert particularly strong influence. This generic pattern treats home as a visual allegory for social integration and belonging in American life. The films *The Wizard of Oz, Cabin in the Sky, Meet Me in St. Louis* (1944), *The Music Man* (1962), and many others engage in this foregrounding of home in order to communicate the ways in which all members of society are intertwined and rooted in place.

Unlike literary idylls, however, the folk musical does not deny the existence of modernity. Film scholars have provided a wealth of documentation on the relationship between the rise of cinema and the modern era. The series of discontinuous "shock effects" and physical "jolts" that Walter Benjamin identified as being the sensory experiences of modernity have found their cinematic expression in different filmic modes of address, such as the "cinema of attractions," sensational melodramas, and the evolution of new reception practices.[13] No less a product of modernity, the musical idylls invariably assimilate forms of modern life into their narratives. In *Meet Me in St. Louis*, the Smith family incorporates, albeit awkwardly, the telephone as a new form of communication that intrudes upon the family dinner hour. In *Summer Holiday* (1948), the Miller family and their friends enjoy a raucous ride in the latest fad, the Stanley Steamer. Similarly, the residents of River City, Iowa, must grapple with the newfangled ideas of traveling salesman Harold Hill in *The Music Man*. In each, the material manifestation of change (the telephone, the car, or the stranger) becomes assimilated into the fabric and rhythms of life through a process that ultimately reestablishes home as a place where life's ongoing, cyclical rhythms are preserved.

In such films, the utopian, pastoral scene shifts to the provincial town or small city. Hollywood musicals such as *Meet Me in St. Louis, Summer Holiday*, and *The Music Man* recast St. Louis, Missouri, Danbury, Connecticut, and River City, Iowa, as typical American towns of the early twentieth century. The films suggest the ways in which the residents have familiarity with one another, engage in the ordinary activities of every-day life—tending to the company store, making catsup on a summer after-noon, giving piano lessons—and generally take pride in the predictability of the town's existence. The connection between the working of the land and the consumption of its bounty in the literary idyll gets reworked into the utopian depiction of small-town American life in which the characters are inherently defined by the ordinariness of the activities in which they take part. In such films, "time here is sunk deeply" not in the earth, but in the lanes and byways of Main Street.

The folk musical's most pivotal encounter with modernity concerns the act of migration. Characters in these films engage in a journey that will take them away from home. Seeking a better life for themselves or for their families, they must decide whether or not to allow this rupture of all that is familiar. The experience of migration takes the form of the physi-cal dislocation of the family/community and a cultural clash of values. It also separates the travelers from the cyclical rootedness of life. Rather than having their lives mirror the ongoing rituals of a stable place, they must contend with time that is organized in a linear fashion, hurried, and bent toward unceasing change. In *Meet Me in St. Louis*, the Smith family considers migration as a means to secure a more comfortable future, but then rejects it in favor of the small-town life that they hold so dear. When migration is a reality, as in *The Wizard of Oz*, Dorothy ventures "beyond the rainbow" in search of a better life, only to realize that the disorienting world of Oz makes her long for her home in Kansas.

The Migration of Musical Film considers musicals as the product of peo-ple on the move. In their production and reception, musical films engage with migration in both explicit and implicit ways. Delving underneath the "epidermic surface of the text," Ella Shohat reminds us, reveals the influ-ence of the ethnic margins on the mainstream. The Hollywood studios' beginnings are intertwined with the immigration of Eastern European Jews in the early twentieth century. As one of the racially "in-between peoples" identified by historians James Barrett and David Roediger, Jews engaged in cultural strategies to gain social acceptance and whiteness. Blackface min-strelsy, as argued by Michael Rogin, was one such route. The creation of the studio system and projections of a staunch Americanism was another. Building upon the theoretical work done by Shohat, Mark Winokur, and

Henry Jenkins on ethnic displacement and immigrant ethnicity in Hollywood film, this book examines how images of the farm/town, the city/stage, and the journeys between them often function as allegories for the migration experience. Instances of displacement or submersion of ethnicity in Hollywood film abound and are a consequence of the diverse society in which we live.[14]

An analysis of the American musical film from this critical position makes clear how the basic duality of American identity—vacillating between the ideal of a classless, collective society and a place of hardship and social disintegration (the *gemeinschaft* and *gesellschaft* of American life, respectively)—gets reworked onto narratives, formal structures, and musical scores. In chronotopic terms, the duality is grafted onto the time-space indicators of the farm/town wherein belonging is a utopian reality and the city/stage wherein individuals must perform new identities in order to survive.

Often, the musical idyll ventures into the territory of another subgenre, the backstage or show musical.[15] Films like *The Jazz Singer* (1927), *The Wizard of Oz*, and *State Fair* (1945) witness a protagonist's journey from the home environment to the world of commercialized entertainment as represented by stage performance. A fundamental material location of the show musical, the stage is the site wherein characters must prove their economic and social worth through the potentially hostile medium of performance. In some instances, the show and the folk are hybridized, as in *State Fair*. While set in the cornfields of Iowa, the fairground simulates an urban space wherein the nightclubs (with their audience-performer interactions), crowds, and sensory thrills of city life abound.

Time in the show musical is linear, verging toward the triumphant completion of a performance. Introducing an outsider to dominant society, such as Jewish immigrant Jakie Rabinowitz in *The Jazz Singer*, the show musical uses the stage-place as a conduit for social acceptance.[16] From *The Jazz Singer* to *La Bamba* (1987), the performer as outsider/Other—Jewish in the first case and Mexican American in the second—becomes assimilated into the American mainstream through the approbation of the applauding audience within the film.[17] Jane Feuer has shown how the Hollywood musical uses this audience-within-the-film as a device that ultimately legitimates the place of entertainment in the film audience's lives.[18] This "myth of entertainment" allows for the identification between diegetic (inside the film) and nondiegetic (outside the film) audiences. The show musical, as a film and as a product of the Hollywood industry, is validated once the audience deems the performance to be successful. As this study will demonstrate, audience acceptance also produces the transformation of the Other on the stage from outsider to insider. This negotiation needs to happen in order to confirm the fluidity of ethnic/racialized identities and the inclusiveness of American society. Furthermore, as Eric Lott, Michael Rogin, Arthur Knight, and Andrea Most have shown, at various moments in American history, social outsiders have used theatrical entertainment forms such as blackface minstrelsy and musical theater to renegotiate their gender, class, ethnic, and racialized positions. Calling attention to the fluidity of American identity rather than its fixity, performers have used the stage as a liberatory space.[19]

As the folk musical migrates between the country and the city, it occasionally ventures into the space of the show musical and so depicts the differences between a pre- and post-migratory existence. Underlying the folk musical's treatment of migration is the suggestion that America is a land of migrants on the move, for whom the process of leaving, staying, and returning home is of paramount concern. The dual experiences of mobility and stasis are multivalent forces in these films. Mobility implies social opportunity, adventure, and romantic freedom as well as deracination, dislocation, and alienation. Conversely, stasis offers the security and comfortable predictability of home at the same time that it harbors the possibility of stifling paralysis, backwardness, and reactionary values.

To be sure, other Hollywood films and genres have explored the relationship and inherent tension between the pursuit of individual happiness and communal prosperity. As Charles Ramírez Berg has demonstrated, John Ford's Westerns evoke the contrasts between frontier glory and the joy of collectivity in moments of macho carousing, song and dance, and military parades.[20] Martin Rubin has noted the abrupt discontinuities in the Warner Bros. show musicals of the early 1930s (*Forty-Second Street*, 1933; *Gold Diggers of 1933; Gold Diggers of 1935*), in which the narratives privilege the rise of an unknown chorine to stardom even while Busby Berkeley's musical numbers reveal a spectacle of aggregation.[21] And in the popular cycle of Astaire-Rogers musicals, romantic integration occurs through the medium of performance, typically in performance-related settings (stages, rehearsal spaces, dance floors), but also in nonperformance places like parks and boudoirs. These musical films follow a trajectory from the individual to the couple, itself a referent for an integrated society.[22] Organized according to what Altman has defined as the "dual-focus narrative," in which both plot lines and aesthetics work first to identify and then to overcome differences between the romantic couple, such films mediate differing ideological positions.[23] It is the folk musical, however, that employs the use of folk song and dance in an integral and integrated fashion. The dual-focus narrative applies less in these films than does the collective's unity of place (and the potential threats against it), which takes primary importance as an organizing schema. Aesthetically, the films reinforce the shared identity of the group, its relationship to place, and the connection to its audience. Fluid camerawork, edited sequences that reveal the passing along of a song, and folk songs and dances that are organic expressions of the natural environment all reveal the ways in which social harmony is rooted in place.

If the folk musical ventures into the show musical world, it does so in order to expose and eventually overcome its alienating and exclusionary qualities. Often, the integrated collective remains intact after the film's characters have made the journey from home to stage. The final sequence of *The Jazz Singer* reveals Jakie's mother in the audience for his opening night on Broadway. And in Luis Valdez's *Zoot Suit* (1981), the theater audience is made up of a cross-section of American society, mirroring the diversity that is given prominence on the stage. In other words, the folk from home are brought into the modern space of popular entertainment.

As Robin D. G. Kelley reminds us, "folk" and "modern" are mutually dependent concepts in American popular culture. They are socially constructed and "categorized in a racially or ethnically coded aesthetic hierarchy."[24] "Folk" in the earliest Hollywood musicals is a representation of the Other. The term ascribes cultural and behavioral qualities to "creatures of feeling," typically African Americans and Mexicans, for whom singing and dancing is proffered as a natural expression.[25] These musical creatures, as I call them, first appear in the Hollywood musicals of the early sound era and extend through the present.[26] *Cabin in the Sky* is part of this cycle, which begins with the black-cast musicals of 1929, *Hallelujah!* and *Hearts in*

Dixie. During World War II, Hollywood cast white communities as folk, indicating the ways in which modernity and migration were being experienced by all sectors of American society.

Rick Altman and Jane Feuer have established the connections between the Hollywood musical and its mission to "pass" as the folk expression of its audience. Offering up "community as an ideal concept," Feuer argues, the folk relations in the musical "act to cancel out the economic values and relations associated with mass-produced art." At its most cynical, the musical can be said to be Hollywood's exploitation of the folk for commercial gain.[27]

An exploration of the folk musical, however, reveals how it has resonated with its audiences in very direct and meaningful ways. The sentimentality of the subgenre, its nostalgia for peoples and places of days gone by, has appealed to migrant audiences hungry for such images. Although film critics have historically dismissed the films as kitsch—Pauline Kael described *The Sound of Music* (1965) as "the sugar-coated lie"—it was the emotional experience that brought audiences into theaters in record numbers.[28] For both ethnic musicals and their Hollywood counterparts, sentimentality has been the primary register through which audiences have chosen to mediate their present circumstances. Far from being "only entertainment," these overly sentimental and romanticized films offer a real social function. As Richard Dyer, Stuart Hall, and Fredric Jameson remind us, forms of popular culture are indeed commodified products. Nevertheless, they present a utopia that is both resonant and desired.[29] The utopian function of the folk musical resides in the form's ability to marry the affective qualities of song and dance to an onscreen representation of collectivity that ultimately thwarts change. Folk musicals are able to mask their calculated, commercial qualities in order to present themselves as an authentic product of the people. As the production of ethnic musicals demonstrates, immigrants and peoples of color willfully participated in this deception. If musicals are escapist, as they are often accused of being, then their audiences have consistently engaged in an active, calculated escapism that addresses the social tensions in their daily lives.[30]

Taking an expansive view of genre formation, *The Migration of Musical Film* delineates the many ways that the concept of "folk" has been defined and applied in the musical film's production and reception. Ethnic cinemas of the 1930s deal with issues of migration and modernity explicitly. Produced for local and regional audiences, ethnic cinemas foregrounded the experiences that were most relevant to their audiences' lives. The migration to and within the United States plays a central role in these films. Often it is not the act of migration itself that receives the most attention, but rather the pre- and post-migratory experiences of the traveler. In the pre-migratory condition, the migrant is surrounded by kin and enjoys a sense of belonging. A decade before Broadway audiences praised *Oklahoma!* (1943) for its integration of music and narrative and its celebration of folk communities, makers of ethnic musicals used song as a mode of self-expression that exalted ties to family and homeland. Ethnic cinemas dwell on the pre-migratory state, innovating the genre by shifting it away from Hollywood's more dominant stage spaces and into Eastern European *shtetls* and immigrant tenement districts, Midwestern farms, and Mexican ranches.

Ethnic musical producers and audiences developed the folk musical idiom as an expression of the migrant experience, in which issues of belonging are determined by a rootedness to place and an ability to express oneself culturally within that space. Drawing on a long tradition of ethnic theater, in which spectators and performers experienced a closeness based on shared expectations and moral attitudes, often blurring the lines between performer and audience members in the process, ethnic musicals translated cultural affinities into cinematic terms. In effect, these films attempted to engage their audiences as inside participants, not outside observers, in their cultural expression. Building upon spectatorship practices in ethnic theater and spaces of early moviegoing, the ethnic film musicals of the 1930s reaffirmed the primacy of performer/audience interaction. Scholars have documented how ethnically and racially marginalized groups have "digressed" at the movie theater. The producers of ethnic musicals encouraged such digressions both aesthetically and by supporting a network of ethnic theater spaces within the United States. The Hollywood folk musical of the 1940s to the present has depended and expanded upon these interactive qualities that are rooted in the margins.[31]

Like the study of folk and folklore, ethnic cinemas are attractive to those who study culture for the ways in which they appear to have emanated from communities that are defined by their homogeneity. Produced by and for members of an in-group, this line of thought follows, folklore is an esoteric cultural form. It is important, however, to consider these ethnic cinemas as products of modernity as well; as such, they are also products of cultural collision. Folklorists Richard Bauman and Américo Paredes have offered alternative ways of understanding the development and sharing of folk culture not as an exclusively esoteric phenomenon, but as an exoteric one as well. Bauman suggests that folk groups experience "differential" identities in addition to shared identities. In its performance, folklore can become "as much an instrument of conflict as a mechanism contributing to social solidarity." Bauman sees such uses of folklore in situations wherein one folk group must define or "perform" itself to another. Such a performance becomes necessary when cultures come into conflict and often lead back to originating acts of migration. Paredes develops this concept in the context of folk cultures in the U.S.-Mexico border region. While *corridos* (Mexican ballads) can express a singular community's cultural values and historical events, reinforcing the cyclical relevance of time and place, they can also arise out of contention over place. Stories of Anglo incursions into northern Mexico occupy a central place in the *corridos* that Paredes studies.[32]

Upon close examination, ethnic musicals created by and for primarily in-group communities of African Americans, Jews, and Mexicans are nevertheless the cinematic embodiment of cultures in conflict. The colliding of Old World and New, South and North, Mexico and the United States drives the narratives and aesthetic structures of these films that seek to secure their communities in the familiar place of home once again. Ethnic musicals operate from a defensive position. They owe their existence to the convergence of different peoples and cultures. For this reason, they attempt to hold at bay and mediate the cultural shifts that their audiences have encountered.

The Migration of Musical Film charts the creation and evolution of the folk musical from the beginnings of sound cinema in the late 1920s to the twenty-first century. Chapters 1 through 3 examine the relationship between ethnic cinemas and Hollywood. Although Hollywood studios dabbled in folk musical production in the late 1920s with the black-cast films *Hallelujah!* and *Hearts in Dixie*, they reproduced power hierarchies that restricted African American mobility and, as a result, rang hollow for contemporary black moviegoers. Ethnic cinemas, including black "race cinema" and Yiddish and Mexican cinema, proved far more adept at addressing the needs and concerns of their audiences. They fashioned an onscreen community for their viewers by featuring the material spaces—the Lower East Side tenement, the Midwestern farm, and the Mexican *rancho*—and the musical cultures that lend them expression. An analysis of these ethnic cinemas and their development of the folk musical reveals the ways in which marginalized peoples had a constitutive role in the genre's formation.

Chapters 4 and 5 demonstrate how the Hollywood folk musical incorporated the content and formal structure of ethnic musicals beginning in the late 1930s with the aim of reaching a mass audience. Films like *The Wizard of Oz, Meet Me in St. Louis,* and *Summer Holiday* did away with stories about the stage and instead offered heartwarming tales about home and family and the joy of cultural identification through communal song and dance. Hollywood producers such as Freed came to recognize the potency of the folk musical, with its ability to conjure and attenuate the stresses of modern life through its formally integrated structure and its nostalgic depictions of home. An analysis of the process by which the folk migrated to Hollywood also charts the ways in which a white folk heritage developed in mainstream cinema during the 1940s and 1950s.

The Hollywood folk musical reached its zenith in the 1960s with *The Music Man* and *The Sound of Music.* Both films elaborate on communities of white persons whose musicality, family loyalty, and ties to the land mediate the challenges of the modern era. White flight to the suburbs, including the upwardly mobile descendants of Jewish immigrants, the nation's abandonment of the cities to African Americans and Latinos, and the conservative rhetoric that blamed the nation's ills on peoples of color continued to make the experience of belonging, the folk musical's most salient and enduring theme, of paramount concern to postwar Hollywood audiences.

Chapter 6 reveals how the desire for ethnic separatism and the ethnic revival among white ethnics produced significant changes within the folk musical of the post–civil rights era. Riding the wave of the ethnic revival, initiated by the success of *Fiddler on the Roof* (1968) among non-Jewish audiences, producers adapted two Broadway musicals, *The Wiz* (1978) and *Zoot Suit,* for the big screen. Funded by the Hollywood studios

and with varying degrees of input from their black and Chicano origina-
tors, *The Wiz* and *Zoot Suit* aimed at a diverse cross-section of society. The
films attempted to articulate the contemporary circumstances of these
groups by shifting their settings from the countryside to the city, hybrid-
izing the rural/home space with the urbanscape and using proscriptive
narratives to suggest paths to self-realization. The folk musical remained
salient, positioning familial solidarity and the search for social belonging
at the center. But rather than cater to an in-group mentality, as ethnic cinemas of the 1930s had done, producers in the 1970s endeavored to trans-
late ethnic cultures for white audiences.

The final chapter reveals how the folk musical continues to resonate in
the twenty-first century. The theatrical distribution of sing-along versions
of musical films, the most popular being *The Sound of Music* and *Grease*
(1978), has met with enormous success in places like the Castro Theatre in
San Francisco and the Hollywood Bowl in Los Angeles. Similar to the appeal
of cult cinema and midnight movies, they offer twenty-first-century audiences a chance to experience community and belonging in the place of the
movie theater. In this way, sing-alongs exaggerate the folk musical's syntax. They extend the integrative quality of the characters' onscreen homes
(Salzburg and Rydell High School) to the theater space itself, thus validat-
ing alternative forms of cultural expression at the movies.

I have chosen an illustrative rather than an exhaustive approach to
the folk musical in American cinema. Rather than documenting every folk
musical ever made, this book instead focuses on significant moments in
the subgenre's development. For this reason, I do not explore Hollywood's
self-reflexive show musicals of the 1950s, including the much-celebrated
films *Show Boat* (1951), *Singin' in the Rain* (1952), *The Band Wagon* (1953),
and *Silk Stockings* (1957). These films, though well known for their seamless integration of musical numbers, are structured around the dual-focus
narrative and, specifically, the union (or tragic separation in the case of
Show Boat) of the romantic couple and the ultimate celebration of making
entertainment. While the adaptation of *Oklahoma!* (1955) would certainly
be a valid selection for inclusion here, I choose to analyze a rarely studied
and original Hollywood production of the 1950s, *Seven Brides for Seven Brothers* (1954). In chapter 5, I explore those musicals of the 1960s that audiences
championed as representing what America should be, *The Music Man* and

The Sound of Music. West Side Story (1961), a film that might on the surface appear to be an obvious choice for this chapter given its treatment of Puerto Rican migration, is not explored in depth. In my analysis, its message of racial tolerance amid the decay of an American city is an exception rather than the rule for folk musicals of the 1960s. The celebration of wholesome and patriotic communities constituted the more dominant trend in folk musicals of that decade, as the reception of *The Music Man* and *The Sound of Music* attests.

The Migration of Musical Film provides a revised history of the American musical film that focuses on one of its most enduring generic patterns. As a concept that has been applied to various groups of people located across space and time, the folk provides a window onto the ways in which Americans and immigrants, insiders and outsiders have negotiated the boundaries of belonging in our society. Characters in the folk musical consistently privilege the collective and its material relation to home and place. In doing so, they resist the experience of the alienated, uprooted individual in modern life. Multivalent in their mediations of the folk past and modernity, such musicals bear the markings of their sociohistorical context. More significantly, however, they reveal the values of a diverse group of cultural producers and audiences for whom migration and the quest for home are central concerns.

1

The *Shtetls, Shund,* and Shows of Musicals

In its publicity for *The Jazz Singer* (1927), Warner Bros. described the film as "a play for all the young who dream of far fields—and for the old, who remember!" Based on Samuel Raphaelson's short story, itself largely drawn from the life of entertainer Al Jolson, the film tells of an immigrant son who dreams of being a success on the American stage. The narrative moves through two seemingly opposed worlds. The first is the Jewish immigrant ghetto of the Lower East Side and the Rabinowitz family home, wherein religion and tradition reign supreme. The second is the world of American popular entertainment, which, though potentially hostile, rewards talent and hard work.

The film and its promotional materials emphasize the duality of American life by juxtaposing the spaces of home/stage and ghetto/Broadway. Jakie (Jolson), the immigrant, bridges these two worlds by journeying between them and shifting his identity accordingly. In this way, the narrative hinges on both geographical and social mobility as symbolized by migration. The relative stability and historical continuity of the Lower East Side represents the immigrant's point of origin. The world of jazz, however, offers dynamic, syncopated rhythms and cultural heterogeneity. Jakie, the immigrant, must grapple with this foreign land, its sights and sounds forming what Raphaelson termed "the vital chaos of America's soul." Immigrants themselves, the film's producers hoped that this story would make Americanized children and immigrant parents "each more tolerant of the other" as they undertake the inevitable journey away from the home and into the world.[1]

Raphaelson believed the immigrant Jew was uniquely positioned to develop and give voice to jazz music. In his preface to the film's souvenir program, he states that "the Jews are determining the nature and scope of jazz more than any other race—more than the negroes, from whom they have taken jazz and given it a new color and meaning." Popular Jewish artists, he maintains, owe their ability to express "the nature of our chaos today" to their "roots in the synagogue." As others have argued, the performance of "jazz" in *The Jazz Singer* is one that denies African Americans their role in creating and shaping this music.[2] The film's use of jazz, however, is in keeping with most Americans' understanding of it in the 1920s, which was associated with Jewish musicians like Jolson and Irving Berlin and white bandleaders such as Paul Whiteman.[3] For Raphaelson and the Warners, the plight of the Jewish immigrant and Jolson's ability to lend it emotional expression were critical to the translation and popularity of jazz music.

Although *The Jazz Singer* has received attention for its self-conscious story of Jewish assimilation, it has not been sufficiently contextualized as one of the earliest examples of what would become the American film musical.[4] To be sure, advertisements for the film do not use any of the terms or phrases that would later be ascribed to the genre, such as "all talking— all singing—all dancing."[5] Nevertheless, the film's promotional materials visually allude to moments of musical performance. The pressbook and souvenir program depict dancing chorus girls and scenes of Jakie performing onstage, serenading his mother at home, and singing as a cantor.[6]

These visual renderings of musical moments in the film also illustrate the spatial conflicts in the narrative. Marketing "catchlines" from the pressbook concisely communicate the two worlds that Jakie must reconcile: "East Side Meets West Side"; "Sparkle and Glitter of Broadway— Sombre Shadows of the East Side!"; "Shall the Show Go On—Or the Dying Father Be Comforted?"; and "Mammy Songs or the Solemn Wistful 'Kol Nidre'?" Such promotional phrases reveal the different types of musical performance in terms of tone ("sparkle and glitter" versus "sombre shadows") and form ("mammy songs" versus Jewish chants). The correlation between the spatial realms of the story and their respective musical qualities is no coincidence. The film narratively and musically explores the dynamics of a journey taken or rejected—to stay home and preserve one's family group or leave home in order to pursue individual success. As one reviewer put it, Jakie's is the "conflict between filial duty and ambition." Even though Jakie eventually finds companionship on the stage, it does not replace the filial relationships that harness him to his past.[7]

The Jazz Singer is in many ways the earliest example of the show or backstage musical film in which an unknown becomes a star on the American stage (*The Broadway Melody*, 1929; *Gold Diggers of 1933*; *Stage Struck*, 1936). The process by which Jakie goes from outsider to insider, immigrant to American, is integral to the film's formal structure, which moves between musical sequences, recorded with the Vitaphone sound system, and silent narrative sequences that are explained with intertitle cards. The musical sequences establish his talent, whereas the narrative sequences explore the conflict with his parents and his relationship with a Gentile girl. The addition of sound makes the performance sequences all the more vivid and persuasive. When he sings, Jakie makes overt pleas to his audience for acceptance, reaching out with his arms in a way that begs for approval. Each performance begins before an audience that moves from anticipation to approbation, effectively demonstrating his transformation.

The film also incorporates qualities and values related to the other dominant strain in the genre, the folk musical. The focus on Jakie's relationship to home, and especially to his mother, indicates that the rise to fame is not an uncomplicated one. Subsequent show musicals do not explore intergenerational dynamics or the places of origin of the chorines on the stage. Rather, the success of their romantic relationships is tied to the success of the "show" that provides the finale of the film. Rick Altman has explored how the "dual-focus narrative" of the show musical renders a parallel conflict between the realization of the show and the happiness of the romantic couple.[8] *The Jazz Singer*'s emphasis on home and family dynamics, especially those set within an ethnic, immigrant context, is more akin to the folk musical's idyllic structure that privileges historical continuity, rituals and holidays, and cyclical time. We see the folk musical being developed in the silent sequences that reinforce an association with the past. Just as silent cinema was associated with a passing era, so too are the traditional immigrant household and the rigidity of the cantor's religious beliefs.

The show musical, with its privileging of the individual, and the folk musical, with its preservation of the collective, fight for dominance in Jakie's struggle between home and Broadway, Jewish chants and jazz. He must journey between both realms in order to find happiness. The film represents a formative moment for the musical film in that it anticipates the genre's preoccupation with migration. Historically specific in its spatiotemporal places of origin and destination, *The Jazz Singer* portrays migration musically and dramatically as a choice between the material spaces of individual and communal expression.

In order to explore fully the evolution of the musical film as it represented Jews and Jewish immigration, it is necessary to look beyond *The Jazz Singer* and, indeed, outside of Hollywood. Produced in New York and Poland for a transnational audience of Jewish immigrants, Yiddish-language cinema engaged with the topics of immigration, assimilation, and intergenerational conflict more directly and consistently than did Hollywood. Its musicals did not revolve around stage performance, but rather focused on the organic musical expressions that defined Jewish home and family life. The first of these, *Mayne Yiddishe Mame* (My Jewish Mother, 1930), vehemently warns children not to stray from the home and seek pleasure over filial duty. This film and the many that followed offer a celebratory vision of resilient families and tradition to an audience that faced the pressures of assimilation daily. Yiddish musicals use song and dance not as a show of talent, but as an organic, emotional expression of a community. When Yiddish musicals do venture into the world of the stage, as in *Dem Khazns Zundl* (The Cantor's Son, 1937), a film that J. Hoberman has called the "anti–*Jazz Singer*," the purpose is to illustrate the perils of an immigrant son's search for fame.[9] A comparison of these Yiddish films and *The Jazz Singer* reveals the parallels and divergences of musical film production as it related to the issue of Jewish immigration and assimilation in this formative moment for the genre.

"They Are Not American"

Despite their success on the stage and in the movies, Jewish immigrants and Jewish Americans occupied a precarious position in 1920s American society. One obvious piece of evidence is provided by the frequent diatribes aimed against them by the celebrated American industrial giant Henry Ford. In 1921 he vented his anti-Semitic prejudices via his weekly newspaper, the *Dearborn Independent*, by attacking what he considered to be the most dire menace to America: the movies. Ford found the Jewish origins of the majority of moviemakers in California and of their financial partners in New York to be a serious threat to the American way of life. In his view, their religion and their race rendered the Jews of Hollywood unfit to entertain the masses.[10]

Ford's position was particularly virulent for early 1920s America, but his message was not uncommon. The Red Scare of 1919–1920 targeted Jewish intellectuals as a domestic threat, and the first immigration quota acts limited the entry of those considered undesirable. The 1924 act, which David Roediger and James R. Barrett call a "triumph of racism," targeted the Jews of Eastern Europe, 1.5 million of whom had emigrated to the United States since the late nineteenth century. Jews, like other immigrants from Europe in this period, were an "in-between people": whiteness was denied them on the basis of certain identity markers, such as skin color, religion, class, language, and culture.[11] This outsider status was a social stigma to which Raphaelson, the Warners, and the makers of Yiddish cinema responded for their respective audiences.

The pervasiveness of new forms of popular entertainment like jazz and the movies was visible particularly in urban centers such as New York and Chicago, where large populations of recent immigrants had settled. Many of these immigrants constituted the first audiences for the earliest movies.[12] Ford and others conflated immigrants and immigration with the perceived breakdown of social mores that they observed in new forms of entertainment. Jews such as Irving Berlin, Al Jolson, and the Warners of Hollywood influenced the direction of popular culture as songwriters, entertainers, and showmen. In response, Ford openly attacked them for willfully destroying what was good and decent about America. "There lies the whole secret of the movies' failure," Ford insisted, "they are not American and their producers are racially unqualified to reproduce the American atmosphere." Pointing to the "falsity, artificiality, criminality and jazz" in current movie fare, Ford concluded that Jewish producers' racial inferiority was inherently linked to the moral laxity of their films.[13]

Apart from direct anti-Semitic attacks, threats of legal censorship plagued the studio heads. Indeed, motion pictures had been attacked by culture critics from the beginning due to their earliest associations with immigrants and the urban slums of major American cities. Many special interest groups fought for censorship, asserting that the movies were "corrupting" the moral standards of the country and spoiling the minds of children. The Jewish background of many motion picture distributors and exhibitors influenced social reformers' perceptions of the movies as a potentially dangerous form of mass entertainment.[14]

Hollywood producers were mindful of the arguments against them. As Michael Rogin has explained, Jews in positions of cultural power experienced pressure to suppress their ethnicity in the interest of becoming American. Blackface and the songs of Tin Pan Alley were two theatrical forms through which Jews allowed themselves expressive outlet as a marginalized people and as aspiring Americans.[15] More subtly, mainstream films can harbor immigrant and ethnic anxieties, as Ella Shohat and Mark Winokur have shown, at the levels of costume or set design or in modes of comedic address.[16]

With its self-conscious subject matter, *The Jazz Singer* provides a rare insight into how the Jews of Hollywood identified themselves. "In the story of America's accomplishments," the film's souvenir program states, "the Jewish race has written many chapters." Lauding the contributions of Jews to American culture, most directly linked to Al Jolson, but also to the Warners themselves, the studio draws a direct parallel between the "humble Jewish homes ordered by the precepts of orthodoxy" and the "talents of boys who were later to become international celebrities—great playwrights, great musicians, great actors."[17]

Harry Warner, the eldest brother, was vocal about his Jewishness in ways that other movie executives were not. His commentary in *The American Hebrew*, a prominent weekly magazine for upwardly mobile Jews, demonstrates how Jewish producers positioned themselves in American society and culture. Labeling himself and his brothers as the "new ambassadors of good-will," Warner explained that he made *The Jazz Singer* because it showed "the sharp and cutting contrast between the new and the old—, and that both are right." He insisted that the film told a pathetic tale about both immigrant parents and children in America. "I find it impossible,"

Warner stated, "to believe that anybody seeing the 'Jazz Singer' could fail to clearly understand and sympathize with the religious and mental attitude of the Jews of the older generation." No doubt referring to the pressures he and his brothers felt as businessmen in America, he observed, "I also feel that an orthodox Jew must surely learn through this picture some of the problems of the younger generation who are thrown into constant business and social contact with Christians every day of their lives."[18]

Some scholars have criticized *The Jazz Singer* for focusing on the intolerance of Jews rather than American anti-Semitism.[19] To be sure, the film focuses on acts of cultural bias by Jews and not Gentiles. It is also important to note, however, that *The Jazz Singer* was not unique in this respect. Themes of intergenerational conflict were common in the literature, theater, and films of the immigrant generation. Moreover, the hostility experienced by Jews in American society, though not overt, is manifest in the structure of the film's musical sequences.

The Jazz Singer (1927)

The form chosen by the makers of *The Jazz Singer* is essential to communicating the different challenges experienced by older immigrants and their children. Its narrative takes place in two distinct realms: the Old World as it is preserved in the Rabinowitz household, with its adherence to custom and prayer, and the outside world of 1920s America, a bustling, syncopated, and secular place. Motivated by his loyalty to his family and his ambition to be a star on the stage, Jakie bridges both worlds through music. An analysis of specific sequences from the film reveals how both the show and the folk musical were being developed in the context of this story about Jewish immigration.

In its fascination with the Lower East Side, *The Jazz Singer* was not unique. A short but significant cycle of Hollywood films met audiences' voyeuristic desires to see the Jewish ghetto of New York. Films like *Humoresque* (1920), *Hungry Hearts* (1922), *Abie's Irish Rose* (1928), and *The Cohens and the Kellys* (1926) explored the sights and themes of Jewish immigrant life. Shots of the Lower East Side's congested streets, filled with pushcarts and shoppers, became conventional occurrences in such films.[20] For Alan Crosland, *The Jazz Singer*'s director, the impulse for authentic representation was crucial to his decision to film on location. As *The American Hebrew* documented, Crosland positioned a camera on the second floor of a restaurant, "taking numerous 'shots' of the welter of Jewish humanity that went about its business wholly unaware that anything unusual was taking place."[21] These scenes hark back to the Progressive Era, when social reformers like Jacob Riis recorded shocking images of overcrowded tenement buildings, poverty, and vice in that area of the city.[22] According to *The American Hebrew*'s account, however, the sequences were intended not to be exploitative, but rather to depict a people and a way of life. Returning to Hollywood, Crosland carried with him "little more than the external appearance of the street" that revealed "tragedy and joy on Orchard Street."[23]

The Jazz Singer attempted to integrate its primarily non-Jewish audience into a position of identification with the members of the Rabinowitz family. For the film's opening, a series of on-location shots gradually moves us into this space. The first high-angle view of a Lower East Side thoroughfare provides the establishing shot of the film, communicating the place and time of the narrative. We see a busy intersection filled with pushcarts, peddlers, and shoppers. The scene dissolves to another perspective, also from a high angle, but this time closer to the action. The third shot positions the audience inside one of the shops, looking out toward the street. In the viewer's sightline stands a Jewish man, humbly adorned with his yarmulke, selling his fabric to passersby. Another dissolve places the audience in front of a spinning merry-go-round full of children, and the final dissolve returns us once more to a high-angle shot of a shopping thoroughfare. In this way, the opening sequence moves its audience from the position of a voyeur who observes the scene at a distance to that of a participant in its daily activities.

Similarly, the film's first narrative sequence begins inside the Rabinowitz household in order to provide the audience with an understanding of the needs and desires of Jewish immigrant parents. An iris shot provides a close-up of the cantor's clasped and wringing hands. The iris opens and we see him pacing the floor of his humble parlor as his wife, Sara, dutifully prepares Yom Kippur supper. Their home is orderly and comfortable. Sara is a matronly woman who moves quietly and gently from kitchen to parlor. As an intertitle card introduces her, she represents constancy: "Sara Rabinowitz. God made her a Woman and Love made her a Mother." The cantor represents a form of constancy that is inflexible: "Cantor Rabinowitz, chanter of hymns in the synagogue, stubbornly held to the ancient traditions of his race." Aligned with the ritual of chanting, a repetitive form of musical expression, and ancient traditions, the cantor seems doomed in the dynamic, secular world around him. A reviewer for *The American Hebrew* took special notice of the cantor's character and commented on his complexity. "He was the man that Alan Crosland . . . and Warner Oland, who portrayed the character, had to understand," the reviewer explained. "When you see Cantor Rabinowitz, you are both annoyed with his bigotry, and compassionate with him because you understand his conflict so well, and that is what makes him a great character."[24] Early in the film we witness the cantor's harsh treatment of his son, precipitated by Jakie's singing of "raggy time songs" in a local saloon. The cantor's attempt to beat the desire out of him prompts Jakie to run away.

As though nothing has changed, the cantor resumes his duties in the synagogue. Shots of the men and women, their heads covered in deference to God, show them chanting together in a call-and-response pattern around sacred objects and texts. The singing of the *Kol Nidre*, occurring at a specific time on the eve of Yom Kippur, is an event rich in custom. The cantor delivers it methodically with sustained and somber notes. The film cuts between medium shots of the cantor and the congregation, united in solemn prayer. This sequence ends with parallel shots of the synagogue, carrying on its ritualistic practices, and Jakie irrevocably breaking with the past.

The film flashes forward, and we encounter an adult Jakie, renamed Jack Robin, at Coffee Dan's in San Francisco. This scene is critical for the ways in which it transforms Jakie from an unknown talent to a successful entertainer. The first shot is a close-up of the Coffee Dan's sign blinking with electric lights. We see a montage of plates of food and people knocking hammers clamoring for more. Jakie is one of them as he bounces in his chair, eats his ham and eggs, and enjoys the syncopated music in the restaurant. Coffee Dan's is a place of movement and rhythm as opposed to the staid sobriety of his home and synagogue. An intertitle card translates the emcee's announcement: "Jack Robin will sing 'Dirty Hands Dirty Face.' They say he's good—we shall see." Jakie shakes a friend's hand, and an intertitle communicates his response: "Wish me luck, Pal—I'll certainly need it." The patrons clap politely as he ventures up to the stage.

The stakes are high in this scene. The patrons, as one teaser for the film explains, treat professional and amateur singers with "silence or the enthusiastic knocking of hammers, with which each guest is provided!" A make-or-break setting, Coffee Dan's determines the fate of the performer. Jakie has made the ultimate sacrifice by leaving home and family for a career in show business. His acceptance into this social world hinges on his ability to sell himself to an audience of strangers.[25]

The scene narratively and musically conveys Jakie's transformation. We see him in medium close-up as he faces the audience and begins to sing. The abrupt transition to sound in this scene exaggerates the significance of the moment. The camera holds the inherent tension in this shot by staying focused on Jakie until the beginning of the second stanza. Jakie dramatically performs the song, expressing every word with his face and hands; but without a corresponding shot of his audience, we are left to wonder about his success. The one subtle indication we have comes from the placement of a female audience member, at the bottom right of the frame, whose attention appears to be held by the performance.

The audience in the musical film is intrinsic to the genre's "ritual function," as Jane Feuer has maintained, which is to "reaffirm and articulate the place that entertainment occupies in the audience's psychic lives." In communicating that the performance is good, the (diegetic) audience inside the film instructs the (nondiegetic) audience outside of the film to respond accordingly. Embedded in this mirroring process is the association of the film's performance and the film itself.[26] The tension in this first shot of Jakie's performance arises out of the absence of the audience. It is not until the second stanza, when the film cuts to a shot from Jakie's perspective, in which we see a young woman and her party enter the restaurant, that we understand that he is doing well. The woman, Mary Dale, and the others sit in rapt attention, entranced by his performance. The sequence then flashes between shots of Jakie, Mary, and the audience. The film's teaser concisely sums up the dynamics of this scene: "*The Jazz Singer* is called on! He responds! Volcanic, emotional, moving—the house is wild! The tiny hammers beat approval!" His emotional rendering of the song, followed by an energetic "Toot, Toot, Tootsie," secures the approval of his new world and sets him on a pathway to success.

The film quickly counters this linear movement forward with a turn backward. As the film transitions to silence, the intertitle that follows declares, "For those whose lives are turned toward the past, the years roll by unheeded—their lives unchanged." Again, the film depicts Jakie's parents as the embodiment of tradition. Sara cooks and maintains the home while the cantor sings in the synagogue and teaches new generations of cantors in the ways of the faith.

The spatial division of the film becomes acute when Jakie gets the chance to return to New York. The intertitles reveal his thoughts in a succession of words that grow progressively larger: "New York!—Broadway!—HOME!—MOTHER!" The material spaces New York/Broadway and Home/Mother are emblematic of Jakie's two loves, his career and his mother. He returns home and finds it unchanged except for the graying hair of his parents. He serenades his mother like a good son, and she sits exuding approval. He sings "Mother, I Still Have You" not just as a performer but

3. Jakie performs for the patrons at Coffee Dan's. *The Jazz Singer* copyright 1927 by Warner Bros. Pictures.

as an expression of his feelings for his home and family. He bemoans that, "Mother, I'm sorry I wandered away, breaking your heart as I did." Referencing the coldness of the world outside, he finds comfort in the "warmth of her smile." Jakie sings this song with great pathos, and the film corresponds with a shot/reverse shot sequence of extreme close-ups. Jakie and Sara have tears in their eyes as they celebrate his homecoming and the unbreakable bond between mother and son. In this sequence, it is clear that Jakie has not lost affection for his home and family. Though he knows he will not stay, he desires to maintain a connection nonetheless. The knowledge that his mother is "still the same" despite the changes in the world outside is a source of supreme comfort. Sara is rewarded for her stalwart support of her son from her permanent position as keeper of home and hearth.

The cantor, however, also remains unchanged. He enters this warm scene between mother and son with horror at the sound of "jazz songs" emanating from his home. Not even the gift of a prayer shawl mollifies him. Once again, he expels his son from his life. Censuring his father's behavior, Jakie declares, "Tradition is all right, but this is another day! I'll live my life as I see fit!" The two worlds, silent and sound, traditional and modern, have repelled one another yet again.[27]

The moment of reckoning occurs when Jakie must choose between starring in a Broadway show and singing the *Kol Nidre*, his father's dying request. Returning again and again to the eve of Yom Kippur, the film is organized as a cycle that in turn organizes the major events of Jakie's life. He must choose between his career and the "songs of Israel." It would seem at first that Jakie refuses his parents' plea. But, after the dress rehearsal, he goes to his father's bedside, where he is persuaded to return to the synagogue. As Jakie sings the *Kol Nidre*, the cantor listens, his wish fulfilled, and dies with his soul at peace. As a review in *The American Hebrew* affirms, Jakie's decision to return to his home and to his Jewish faith was the correct one. "The boy is won over in 'the end,'" the reviewer notes, "to remain true to his Jewish traditions." The reviewer chooses to ignore Jakie's ultimate return to the stage, instead focusing on his devotion to the "Jewish congregation to which he belongs."[28]

Most interpretations of the final scene in *The Jazz Singer* agree that Jakie has rejected his Jewish past in favor of assimilation into an American present.[29] Although he ultimately does return to Broadway, it is important to note how his assimilation is attenuated by loyalties to home and family. The film suggests that Jakie can strike a balance between both worlds.[30] Returning to his father's bedside, Jakie listens to the pleas from his mother and from Mary Dale and the Broadway show's producer, pulling him in opposite directions. Ultimately, he heeds the advice of his mother to do what is in his heart, since his father will know if he sings without "God in his voice." Jakie delivers the *Kol Nidre* from the same physical space formerly occupied by his father at the synagogue's pulpit, singing with his congregation and with his father superimposed behind him. As a result, the show does not go on. Quite remarkably, the famed Winter Garden Theatre closes for Yom Kippur, as Mary, the show's other star, and its director listen intently to "a jazz singer—singing to his God."

The film reveals, however, that the "season passes" and that the show eventually continues. Positioned on the stage of the Winter Garden, Jakie sings "My Mammy" to a packed house. It is clear that he has found acceptance in the New World, which includes the genuine affection of Mary Dale. The film prominently situates Sara as part of Jakie's modern family as well. Again praising the constancy of a mother's love, Jakie directs "My Mammy" to Sara. Through the allegory of the black experience, the song recounts the journey that Jakie has made during the course of the film. It takes him from his youthful days of wanderlust in the ghetto ("Everything is lovely when you start to roam") to his hardships as a young, traveling entertainer ("But later when you are further away / Things won't seem so lovely / When you're all alone"). In the end, what sustains him is not the love of his American girlfriend or even the success of the Broadway show, but his mother's enduring affection. Celebrated by the film, she is the character who delivers the Warners' message of tolerance most keenly. Sara ensures Jakie's connection to home, but also provides him with the support that he needs in order to pursue his dreams. As long as he has her pride and approval, he can take the Old World with him into the New. The film conveys this message with another shot/reverse shot pattern that foregrounds not the audience of strangers, but an audience of one: his mother. As Jakie sings to Sara with outstretched arms, the camera reveals her tears of joy. In this cinematic space, the desires of the old generation and the needs of the new enjoy a harmonious existence.

The story of intergenerational strife told with great melodramatic fervor suggests that a stronger connection exists between *The Jazz Singer* and Yiddish culture than has been presumed. Depictions of mother-child devotion and father-son conflict were central to the popular entertainment of Jewish immigrants in the early twentieth century. In his observations of the Jewish ghetto in 1901, for example, Hutchins Hapgood described how in the Yiddish theater "the pathos or tragedy involved in differences of faith and point of view between the old rabbi and his more enlightened children is expressed in many historical plays." Classified by Jewish audiences as "one-handkerchief, two-handkerchief, or three-handkerchief ordeals," such stories predated *The Jazz Singer* by decades.[31]

The film also signals Jakie's enduring connection to his Jewish origins through his emotive style of performance, the hallmark on which Jolson built his career. Press materials for the film conflate the narratives of Jakie and Jolson by establishing how both came from immigrant families headed by fathers who were cantors. Like Jakie, Jolson broke from that tradition to find success on the American stage. Nevertheless, it was the "sob in his

4. Jakie sings to his mother. *The Jazz Singer* copyright 1927 by Warner Bros. Pictures.

voice" that distinguished Jolson's performance, the American Jewish press asserted, a quality "that comes from singing mournful Jewish melodies and Hebrew chants in the synagogue."[32]

Franklin Gordon, writing for *The American Hebrew*, emphasized this association between Jolson's performance appeal, his emotional capacity, and his Jewishness. Calling him an "alchemist of emotions," he declared that Jolson had "become a synonym for all that is warm and throbbing and direct in human intercourse." Gordon pointed to a direct, mutually constitutive connection between Jewishness and Jolson's emotionality: "The gift he possesses of feeling emotions poignantly, and being able to communicate them to this fellowmen, he undoubtedly owes to his Jewish heritage." This gift is innate, Gordon continued, "it wells from his unconscious, floods to the surface from deep unsounded wells of past sufferings that are racial and ineradicable."[33]

Jewish audiences of *The Jazz Singer* recognized the pathos of Jolson's musical expressions as being rooted in suffering. Linking the Jewish past of dispersal and deracination to the African American experience on the plantation, blackface liberated Jolson to express his angst both emotionally and physically. Jolson's "construction of racial feeling," Linda Williams notes, is in keeping with an American melodramatic tradition in which "singing Black" and "feeling Black" becomes a path to "white virtue."[34]

Contemporary critics of popular Jewish entertainment used the term *shund* (trash) to describe the overt sentimentality and emotional excess with which performers played their roles. As the emotionally excessive numbers "Mother, I Still Have You" and "My Mammy" indicate, the invocation of mothers in "mother songs" was especially acute in Jewish immigrant culture of the late nineteenth and early twentieth centuries.[35] Immigrants expressed feelings of homesickness and nostalgia for the land left behind through songs that expressed devotion to the mother figure, assuring audiences of the permanence of the family in the face of change. The Warners exploited this aspect of their film's narrative by suggesting that theaters arrange a "reception for mothers" where tea would be served and local talent would sing "Mother, I Still Have You." At the premiere in Los Angeles, Jack Warner gave a speech that implored the audience to remember the most important of biblical commandments: "Honor thy father and thy mother."[36]

Lessons of filial conflict and piety and Jewish expressions of emotion are central to *The Jazz Singer*'s narrative and reception. Unlike Yiddish-language productions, however, *The Jazz Singer* operates in the context of mainstream, commercial cinema and its primarily non-Jewish audience base. Here again, the show musical sequences in the film are instructive for understanding the ways in which Jakie/Jolson "wins over" his audience and achieves acceptance by the dominant culture. Jolson was the most appropriate entertainer for such a task precisely because of his ability to, as critic Alexander Woollcott put it, "hold an absolute dictatorship over his audience." Positioned at the edge of the stage and reaching outward in numbers like "My Mammy," Jolson establishes a connection to his audience that works to break down the separation between them. "This is not essentially a motion picture," another critic observed, "but rather a chance to capture for comparative immortality, the sight and sound of a great performer." The same reviewer recounted the opening of *The Jazz Singer* at the Warner Theatre in New York: "Last night whenever the shadow of the actor sang 'Mammy' or 'Mother O' Mine' the audience listened enraptured and applauded ecstatically, just as though he were being observed in what is accurately enough termed the flesh."[37] Aided by synchronized sound, editing, close-ups, and Jolson's direct address to the audience, his songs assume a live quality, transforming the impersonal experience of watching a film into a highly personal one. Robert Benchley, the drama reviewer for *Life*, reflected, "He trembles his under lip, and your hearts break with a loud snap. He sings, and you totter out to send a night letter to your mother."[38]

By invoking the importance of parental figures, especially the mother, the Warners positioned *The Jazz Singer* as a film about the sanctity of home and family. Even though Jakie ventures into the world of Broadway and jazz, he remains, first and foremost, Sara's son. He celebrates and devotes himself to Sara, who represents the link to his past and his source of strength for the future. *The Jazz Singer* reaffirms the endurance of motherhood, family, and tradition. In doing so, the film shows the desire to overcome alienation in American life.

Mayne Yiddishe Mame (My Jewish Mother, 1930) and the Yiddish Musical

The Jazz Singer's investment in maintaining familial relationships tempers the film's assimilationist thrust. This thematic concern was of central importance to Yiddish cinema, which drew upon various forms of Yiddish culture, including theater and literature, more overtly. It was a cinema made up of small production companies that existed on the margins of mainstream American society. From its production bases in New York and Poland, Yiddish cinema appealed to audiences whose lives were marked by the experience of migration, including those who had emigrated to the United States and those who remained behind in Eastern Europe.

Yiddish films referenced immigrants' sense of displacement and anxiety as a result of leaving the insular life of the Eastern European *shtetl*. Most of Yiddish cinema's audience was composed of people from the Russian Pale of Settlement who had fled the pogroms that followed the assassination of Tsar Alexander II in 1881.[39] The first immigrants to settle in the United States mythologized the *shtetl* almost immediately. For them and their children, it came to represent the traditional ways of Jewish life and culture that had dissipated over time.[40] Yiddish cinema, as literature and theater had done before it, engaged in the romanticization of the *shtetl* by locating its narratives in Eastern European communities or by re-creating their dynamics in the Jewish ghettos of the United States. The films operate on an overtly emotional register in order to conjure an idealized folk community.[41]

Yiddish cinema did not look only backward. Many of its films acknowledged the differences between traditional Jewish life and modern life in America. With rare exceptions, the films portray these changes as pressures to be warded against.[42] Often, the older generation understands immigration as a necessary evil while the younger generation becomes seduced by American ways. The crisis stems from children who disobey their parents, leave home, and shirk their filial duty. Typically, the films offer a happy ending by showing the reunification of the family. The wayward children see the error of their ways, apologize to their parents, and return to the sanctity of the family home. In the process, as J. Hoberman has explained, the films convey the "dislocation between the Old Country and the New World, parent and child, folk community and industrial society, worker and *allrightnik*."[43]

On the surface, there appears to be significant overlap between *The Jazz Singer* and *Mayne Yiddishe Mame*, the first Yiddish film musical. Their narratives center on a Jewish immigrant family named Rabinowitz. Both films are set in the Lower East Side of New York. And they share a fixation on the differences between parents and children.[44]

There was little to no overlap, however, between the targeted audiences for the two films. The Warners reached out to American Jews, as the commentary in *The American Hebrew* suggests; but ultimately, they sought to appeal to a mass, non-Jewish audience. With the exception of Jolson's performance of the *Kol Nidre* in the synagogue, American English dominates both the silent and the sound sections of the film. Setting the parameters between spoken dialogue and musical performance, the silent and sound sections would seem to offer a cultural break between Yiddish (inside the Rabinowitz home) and English (in the American city). Catering to their largely non-Jewish audience, however, the filmmakers used English-language intertitle cards to explain the dialogue between Jakie and his immigrant parents. The Warners even went a step further to cater to their non–Yiddish-speaking moviegoers: a Yiddish-English glossary in the souvenir program provided translations of Yiddish words and explained practices of the Jewish faith. The glossary defines "kibitzer" as a "busybody," a "cantor" as a "Chanter of Sacred Hymns," and the *Kol Nidre* as a "sacred hymn chanted only on eve of Yom Kippur 'Day of Atonement.'"[45]

In *Mayne Yiddishe Mame* and the multiple musicals that were to follow, the Jewish filmmakers, many of them immigrants themselves, served an audience that was immersed in Yiddish culture. Combining multiple languages, including German, Hebrew, and Slavic idioms, Yiddish was "a migratory and international language, a tongue without a national home." In their studies of the Yiddish cinema, Joseph Cohen and J. Hoberman have stressed the symbolic qualities of this language: its words, sounds, and gestures indicate the pain of departure and resettlement. In their prominent use of Yiddish, filmmakers redirected the cinematic narrative of Jewish immigration from one that celebrated the idea of American mobility to one that insisted on cultural retention.[46]

5. The cast and crew of *Mayne Yiddishe Mame* pose for a publicity still. Copyright 1930 by Judea Pictures Corporation. Courtesy The National Center for Jewish Film.

Yiddish cinema drew heavily upon the well-established tradition of Yiddish theater in New York, in which audiences were culturally inter-twined with the plays and the actors who performed them. As Nahma San-drow has observed of this community, "theatergoing took over some of the functions of the traditional community institutions back home." Jewish immigrant audiences supported such spaces, wherein their language and culture were upheld. Fans of Yiddish theater stars formed clubs that regu-larly interacted with the performances on the stage and organized benefits for charitable organizations. Significantly, the theaters also assisted in the maintenance of a "calendar separate from the rest of the world" that cel-ebrated Jewish holidays and commemorated the lives of Jewish cultural figures. Fueled by these fan clubs and often sponsored by a *Landsmannshaft* (immigrant benevolent association) or a politically oriented organization like the Workmen's Circle, Yiddish theater flourished as an expression of the Jewish immigrant community.[47]

Yiddish cinema worked to maintain that relationship in the new medium. Unlike *The Jazz Singer*, *Mayne Yiddishe Mame* does not qualify its musical sequences with a show business narrative in which an outsider, having entered a new world, struggles for inclusion. Instead, it features song in an integrated fashion that gives lyrical expression to the characters' thoughts and feelings. In this way, musical sequences in Yiddish cinema articulate the folk communities both on and off the screen. They rely heavily on the symbolism of the family home, either in the *shtetl* or in the tenement dwellings of the Lower East Side. Home is safe and familiar, and reinforces social cohesion; the world outside is unknown, potentially menacing, and deleterious to familial harmony. In films like *Mayne Yiddishe Mame*, the protagonists are folk who, having arrived in the New World, cling to the traditions and values they have brought with them. They uphold those ritualistic behaviors as a means of thwarting the change that American life represents. In this way, such Yiddish musicals reject *The Jazz Singer*'s example of how the pursuit of individual ambition can be reconciled with the endurance of the collective.

At five reels (approximately fifty-five minutes), *Mayne Yiddishe Mame* is noteworthy for its feature-length running time and its sound synchronization. In the early years of sound cinema, cameraman Joseph Seiden realized that there existed a cultural niche for Yiddish talking pictures. Trained in discerning audience tastes at his father's nickelodeon theater in Greenpoint, Long Island, Seiden used the capital he had accumulated as a cameraman of boxing films to establish the first motion picture sound equipment rental house in New York City. In 1929, he incorporated Judea Pictures and relied on his theater contacts to reach his targeted audience. With films like *Mayne Yiddishe Mame*, Seiden created a unique product that spoke to immigrant concerns. Although no print survives, the film's script and limited promotional and exhibition materials remain to indicate the content and form of this landmark work.[48]

The film opens with a prologue about filial sacrifice. A grandfather recounts to his grandchild the biblical story of Abraham and Isaac. Tested by God, Abraham agreed to kill his only son, Isaac, as a sign of his devotion. Obeying their fathers, the grandfather explains, Abraham followed God's will and Isaac submitted to Abraham. When the child asks what happens if "one does not obey," the grandfather responds, "Then one does not live a full life." The holiest of all God's commandments, he continues, is to "Honor thy father and mother." The child takes this lesson to heart, turns toward the camera, and implores "all the children of Israel, the world over, gather ye and vouch that thy biggest deed should be to honor thy fathers and mothers." He then begins a song about filial devotion that details instances of parental sacrifice for the sake of their children.

The next scene shows immigrants David and Mae Rabinowitz in their home hosting a surprise birthday party for their beloved son Eddie. The children, Helen, Seymour, and Eddie, are gracious to each other and happily assist their parents in making tea and cake for the occasion. The festive day quickly turns tragic, however, when David is killed on his way to exchange his son's birthday gift. With the primary breadwinner gone, Mae must begin work in a sweatshop. Her absence from the home leaves her children vulnerable to the vices of the city. Mrs. Greenzeig, the family's neighbor, admonishes the children, "When your father lived, you worked, and your mother could watch over you. And now your poor mother must work all day in a shop that she may feed you, and you go around having good times." Helen spends time away from the home with a boyfriend who teaches her to smoke and lie to her mother. Seymour gambles his mother's hard-earned money in crap games. And Eddie, the youngest, plays in the streets. Left unsupervised, he soon disappears. Significantly, the film maintains its unity of place inside the tenement. David's death and the misdeeds of the children happen entirely off-screen.

The film flashes forward and shows Eddie, married and with a son, in his new home far from the Lower East Side. He has become a successful lawyer, but has lost touch with his family. An older Mrs. Greenzeig pays him a visit to ask if he will accept a case that charges ungrateful children for abandoning their mother. When she reveals that the abandoned mother is in fact his own, Eddie begs forgiveness. Correcting the wrong that he committed, he returns to Mae. She welcomes him back into her arms, and the film ends with parent and child reunited.[49]

Emphasizing the strength of the family over individual advancement, *Mayne Yiddishe Mame* reveals the immigrant's struggle in the New World. As Mae declares at the beginning of the film, she desires that her children be successful in America, but it is understood that any gains enjoyed by one will be shared by all. The parents seek security and comfort in the New World, but not at the expense of the family. The arc of the film indicates the keen insecurity felt by immigrant parents that their new home will result in the loss of their children. The film's narrative realizes this fear, but then demonstrates how the family can recover in the end.

Mayne Yiddishe Mame also fortifies community by integrating its audience into the world of the film. Seiden produced a trailer that, in keeping with other Yiddish films, was shown in theaters between live acts. Building upon the interactive and intimate relationship between the Yiddish stage and its audience, the trailer features Mae Simon and other members of the film's cast speaking directly to the audience: "My dear friends, I have the honor of announcing to you that in the near future you will be able to see me here in a Yiddish talking and singing picture, made by Judea Films, Inc. and I hope that in this picture I will please you as much as I have tried to during all these years on the stage."[50] Simon positions her role in the "talking and singing picture" as an extension rather than a departure from her work in the theater. With her warm and inviting address to the audience, she lends a personal touch to this new form of entertainment and suggests that the film will serve its audience in the same way that Yiddish plays have done in the past. The film reinforces this connection by using the actors' real names for their onscreen roles.[51]

Following her introduction, the actors who play her children join her in front of the camera and introduce themselves to the audience one by one. Simon tells the audience that though these are not her real children, she "would not refuse having a family like that." She then invites the audience to get acquainted with each of them by seeing the film.

Near the trailer's end, Simon announces that they will enact a scene from the film. They abruptly shift into character. Mae Rabinowitz tells her children that if they do not behave, they will lose her. Seymour responds that she should not talk that way and that he does not want to lose her. Turning to the camera, he breaks character to announce, "I sing now." He begins, "Devoted mothers are all alike, nobody doubts that. . . ." But Simon interrupts him saying, "Enough of singing. If you sing now they will not come to the theater." She addresses the audience, "Therefore I tell you, my friends, 'My Yiddishe Mama' will be shown in this theatre shortly and I know that you will all come to see the picture and hear Seymour Rechtzeit sing 'My Yiddishe Mama.'"[52]

The trailer suggests that the anticipation for *Mayne Yiddishe Mame* was due in large part to its musical sequences, a novelty in the early period of sound cinema. In particular, "My Yiddishe Mama" engages with the celebration of Jewish mothers that had made other mother songs popular among Jewish immigrant audiences. It references an earlier popular song, also called "My Yiddishe Momme" that Sophie Tucker had made famous on the Jewish stage. Projected at the immigrant for whom American and Jewish cultures collided, the song often appeared on the same disc in both Yiddish and English. Musical references to the Jewish mother invoked nostalgia for a time and place left behind and resonated deeply with listeners.[53]

The film extends the emotional appeal of the song by integrating it firmly within its narrative. Seymour first sings in response to his mother's warning about losing her. The children are bickering, a stark contrast to their harmonious state at the opening of the film. Thus admonished, Seymour opines, "I don't want to lose my good, Yiddish mother," and he begins to sing. The scene takes place in their home and provides a moment that reconvenes the family when they are at their most vulnerable. Mae joins in the song, reinforcing her desire for the "happiness of her children" and again warning that only "when the mother dies, they first sense her worth." It is significant that mother and child share this song. Rather than have one character perform for an audience of strangers, *Mayne Yiddishe Mame* demonstrates how music is a communal activity. This integrated musical sequence creates an emotional point of entry for the film's audience in which they are welcomed to share in the narrative moment. The song is reprised at the end of the film when the family has been reunited.

Another instance of musical integration occurs when Mae teaches Eddie a special prayer for his father on the anniversary of his death. The birthday scene and its subsequent anniversaries provide the organizing structure of the film and emphasize how cyclical events render life meaningful for the family. On the first anniversary of Eddie's birthday/David's death, song functions to educate and instruct the younger generation. With a call-and-response pattern, Mae sings the lyric that is repeated by Eddie ("Praise, praise / holy, holy / Is your name, Is your name"). The final chorus ends with Eddie again expressing his devotion to his mother.[54]

The film's integration of musical sequences in which multiple characters join in the song was still quite rare in Hollywood in 1930. After *The Jazz Singer*, the Hollywood studios, including Warner Bros., produced show musicals that featured stories about the making of entertainment. Jolson's subsequent features, such as *The Singing Fool* (1928) and *Say It with Songs* (1929), and MGM's Academy Award–winning *The Broadway Melody* (1929) follow the transformation of singers and dancers from unknowns to marquee headliners. Hollywood did experiment with folk musicals in 1929 with two black-cast films set in the cotton fields of the South. These films justified their musical sequences in non-stage settings with the mutual association of blackness and musicality.[55]

Ethnic cinemas also developed the folk musical, albeit in direct counterpoint to Hollywood's depictions. *Mayne Yiddishe Mame* eschews the stage narrative of *The Jazz Singer* and instead features an immigrant family that struggles to stay together in America. The family sings together as a form of organic communication that ultimately strengthens their bonds in the face of external pressures to break them. Produced for a Jewish immigrant audience, *Mayne Yiddishe Mame* wields the folk musical's form in order to reinforce social relationships, not to adapt them to new cultures and values. Countering the message of *The Jazz Singer, Mayne Yiddishe Mame* foregrounds the immigrant struggle as one that is resolved only when the children return home.[56]

The Jazz Singer adopted the theme of intergenerational conflict in order to portray the immigrant son's confusion about where he belongs. In the Yiddish sound cinema that followed the Warner Bros. release, the films leave no room for doubt that the immigrant belongs with his family and not on the American stage. In the Yiddish musicals produced throughout the 1930s, including *Der Lebediker Yusem* (The Living Orphan, 1937), *Dem Khazns Zundl* (The Cantor's Son, 1937), and *Kol Nidre* (1939), the stage itself becomes symbolic of the loss of tradition and the rupture of family ties.[57] It is telling that the stage to which immigrant Jews are lured in these films is the stage of Second Avenue, the hub of Jewish American entertainment in New York for much of the twentieth century. Such films suggest that any endeavor that privileges individual stardom over the welfare of the family, even if Jewish in orientation, is suspect. This theme is most overtly explored in *Der Lebediker Yusem*, in which the parents of a newborn baby are entertainers on Second Avenue. When the child becomes ill, the father sacrifices his career to tend to his son. The mother, however, makes no such compromise. Her blind ambition divides the family and denies the son the loving comfort of his mother for many years. It is telling that in the film's conclusion, the mother recognizes the error of her ways and decides to become a housewife while the father resumes his career where he left off. In *Kol Nidre*, another woman is led astray by the stage, but this time in the form of an actor who impregnates and leaves her. The cautionary tale communicates that she would have been happier if she had married a rabbi and rejected the lure of the stage entirely. In both films, the archetype of the Jewish mother is imperiled by American entertainment.

Ironically, the success of these films hinged on the merits of the professional performers who starred in them. The fame of singers like Moishe Oysher and the husband-and-wife acting team Leon Liebgold and Lili Liliana contributed to the films' popularity, but also undermined the proscriptive messages they delivered. The performers' real-life stories modeled the individual rise to stardom promised by the American stage, which the films vehemently warn against. Yiddish musical productions of the 1930s therefore encapsulate the diverging cultural currents at work in the Jewish immigrant world: to maintain tradition and family or to climb the ladder of success.

Dem Khazns Zundl is particularly noteworthy for the ways in which it merges the conventions of the show and the folk musical to indicate the cultural divide between home and the world of entertainment. Produced by Joseph Seiden and based on the career of former cantor Moishe Oysher, *Dem Khazns Zundl* places the act of migration, and the itinerant life of the entertainer, at the center of its storyline. In the *shtetl* of Belz, young Schloimele shirks his duties as the cantor's son in order to sing with a troupe of performers who are passing through the village. Even though the performers insist that they are a respectable group of "Jewish entertainers," Schloimele's parents are horrified by his activities. Much like Jakie in *The Jazz Singer*, Schloimele longs for the stage while his parents forbid it. The young boy runs away in the night and joins the entertainers.[58]

The entertainers travel endlessly in search of work. A montage shows superimposed images of the countryside and changes in the season over their wandering horse-drawn wagon. The troupe sings as they go, "Aimlessly we wander, not sure of tomorrow, not sure of today." A migrant's lament, the song expresses weariness and uncertainty. Once they are able to emigrate to the United States, they hope for better times, but the senior actress in the troupe falls sick. At her deathbed, a teary-eyed Schloimele longs for his homeland. He turns to the camera and sings, "I long to go home / To my old home village / I long for a peaceful life back home." It is not until Schloimele is grown and renamed Saul Reichman that we see him perform for an audience. He first proves his talent in a middle-class Jewish nightclub that features Yiddish folk songs. Performing "Mayne Shtetle Belz" (My Little Town Belz), Saul easily wins over the audience. The performance propels him to stardom, setting him adrift once again as he tours the country. When summoned by his parents to the celebration of their golden wedding anniversary, he does not hesitate to leave all behind, including a Jewish American girlfriend, and return home. Again, the film features a series of folk songs that express the joy of family and community life. Schloimele returns to Belz singing "Mayne Shtetle Belz" and arrives at the anniversary party by musically invoking the village: "My dear friends, I am truly happy / I traveled across the sea to see my mama and papa / To honor this dear old couple / May God bless you and them many times over." He then sings the chorus, "Golden Wedding anniversary—Mazel Tov," to which all the villagers respond in unison. The sequence alternates between medium shots of Schloimele with his parents to long shots of the attendees singing in merriment. He commands, "Mama! Papa! Dance! . . . Musicians, play!" and the group responds with a rousing and spontaneous folk dance that communicates the happiness and solidarity of the group. As indicated by this joyous scene, Schloimele finds his true self at home in the *shtetl*. The film ends with his acceptance of his calling as a cantor and his marriage to a childhood sweetheart.

Yiddish musicals such as these use the stage, and profit-driven musical performance, to demonstrate what is lacking in American life. Although Schloimele is not unhappy as an entertainer, that life pales in comparison to the rewards he finds in his village. *Dem Khazns Zundl* deftly interweaves folk numbers with stage-bound sequences in order to reveal a fundamental difference in culture and values. The stage promises prestige and material comforts, but life in the *shtetl* offers the pleasures derived from filial duty and familial love.

Mayne Yiddishe Mame and *Dem Khazns Zundl* developed the folk musical with an emphasis on the experience and effects of migration. Long before Dorothy sang "Over the Rainbow" on her farm in *The Wizard of Oz* (1939), Yiddish films moved musical numbers away from stage settings to places that were relevant to immigrant life. Unlike the Nelson Eddy and Jean-nette MacDonald operettas, these Yiddish musicals set their narratives in modern, realistic locations, such as the villages of Eastern Europe and the tenements of the Lower East Side. Their extensive folk sequences, such as those between mother and son in *Mayne Yiddishe Mame* and the villag-ers in *Dem Khazns Zundl*, reveal the extent to which musical film could be adapted to portray the concerns of immigrants and their collective expres-sions of emotion.

When Henry Ford published his anti-Semitic diatribes against the mov-ies in the 1920s, he identified a concern that many Americans shared at that moment: the breakdown of the family. He observed a moral laxity in Holly-wood films that he feared was undermining a fundamental social institution. As he put it, the Jew "has not as yet been able to understand what American domesticity means." Indicating that home life was unique to the Western world, Ford insisted that it is "an almost unknown quantity to foreigners of the eastern races." While he conceded that "it may not be strictly true that the majority of movie producers do not know the interiors of American homes," he concluded that "there is certainly every indication that they have not caught its spirit, and that their misrepresentation of it is more than a false picture, it is also a most dangerous influence."[59]

What Ford did not realize was that Jewish immigrants were just as committed to preserving the sanctity of the home and its relationships. We see the centrality of evocations of home both in Hollywood, with *The Jazz Singer*, and in Yiddish cinema. In *The Jazz Singer*, the importance of Jakie's bonds to his parents and the proliferation of "mother songs" emphasize this theme. Foregrounding Sara's presence at the Winter Garden Theatre allows the film to demonstrate that the theater can also be a space in which familial relationships can be upheld. By contrast, *Mayne Yiddishe Mame* and many other Yiddish musicals prioritize filial piety as a corrective to way-ward immigrant children who desire fame and fortune. In the early sound era, Jewish immigrants in both Hollywood and Yiddish cinema found ways of strengthening the bonds of the familial collective with their films. *The Jazz Singer* and the Yiddish musicals of the 1930s demonstrate the ways in which American life could be managed and mediated in service to the endurance of the Jewish family.

2

The Musicals of Black Folk

Race Cinema and the
Black-Cast Musicals of 1929

Hearts in Dixie, one of the two black-cast musicals from Hollywood in 1929, begins with an initial address to the audience: "My friends—I trust that in this theatre you are forgetting for a brief hour the cares and troubles of everyday life. If the motion picture which follows helps you to forget and to relax and to enjoy yourselves, it will have served its purpose." The lengthy prologue does not explicitly reference the novelty of an all-black cast, but instead insists on the film's universal relevance and appeal. "Our manners and our civilizations change," it explains, "but our emotions remain the same in all ages—in all countries—in all climes." Even as it highlights stark distinctions between time and space, the prologue nevertheless emphasizes the continuity that binds all peoples: "The same feeling that made our prehistoric father and mother brave the wild beasts of the forest to get food for their baby, makes them today risk their lives to snatch their child from the path of a speeding automobile." Human expressiveness and emotion are unifying forces: "We all laugh when we're happy; we cry when we are sad; we sing—we dance—we play—we work—we love—we're all brothers and sisters in our emotions." The story to follow, the opening insists, is merely a "slice" of this life, "the life of a race of humans."[1]

Along with *Hallelujah!* (1929), which was released by MGM soon afterward, *Hearts in Dixie* represents a pivotal moment in the history of American musical film. Employing sound technology to capture and commodify black voices in song and speech and black bodies in movement, the Hollywood studios inaugurated a new era in musical film production. After

The Jazz Singer (1927), the studios released films about backstage romances between aspiring performers (*The Singing Fool*, 1928; *The Broadway Melody*, 1929). As discussed in chapter 1, Al Jolson's first feature-length film structured its basic thematic duality, the world of jazz and the world of Jewish tradition, along a spatiotemporal axis that divided individual success on the American stage from family and community life in the home/synagogue. Thus incorporating elements of what would be the two dominant strains in musical film production, the show and the folk, *The Jazz Singer* mediated the conflicted world of the immigrant.

By contrast, Hollywood's black-cast films jettisoned the prevailing show musical structure for one that featured folk communities far away from the American stage. This simultaneity of black casts, folk communities, and integrated song and dance is no coincidence. In this instance, the association of black peoples as "folk," possessors of a spontaneous and authentic culture that allowed for collective, emotional expressions of musicality, inspired the first folk musicals in Hollywood. Whereas stories of white persons and ethnically marginal groups like Jews allowed for musical narratives about social mobility via the American stage, narratives about black persons prompted an emphasis on historical continuity and rural settings. Early in the genre's inception, Hollywood distinguished between different kinds of musical films using racial logic.

Hollywood's black-cast musicals were "antebellum idylls," according to Paula J. Massood. They restricted the mobility of their African American subjects at a time when migration was a reality of black life. Limiting them to a pastoral existence in which they seasonally pick and sell cotton, the antebellum idylls denied the black presence in urban spaces of the modern era.[2] As Jacqueline Najuma Stewart has revealed, this onscreen restriction and denial of mobility was one that began in the first decades of film production.[3] These earliest productions, however, prompted discussions among black filmmakers, actors, critics, and audiences that revolved around the question of where black folk belong. The conflation of race, folk, and musical expression in these early folk musicals was therefore linked to the effects of migration on society. This chapter provides an analysis of the production and reception of these black-cast musicals as well as the first feature-length black-produced musical, *Georgia Rose* (1930). The makers of this latter film sought to provide a corrective to the imagery of black life featured in *Hallelujah!* and *Hearts in Dixie*. As part of race cinema's small but significant output in this period, *Georgia Rose* foregrounds the experience of black migration out of the South while preserving black folk life. A comparison of these three films and the reactions of their black audiences reveals the ways in which a discourse of mobility and belonging was at the center of musical film production in the early sound era.

Race Cinema and Migration

Georgia Rose was an outgrowth of the race film production company Lincoln Motion Pictures, which made its first film, *The Realization of a Negro's Ambition*, in 1916. Actor Noble M. Johnson founded Lincoln, his younger brother George would recall, "not so much as a money-making proposition," but just to "make a colored picture."[4] Although he was proud of his starring roles in his company's films, Noble made his living by playing minor parts and doing stunt work for Universal Studios serials, such as *The Last of the Night Riders* (1917) and *Bull's Eye* (1917). They offered significantly lower billing and static roles (he most often played stock Indian or Mexican characters), but the serials provided steady work.

Noble's two film careers eventually came into conflict on Chicago's State Street. In 1919, a theater featured Universal's *Bull's Eye* at the same time that the theater next door was showing one of Johnson's Lincoln films. George Johnson recalls how both theaters had large, colorful posters advertising their films, but the Lincoln poster featured a prominent photograph of Noble as the star. When black moviegoers overwhelmingly chose to see the Lincoln picture, the exhibitor of the Universal film complained to the studio: "Here we are paying five times the amount for the Universal pictures with Noble Johnson in them, and here you let a colored house come next door. They are all leaving our house and going into the colored house to see the same star. We can't do that."[5] Universal responded with an ultimatum: if he wished to remain with the studio, the actor would have to quit his work with the Lincoln Company. He gave his resignation to the Lincoln board of directors soon afterward.

The Chicago incident demonstrates the inequalities that existed in early American film. The Hollywood studios' wealth of labor and capital, including its vertically integrated structure that guaranteed the exhibition of its films, vastly overpowered independent black filmmaking efforts. Nevertheless, black audiences desired films that countered Hollywood's erasures and misrepresentations of black life, which relegated black actors to comical and often servile roles.[6] Noble's celebrity among black audiences indicated that there existed a demand for substantial and nuanced black characters on the screen. Such demand encouraged members of the Lincoln Company to continue to make "race films" for the black community even after the company disbanded in the early 1920s. Their films traveled an exhibition circuit that offered an alternative to the degrading treatment black moviegoers experienced in mainstream theaters, such as separate seating and separate entrances for white and black patrons.[7]

As booking agent for the Lincoln Motion Picture Company, George Johnson counted more than fifty race film companies operating between 1916 and 1924 alone.[8] Of these, the most prolific were the Lincoln Company based in Los Angeles, the Norman Film Manufacturing Company of Jacksonville, Florida, and the Micheaux Book and Motion Picture Company in Chicago. Upstart race film companies often pointed to unequal treatment in mainstream theaters in order to entice potential stockholders among the black middle class. Entrepreneurs like E. C. Brown created their own films and built theaters in which to watch them free from discrimination. An advertisement recounted Brown's personal experience of being denied a seat at the Forrest Theatre in Philadelphia. "Disgusted, disheartened, and embittered," he decided to erect "a place of amusement where his people could have equal accommodation—a place where any respectable person could get what he paid for—a thing that legislation in the North, as well as the South, could not, or rather, would not enact."[9]

Remarkably, these companies were able to accrue enough capital to make their films and then find a means to distribute them. The Lincoln Company's films were made in one week, a relatively luxurious shooting schedule for race films, largely because Lincoln had access to the many resources of the motion picture industry in Los Angeles. The Johnsons rented Crosby Studios in Hollywood and made use of its equipment and props.[10] George described the process of making and distributing the Lincoln Company's films: "Now, we had to make a picture and then we had to close down everything and take the same man we made the picture with and go out and spend money traveling all over the United States, trying to get money enough to make another picture."[11]

He believed that the company's difficulties in distributing "colored pictures" were the result of the type of films Lincoln was making. He suggested that white companies might have facilitated distribution if Lincoln "had started out and made a lot of slapstick, chicken-eating, watermelon Negro pictures like they had been making, and then gradually gone into our type of picture." Biograph's adaptations of Harrison Dickson's "darky" stories in the *Saturday Evening Post* depicted black southerners as lazy, dim-witted, and clownish. Dramas with serious storylines about African American success and struggle, George insisted, "had never been made before" and did not appeal to white audiences.[12]

Setting out "to picture the Negro as he is in his every day life, a human being with human inclination, and one of talent and intellect," the Johnsons produced their first film, *The Realization of a Negro's Ambition*.[13] The Lincoln Company made the bold decision to employ black actors in its films, not white actors in blackface. Just a year earlier, D. W. Griffith's epic *The Birth of a Nation* (1915) had featured white actors in blackface playing morally depraved and sinister former slaves in the Reconstruction South. With its story about a Tuskegee Institute graduate who migrates to California in search of work, *The Realization of a Negro's Ambition* resonated with a critical experience for African Americans. These were comparatively positive images of black life, although they fell far short of critiquing the entrenched racism of American society and culture. Instead, they insisted on the ability of black people to better their social situation by enduring with tenacity and showing themselves to be good Americans.[14]

A number of scholarly studies have emphasized the separateness of race cinema from the mainstream, an argument that certainly has usefulness for understanding the extent of Hollywood's hegemony. But Noble Johnson's conflict with Universal Studios demonstrates how interaction with the mainstream was in many respects unavoidable, especially for the more successful race film actors and companies. In order to secure the exhibition of their films, race film producers strategically collaborated with the movie industry. They created interracial networks of production and distribution by working with white and Jewish Americans who were part of the larger filmmaking community. Some examples include David Starkman, who directed and produced for the Colored Players of Philadelphia, and Frank Schiffman, who functioned as both a financier and an exhibitor for the Micheaux Film Corporation.[15]

The Lincoln Company was no exception. Having met cameraman Harry Gant on the set of the Universal serials, Noble Johnson asked him to join his film company. Gant served as cinematographer and director for many of Lincoln's films. Importantly, he also operated as a liaison to the Hollywood studios. In one instance in 1918, Gant gained access to a closed meeting of Hollywood executives in order to discuss the possible appropriation of government funds to make films for American troops abroad. In his role as representative for the Lincoln Company, Gant insisted that part of the monies should go toward the production of "Negro films for Negro troops." The funds were never appropriated for the project, but the incident demonstrates how the Lincoln Company penetrated and navigated the industry.[16]

The interaction between race films and the dominant industry's output has also received less attention, perhaps because of the relatively few race films that are known to have been directly influenced by mainstream productions. One example is Oscar Micheaux's *Within Our Gates* (1920), a film that effectively transforms the black menace in D. W. Griffith's *The Birth of a Nation* into a lascivious and predatory white landowner. Its overt politics, rare in race films, have prompted Cedric J. Robinson to label *Within Our Gates* "the only Black film of the silent-film era."[17]

In the first decade of sound a number of race films used music and musical numbers in ways that diverged from Hollywood caricature. The first of these was a film now considered lost, *Georgia Rose*.[18] After Noble M. Johnson stopped acting for the company's films, actor Clarence Brooks took the lead and went on to collaborate with Gant long after Lincoln disbanded in the early 1920s. Together, they produced *Georgia Rose* as a response to Hollywood's black-cast musicals of 1929. Although the film did not take on racial discrimination directly, neither did it participate in the narratives of racial uplift that characterized previous race films. Instead, *Georgia Rose* offered a nuanced portrayal of black life in a context that was familiar to many in its audience: the migration out of the South.

Persistent racial violence, a crippling boll weevil infestation in the cotton fields, and the demand for cheap labor in industrializing cities precipitated the massive exodus of nearly two million African Americans to places like New York, Chicago, and California.[19] Northern black newspapers like the *Chicago Defender* assisted the exodus by printing train schedules and listing accommodations and employment opportunities in the North. Neighborhoods like Harlem in New York, Central Avenue in Los Angeles, and the South Side of Chicago offered thriving communities in which numerous social outlets like churchgoing, sports, and the movies could be enjoyed.

Change and transition, and what black writers and critics termed the "New Negro," were dominant and successful themes in migrant literature in this period. Most attention has been paid to the effects of regional black migration out of the South to the North and West. Still, localized movement, from rural areas to urban centers of the South, also affected black society in the early twentieth century. Capturing the migration experience broadly, rural and urban spaces figure prominently and in multivalent ways in forms of migrant culture.

As Farah Jasmine Greene has found in migrant literature, the city simultaneously held the promise of opportunity and presented new threats to the culture that the migrants brought with them. Migrant narratives of this era revolve around these new city spaces and the behaviors of adjustment that take place inside of them. Public spaces like dance halls were at once places where migrants could be "healed, informed, ministered, and entertained" and sites where they might encounter strangers with devious intentions. Nightclubs often appear as dangerous, uniquely urban spaces where gambling and loose women could hinder the migrant's efforts to prosper. With such conventions, migrant narratives attempt to address the complexities of past and present life on the path to securing a better future.[20]

In keeping with the tradition of these narratives, the black-cast musicals of 1929–1930 order their narratives according to a spatial divide. Home and the city represent the pre- and post-migratory act, respectively. They are also spatiotemporal constructs that predetermine the values and behaviors of those who dwell within them.

Hearts in Dixie (1929) and *Hallelujah!* (1929)

The coming of sound did much to alter the "darky" narratives in Hollywood's depictions of African Americans. The studios' interest in using the new technology to feature popular forms of song and dance indicated to some that the moment was auspicious for black performers. "Vitaphone," the amusements editor of the *Chicago Defender* announced in 1929, "is crowding incompetent actors off of the stage and is bringing to the fore those among the Race who possess real talent."[21] The newspaper solicited the perspective of Hollywood directors like Monte Brice, who specialized in "all-Colored comedies" at Pathé Studios. "The Negro belongs in sound pictures just as much as sound belongs in films," declared Brice. The realms of performance in which they do well "have not been needed in silent pictures," he claimed. But "the melody of the Negro voice, his skill in dancing and his mirthful laughter . . . have proven a great thing for the talkies."[22]

Brice subscribed to the common assumption in white America that African Americans had a natural ability for song and dance. Implicit in such a belief was that black people were driven by their natural instincts rather than their intellect. Such associations had deep roots in American society and culture by the time sound cinema developed. In describing the appeal of minstrelsy, Eric Lott shows how nineteenth-century audiences understood African Americans as "creatures of feeling" who were intellectually inferior because they were "in thrall to the emotions." And Jon Cruz has documented the ways in which the historical development and reproduction of spirituals was intertwined with a "budding spirit of ethnosympathy" among whites. This cultural current stemmed from both antimodernism and the study of folklore in the nineteenth and early twentieth centuries and justified the equation of black song with the innate cultural expressiveness of its authors. In Brice's observations about the black voice and its suitability for sound cinema, we can detect these same impulses, but for commercial ends. Therefore, the process by which more African Americans entered into Hollywood sound films was a double-edged sword. On the one hand, they increased their presence on the screen. On the other hand, that presence was the product of and contributed to deeply held assumptions about black primitiveness.[23]

Influential members of the black entertainment community took advantage of these assumptions for their own advancement in the industry. Salem Tutt Whitney, a prominent vaudevillian and contributor to the *Defender*, agreed with arguments about "Negro essentialism" shared by many in middle-class black society. "There is a quality about the Negro's voice that makes it peculiarly adapted to talking pictures," he observed, "it has to do with vibration." Like Brice, Whitney insisted that this quality was a uniquely racial attribute, remarking, "it is a fact that nine out of ten Negroes without any training pass the test, while seven out of ten whites, no matter what their culture or training, fail to make the test." He predicted that African Americans "will figure about 25 per cent in that business if singing and dancing have their say, so it is evident that now, if ever, is our golden opportunity."[24]

The two black-cast musicals of 1929, *Hearts in Dixie* and *Hallelujah!*, capitalized on the notion that African Americans were musical creatures and structured their narratives accordingly. *Hearts in Dixie*, the *Chicago Defender* reported, is "an unpretentious narrative of a little cotton town on the banks of a stream in old Virginia. There are spirituals and camp meeting tunes, there is dancing in the dust and lovemaking and just to be true to the life there, sickness and sorrow creep in and added to this the lonesomeness of the old men when their chillun go northward in search of 'learnin.'"[25] Like the film's prologue, the narrative features an organic community, primitive in its experience of emotion and natural in its cultural expression. Unlike Hollywood's show musicals of the era, *Hearts in Dixie* takes place far from the world of the stage and insists on the intrinsic relationship between its racialized subjects and the land of which they are a part, the rural South.

Central to the narrative of *Hearts in Dixie* is the relationship between grandfather Nappus (Clarence Muse) and his children. When swamp fever takes the life of his granddaughter, Trailia (Mildred Washington), Nappus realizes that folk medicine is inadequate. He sells his possessions so that his only grandson, Chinquapin (Eugene Jackson), can go North, where he might have a chance to prosper. Nappus knows that his small, insular community offers no opportunities for his family, but he cannot bear the thought of being separated from his loved one. A crucial scene comes at the end, when, after being warned about what might happen if his grandson leaves and gets an education, Nappus stands on the banks of the Mississippi and watches a passing steamboat. The pulse of the engine seems to say "Up North." Ultimately, Nappus sacrifices everything and arranges for his grandson to leave. As described by the *Defender*, "He manfully keeps up his surface bravery until the boat pulls out into the stream with his very heart and soul as its cargo, and while the plantation workers sing their plaintive melodies in the distance he sits, broken and alone, as great and noble as any father who ever sacrificed his all for the love of his son."[26] Much like *The Jazz Singer, Hearts in Dixie* tells the melodramatic tale of parental sacrifice for the good of the children and the estrangement that occurs between the generations as a result. By not portraying the grandson's migration North, however, the film restricts its depiction of black life to the South. Unlike *The Jazz Singer*, the emphasis is not on individual success, but on the endurance of the family members who remain behind. For them, life's activities will go on unchanged.

With this final sequence, *Hearts in Dixie* distinguishes itself from *Hallelujah!*. Chinquapin's departure for the North admits to both the reality and the necessity of black migration. While it explains migration as a quest for progress and uplift rather than escape from racial persecution, it nevertheless indicates that change is a part of black life. In this way, *Hearts in Dixie* is the more progressive of the two black-cast musicals of 1929. Since the time of its release, however, it has received less attention because of the relatively high critical esteem for *Hallelujah!*'s director, King Vidor. A southerner, Vidor desired to capture the black South as he remembered it and insisted on shooting on location, a decision that added realism to the depiction of the film's black subjects. But ultimately, *Hallelujah!* denies that social and cultural phenomenon of contemporary African American experience, the Great Migration.

Like *Hearts in Dixie, Hallelujah!* privileges the black home of the rural South. Eva Jessye, an African American composer and choral director who took part in the film, described the narrative trajectory in the black press. It begins with an image of "sweet security" of the son's home and then follows him on his wayward journey, only to return him to "the old home and those most dear" at the end.[27] *Hearts in Dixie* admits to the possibility of black success in the North by sending the grandson away at the end, a necessary, but painful act for the family left behind. *Hallelujah!*, by contrast, disavows the merits of migration outright and instead reaffirms the rightful place of its subjects in the rural South.

The first image that Jessye describes was shot on location in the South. Wafting over the opening credits and a montage of black laborers in the cotton fields, black spirituals appear to arise organically from the land. The film follows the montage of actual laborers with a shot of the cast of characters, a family composed of Mammy (Fanny Belle DeKnight), Pappy (Harry Gray), Zeke (Daniel L. Haynes), Spunk (Everett McGarrity), three smaller children, and their adopted sister, Missy Rose (Victoria Spivey). When their work is finished, they leisurely make their way back to the cabin. Zeke sings a phrase, "Oh, Cotton," and the family repeats it. Together, they mark the ending of the day with enjoying a meal, reading the Bible, and playing the banjo. Pappy conducts an impromptu marriage ceremony for a neighboring family, after which everyone celebrates with more festivities. Later that night, Mammy takes her usual place in the rocking chair and sings the smaller children to sleep.

The songs and dances in this opening sequence mark the phases of the day and indicate the continuity of life. The most natural expressions of black folk, the film suggests, emerge from the relationship to place. The film uses music to reveal how kinship is fostered by a shared commitment to the land and nature. Spirituals and banjo music are spontaneous evocations of their daily activities, labor and rest, that emanate from the land. In this way, the film establishes the cyclical nature of existence and the inherent stability of this world.

The film offers this image of domestic harmony only to rupture it. When Zeke and Spunk take the family's cotton to a nearby mill town, they embark on a localized migration from country to city. In this sequence, the two sons encounter a world governed not by devotion to family and the land, but by a market economy that promises material goods and bodily pleasure. After getting paid, Zeke comes upon a shady group of characters shooting craps and is lured into a nightclub. As the camera pans this dark space, it reveals men and women gambling, drinking, and smoking. Opposed to the quiet tranquility of Zeke's home, this space is loud with raised voices and syncopated jazz music. Chick (Nina Mae McKinney), an attractive and wily young woman dressed in flapper style, schemes with her boyfriend, Hot Shot (William Fountaine), to rob Zeke of his money. When Zeke realizes he has fallen for their ploy, he scuffles with Hot Shot and mistakenly shoots Spunk rather than his target. Spunk dies as a result of the wound, and Zeke falls into despair.

Though not set in the North, this scene references the urban experience of the migrant, with its signs of the vices of modern life, such as crap shooting, bars, and loose women. The people in the club are strangers who befriend and betray Zeke, a gullible man of the country. He is easily seduced by Chick's suggestive performance. As she writhes and contorts her body, the film cross-cuts to the faces of Zeke and others in the audience who cheer her on. Zeke has entered a space wherein the music does not arise organically from the spirit of the land; rather, it contributes to the desire for profit and hedonistic pleasure.

This urban space precipitates Zeke's downfall. Out of repentance for Spunk's death, Zeke seeks out religion and becomes a preacher. At a camp revival meeting, he reunites with Chick, who seduces him once again. She is soon dissatisfied by the simple life that he offers her and arranges to run away with Hot Shot. Her escape leads to death, however, when she is injured in her getaway. Zeke takes revenge on Hot Shot by strangling him in the swamp. The film then flashes forward and shows Zeke working in a prison camp. After serving his time, he is able to return home. In a montage sequence that charts his journey, Zeke sings "Goin' home, goin' home, I'm a goin' home" as he crosses a river on a barge, rides a train, and walks through fields. He comes upon his family in the cotton fields and they heartily welcome him back into the fold. Zeke realizes that what he most truly desires is to be surrounded by his brethren and to marry his childhood sweetheart, Missy Rose. The film ends as it started, with the family united and taking their cotton to the cabin to the musical accompaniment of black voices singing "Goin' Home."

As *Hearts in Dixie*'s prologue communicates, these films about black life were first and foremost produced for the entertainment of Hollywood's mainstream audience. Similar to the commodification of black spirituals, black-cast musicals were profit-oriented vehicles that met the demand for idealized images of a simpler time. Romanticism, Jon Cruz reminds us, is not restricted to a moment in the past. It serves as a "countersensibility to a modernity that constantly threatens increasingly fragile notions of identity and authenticity." Ministering to white needs and desires, the black-cast musicals of 1929 projected bucolic visions of black people far away from the cities and relegated to a rural existence in the South.[28]

Romantic notions of black life were not confined to white audiences. They also informed the thoughts and activities of black intellectuals, critics, filmmakers, and actors. As Cruz posits, even W.E.B. Du Bois believed in the "primitive folk" sensibility of the slave. The desire to see "black folk"

6. Zeke reunites with his family. *Hallelujah!* copyright 1929 by MGM.

projected with authenticity on the screen was something that black writers and critics applauded and encouraged. This impulse accounts for the favorable reactions of many in the black community to Hollywood's folk musicals of 1929.

Critics Alain Locke and Sterling Brown published an essay about the two films in 1930. Locke and Brown were supportive of these productions, understanding sound cinema as a propitious moment and lauding the musical contributions of the black actors. According to Anna Everett, these writers and many others in the black press were "accommodationist" in their assessment of Hollywood's black-cast productions and advanced arguments that were as essentialist as those made by white critics. She concedes that Locke and Brown were nevertheless in step with the majority of black audiences who applauded the films. The essentializing arguments made by these and other writers, both black and white, are indeed problematic for the ways in which they further entrenched notions of the presumed inferiority of black peoples. They are also indicative of the powerful seduction of the folk, an invention of romanticism that withstood the effects of modernity. In the folk, these first folk musicals suggested, could be found an authenticity and spontaneity that was lacking in contemporary society.[29]

Locke and Brown identified the moments in both films that exhibited "true folk values." The expression of these values, they asserted, was made possible by the use of "real flesh and blood Negroes evoking a spontaneous and genuine human interest." Previous films, including the multiple adaptations of *Uncle Tom's Cabin*, featured caricatured depictions of black characters with white actors in blackface. The new musical productions, the writers pointed out, include black actors on the screen and therefore have the potential to provide "spiritual revelations of some fundamentals of Negro folk character." Actors Stepin Fetchit, Clarence Muse, and Eugene Jackson offer "spontaneity, naturalness, and unself-conscious charm," qualities that allow for a spectrum of representations, from humor to pathos. In particular, the writers commented, Fetchit is a "vital projection of the folk manner, a real child of the folk spirit." In this assessment, the authors were in agreement with others in the black press who admired how Fetchit "'ad libbed' the conversation for the scene with the girl in the road whose bundle he evaded carrying in 'Hearts in Dixie.'" The "folk," as these authors understood it, is a representation of black spontaneity in the hands of black actors, the depiction of a cross-section of characters and emotions, and the sense of a shared identity rooted in a common experience.[30]

The authors drew a sharp distinction between *Hearts in Dixie*, which they understood to be an authentic expression of the folk, and *Hallelujah!*, which they accused of relying on "the usual claptrap," a "potpourri" of "Berlin's mammy songs and the spirituals." They provided further explanation of what they meant by "folk" in their criticism of *Hallelujah!*'s "trick plotting" narrative, which is "hardly folk but Hollywood": "the hero, lured by the vamp, who deserts him for the roué, expiates and returns chastened to the waiting girl, 'at the end of the road.'" Although encounters with sirens and villains are not completely outside of "a folk situation," the critics found that this plot in particular "smacks too much of Hollywood." By contrast, the characters Missy Rose and Mammy, types rooted in the countryside, "identify themselves with folk material."[31]

Locke and Brown assigned spatial and musical qualities to the folk, which, they insisted, are located in the spirituals sung against a rural backdrop. The "mammy songs" that Chick sings in the nightclub are decidedly not folk, but rather Hollywood constructions of black life. The writers took particular offense at the inclusion of an Irving Berlin song, "The End of the Road," which has "no connections with any point farther south than the lower East Side." In these comments, we see the writers' discomfort with the ways in which black song and representation have been commodified by the dominant culture and passed off as authentic. *Hearts in Dixie* has a truer folk sensibility because it takes place entirely in the South, with only a final allusion to the North. *Hallelujah!*, on the other hand, falsifies its depictions of black life by moving from country to city (with its corruption of black culture) and back again.

Nevertheless, the writers insisted that the black actors' voices invest even *Hallelujah!*'s "The End of the Road" with the folk spirit. "Here are mellow, full voices, spontaneous and enthusiastic," they wrote approvingly. The musical productions allowed for black song to be married to its source, the black body. The "Negro voice achieves an artistic triumph and becomes a more purely Negro thing, for once—," they asserted, "a true peasant gem in a genuine setting." The identification of black song with black bodies suggested a relatively authentic representation of black life for the authors. They highlighted this positive cinematic development to make the claim that "great things" might come in the future from those familiar with the "Negro folk genius."[32]

The essay reveals the folk as a contested terrain of cultural representation in early musical film production. The authors make the political argument that the folk has the ability to minister to modern audiences who desire something genuine. A true "folk spirit" can be achieved, however, only by casting black actors to give it voice. Locke and Brown made this political statement as a means of wresting control of the cinematic black image. Central to their argument was the significance of black song as emanating from its source, a development made possible by the creation of the musical film.

While critics like Locke and Brown grappled with the significance of folk depictions in the two films, the actors and musicians offered their own interpretations in the pages of the black press in anticipation of the films' release. Although they expressed frustration at not being treated the same as white actors, they nevertheless asserted a profound and steadfast commitment to assuring the success of these black-cast ventures. Above all, they saw the production of such films as a chance to alter the image of black persons in film. Actor Clarence Muse is a case in point. His opportunity to play Nappus in *Hearts in Dixie* came after a long career as an actor on the New York stage and as a producer of stage shows in Chicago. After completing production of the film, Muse wrote that audiences "who have been taught to know the Negro as a conventional type of fear and ignorance, with immoral tendencies and criminal proclivities, would be keenly surprised to know that there is a beautiful, impressive and creative genius among the Black folks of America that would inspire the most ordinary or highly trained American mind to lofty heights or idealistic dreams." Muse attempted to reconcile the portrayal of southern, rural black life in *Hearts in Dixie* with the "respected, thinking, ambitious modern Afro-American" of the city. He asserted that the film is accurate in its representation of "an element or phase," not the whole of black life. Muse's careful distinction of his character as "an old man" and "not an Uncle Tom" indicates a certain defensiveness on the actor's part for the ways in which his role could be interpreted.[33]

Where Locke and Brown emphasized the naturalness and spontaneity of the performances, the actors themselves focused on their labor. One of the most vocal spokespersons for *Hallelujah!* was Eva Jessye, King Vidor's musical director and conductor of the Dixie Jubilee Singers, who were hired for the film. Jessye was the first African American to be employed as musical director by a major studio.[34] Not only did she have the responsibility of composing and arranging for *Hallelujah!*, but she also coached the singers and conducted all rehearsals. Like Muse, Jessye emphasized the universal quality of the story, observing that "it is a faithful reproduction of a phase of American home life which will appeal to the public and strike a tender chord in the breast of all who witness it."[35]

On the other hand, Jessye did not deny the racial politics involved in making the film. In a four-part editorial for the *Baltimore Afro-American* called "The Truth About *Hallelujah!*," she revealed the subtle and overt forms of racism that she witnessed on the film's set. Salaries of the cast, including her own, were one-fifth to one-tenth of the standard. With "the plea that the picture was a costly experiment, appeals to their race pride and the promise of much publicity," MGM studio executives were able to secure the cast with one lump sum. Other grievances included separate lunches for the white and black crews and being asked to work extra hours with no pay.[36]

Nevertheless, according to Jessye, the entire cast recognized what the success of *Hallelujah!* could mean for the black actor in Hollywood. The high stakes of their presence in the studio production led them to bypass certain objectionable elements in the film's script. Jessye called attention to King Vidor's white, southern background (his idea for *Hallelujah!* came from his boyhood memories) and his free use of the term "nigger" on the set. Cast members did not feel they could criticize him on this issue. Conscious that their behavior on and off the set was being closely scrutinized by Hollywood personnel, the cast was "as sensitive as high strung racers shying at shadows, sensing even in their inexperience where certain sequences would lead and what conclusions would be drawn by the waiting and suspicious public."[37]

It is clear that the actors in *Hallelujah!* were aware of the full import of their characterizations on the screen and recognized how the film could be manipulated. Jessye documented how they actively determined the content and performance of certain scenes. "There were times when Vidor was at a standstill," she wrote, "and the proper dialogue was hard to conceive." It was then that "the ingenuity of the actors put in little touches . . . Negro mannerisms, phrases that could be written by no white man." Jessye herself was instrumental in the musical sequences, orchestrating hundreds of extras for the camp meeting and baptism scene. Vidor would later describe the success of these takes as the result of the "natural" expressiveness of the "Negro as an actor." In fact, Jessye had carefully planned and rehearsed the scene on her own.[38]

In some cases, the actors were able to resist the use of overtly objectionable material. William Fountaine, who played the villain of the picture, was rehearsing the dialogue for one of his scenes in the studio projection booth when a line prompt appeared: "A big coon like you ought to be carrying dar donkey 'stid a ridin' him." Jessye recalled, "When this line flashed on the screen, Fountaine, who had been enjoying [the movie] hugely up to that point, yelled out in excited protest, 'O, my God! You don't mean for me to say that, I know. Not me. Why, man, I wouldn't dare go back to Harlem.'"[39] In the end, the producers did not include those exact words in the final film. Fountaine's reaction reveals the cast's concern with how the black community would receive the film.

The actors' experience also conveys the wide disparity between contemporary black life in Harlem and the southern community depicted on the screen. The difference became apparent while shooting on location in Memphis. Jessye recalled that when "scenes were taken on the wharf and public ferries many mouths gaped with amazement at the modish attire of the ladies of the cast, who adopted snappy trench coats, oxfords or boots and the Dobbs sport felt." Some local onlookers took great offense at the cast's appearance and behavior and even interrupted the shooting by yelling racial slurs.[40]

For the cast, the changes wrought by mass migration were starkly apparent. For some, filming on location in the South was an entirely new experience. Most, like Jessye, came as outsiders. She recounted, "We got a great kick out of crossing the river in the picturesque ferry boats and drank in the quaint sights of the cabins, cotton fields and Southern life thirstily; for it is one thing to hear about the South and still another thing to see and feel it." Although "comparatively all the cast was Southern born they had spent most of their lives up North and it was like returning to the scenes of one's distant childhood—to scenes that are strange, and stir in the memory like a dream." For those who "had never seen cotton grow," she conjectured, "it must have been an old canvas come to life."[41]

The discrepancy between the actual experiences of *Hallelujah!*'s cast and the film's idealized southern narrative was apparent to the actors and to their black audience. The inherent contradiction between reality and fiction came to a head at the film's opening in New York. Exhibitor Frank Schiffman arranged to have *Hallelujah!* premiere at his Lafayette Theatre in Harlem simultaneously with its opening on Broadway.[42] No other film had ever had a double premiere in New York. Schiffman, a long-time owner of Harlem theaters, thought that he could capitalize on the black community's interest in the picture by offering them their own premiere, complete with a red carpet and klieg lights. Many in the Harlem community took offense, however, declaring that it was an attempt to keep "our people from mingling with the whites on Broadway." Protest took various forms, including the picketing of the film's opening.[43]

Others in Harlem used the premiere to showcase the progress and achievements of black people since the end of slavery. Oscar DePriest, the newly elected African American congressman from Illinois, attended the event, as did tap dancer Bill "Bojangles" Robinson, who served as master of ceremonies. After the screening, Robinson introduced members of the cast and welcomed them back home after their time spent in Hollywood and the South. Congressman DePriest addressed the crowd: "We are standing on the threshold of civil and cultural emancipation in America." "Tonight," he declared, "we have seen how far our race has progressed culturally and artistically since the Emancipation Proclamation."[44] Harlem's community took advantage of the opening to foreground black achievements that were obscured by the film's narrative.

Exhibitors in the South rejected the film outright, largely because of the ways in which it indirectly indicated black advancement. At a 1929 convention of the Southeastern Exhibitors, held in Georgia, theater owners voted to "'restrict or entirely forgo' the making of pictures exploiting the Colored race." As reported in the *Chicago Defender*, this meeting posed potentially grave consequences for black-cast films then in preproduction.[45] The harsh reaction perplexed black critics, who recognized that the film "shows Race folk doing things that are generally conceded to be indigenous to them; such as picking cotton, singing spirituals, living in cabins, shooting craps, seeking God in churches with much loud shouting." *Hallelujah!* does not depict "some of the real activities of the Race, such as conducting banks, driving expensive motors, wearing evening dress at swanky parties, or going to college." This reviewer concluded that the white southern exhibitor merely objected to showing films in which black actors have substantial roles. Accepting Hollywood's black-cast musicals also required white southerners to acknowledge the existence of modern black life, of which *Hearts in Dixie* and *Hallelujah!* were an intrinsic part.[46]

Georgia Rose (1930)

Race film producers capitalized on the coming of sound to feature black voices. In 1930, Harry Gant collaborated with former Lincoln Motion Picture Company actors Clarence Brooks and Webb King to make *Georgia Rose* under a new company, Aristo Films.[47] An "all-Talkie of Southern

Migration," the film begins with the journey of Reverend Hoskins and his two children, Rose and Ezra, from Covington, Georgia. Singing hymns as they travel, such as "Will There Be Any Stars in My Crown," they reaffirm their faith in God as they venture to the North. The family's goal is to reach Chicago, but along the way they encounter Mrs. Barnett, an elderly woman who owns a farm on the outskirts of the city. Believing that they would "be better off working on a farm than going to a big city," the parson accepts Mrs. Barnett's offer to work for her as a tenant. Rose initially objects, "Oh, Daddy, who wants to come all the way from Georgia up here just to work on a farm?" The parson accepts the arrangement despite Rose's desire for the excitement of the city.[48]

The narrative space of *Georgia Rose* moves between the country and the city, as shown by two diagonally positioned shots on a lobby card from the film. The shot in the upper left-hand corner shows Rose and Mrs. Barnett's educated son Ralph dressed for a night in the city. In the lower right-hand image, by contrast, farm workers relax on Mrs. Barnett's porch. In between the two images is a series of portraits of the various characters. Shots from the film that appeared in the black press also emphasize this country/city dichotomy by indicating the innocence of life on Mrs. Barnett's farm and the titillation offered by the urban nightclub.[49]

The narrative of *Georgia Rose* highlights these distinctions. It portrays country life as socially harmonious. Mrs. Barnett, the parson, and their children live in a contented state of tranquility. The family members gather around the organ to sing hymns, collectively demonstrating their connection to each other and their faith in God. These activities appear as a matter of routine and are natural like the world around them.

In the city, however, Ralph and his friend Bob patronize cabarets where they encounter loose women, jazz, gambling, and liquor. Their activities are self-indulgent and pleasure-oriented rather than productive.

Nevertheless, Ralph and Bob traverse both the city and the country. They "come down" from the city to visit Mrs. Barnett, and there they encounter Rose, whose voice captivates both of them. Ralph falls in love with her and desires to make her his wife. In the country, he sings love songs to her in appreciation of her beauty and innocence: "You're just a rosebud, like a rosy little flower, that came to me from a garden down in Georgia." Rose returns his love, and the two seem destined for a happy life together.

7. *Georgia Rose* copyright 1930 by Aristo Films. Department of Special Collections, Charles E. Young Research Library, UCLA.

Bob has different plans. He wants to lure her to the city, put her in a cabaret act, and be her manager. Offering her this option, Bob assuages her concerns about leaving her family: "After you have become famous they will all be proud of you." He urges her to focus on her own future and happiness and promises money and clothes if she comes to the city. She consents and becomes the next star of a cabaret in Chicago, appearing on stage as "Miss Georgia Rose of New York," a commodified version of her true folk self. In sharp contrast to the spontaneous and organic hymn singing that she enjoys at home, her act for the cabaret is calculated work. She promises Bob that she will "work hard" at learning her song, and the film shows her diligently practicing the number in rehearsals.

On her opening night, Ralph appears at the cabaret with the intention of taking her home. He witnesses her transformation into a blues singer who performs "Come Back to Your Little Mama" provocatively for an audience of strangers. Rose is no longer an innocent young girl, but a worldly, sexualized being. She sings, "I've made up my mind, since you been away, I'll be good and kind if you come and stay." After the number, Ralph orders, "Put your clothes on that you come from the farm in. I'm going to take you home."

Rose initially resists Ralph's efforts, but ultimately agrees to return home, despite her fear that she will no longer be welcome on the farm. When Ralph reveals that he still wishes to marry her, the parson forgives her and expresses his joy by singing the title song, "Georgia Rose." With his daughter returned to the fold, the parson celebrates their union of North and South: "Northern girls may be fairer, but no sweeter flower grows, than my little Georgia Rose."[50]

Unlike the common migration narrative that moves from the South to the North, *Georgia Rose* settles its characters in the space between those two extremes. In publicity for the film, Gant located Mrs. Barnett's farm in Illinois or Indiana.[51] Although leaving the South is necessary, the film suggests, black migrants need not commit themselves to the city, where the lure of money and success breaks down family bonds. In the country outside of the northern city can be found a virtuous existence that reinforces rather than imperils kin relations. The film demonstrates these differences through the character of Rose, who finds joy in filial devotion while on the farm, but seeks self-advancement in the city. Engaging with the form of the show musical, wherein individual success is linked with show business, *Georgia Rose* conveys how the American city fosters values that are opposed to family and community. Restoring Rose to the farm also restores social harmony.

As one review put it, *Georgia Rose* "is a story epic of the modern Negro." "Devoid of the usual racial propaganda," the film "unravels a story beautiful in its simplicity." Unlike *Hearts in Dixie* and *Hallelujah!*, which are set in an undetermined pastoral past, *Georgia Rose* takes place in the contemporary moment. It engages with the "exodus of southern Negroes migrating north." For race film audiences, migration and its effects were a daily reality. *Georgia Rose* shows how the "simple folks of everyday life" struggle to sustain their community and cultural values, an important source of conflict in these musical films of family life and migration.[52]

The *Baltimore Afro-American* praised *Georgia Rose* as "by far the best effort put forth by Negroe [*sic*] producers to date."[53] Advertised as "100% Talkie," *Georgia Rose* featured an "all star Negro cast" drawn from both stage and screen. The professional backgrounds of the actors represent the full spectrum of black performance. Irene Wilson (Rose) was the only newcomer to the cast. Brooks (Ralph) was a veteran of both race cinema and Hollywood films. Evelyn Preer (Grace) had been a leading actor for the Lafayette Players, the prominent black theater in Harlem.[54] Dora Dean Johnson (Mary Barnett) had been part of the dance team Dean and Johnson that, according to the *Chicago Defender*, "introduced the 'cakewalk' to the nobility of Europe." Edward Thompson (Bob) had also been featured in lead roles for the Lafayette Players and had appeared in comedies along with costars Roberta Hyson (Helen) and Spencer Williams (Ezra). Bringing actors together from both black and white productions, dramatic and comedic forms of entertainment, *Georgia Rose* promised to be of "tremendous interest" for critics and audiences.[55]

The premiere at the 1,960-seat Lincoln Theatre on Central Avenue in Los Angeles was a much-anticipated event. The *California Eagle* reported that "capacity crowds" were expected on opening night and that preparations were being made for the "biggest crowd in the history of the Lincoln theatre." The theater was located in the black neighborhood of the downtown area and served as the new home for the Lafayette Players' productions. Live acts supplemented the premiere, including the King Minor's Minstrels and several "clever and captivating acts of vaudeville."[56]

Despite the fanfare that surrounded its opening, *Georgia Rose* suffered the fate of many race films. The producers lacked the budget and distribution network to ensure a successful theatrical run. Brooks worked to promote the film by making personal appearances in theaters in Chicago, Washington, DC, and cities throughout the South. Following his travels, the black press announced that Aristo Films would soon release another all-talking picture, but it never materialized.[57]

The film also suffered from some negative press. In response to a review that criticized both the narrative and its execution, Harry Gant explained that he and Clarence Brooks made the film "primarily and principally for colored people." Dismissing the representations of black life in *Hearts in Dixie* and *Hallelujah!*, Gant insisted that he showed "the Negro as he really is in all walks of life." Gant and Brooks rejected the stereotypical images of the "Negro singing spirituals, eating

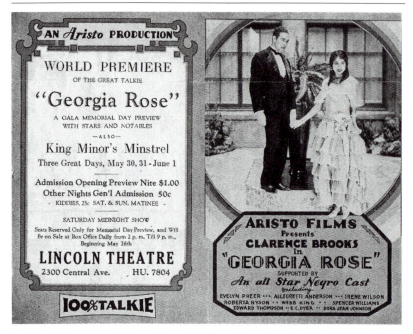

8. *Georgia Rose* copyright 1930 by Aristo Films. Department of Special Collections, Charles E. Young Research Library, UCLA.

watermelon and shooting craps," which, he explained, would not "please colored audiences." Gant reminded critics that his company had to make *Georgia Rose* for "much less money than the big white companies . . . on account of the limited number of theaters that cater to colored trade." Nevertheless, *Georgia Rose* offered black moviegoers a rare image of modern black life, one that emphasized the migration experience and its consequences.[58]

Georgia Rose reveals how the folk musical also developed on the margins of Hollywood in the early sound era. Hollywood's black-cast musicals of 1929 had firmly linked black life with a primitive, rural past. Beginning with the act of migration, *Georgia Rose* countered Hollywood's narrative and provided an alternate vision for black audiences. The film admits to the black presence in northern cities, but also warns against the loss of cultural values that can come with urban living. Alternating between folk and show sequences, the film negotiates the spaces of black life from the countryside, where music is a form of collective expression, to the city, where song is commodified for self-advancement. Significantly, the show musical sequence serves as a cautionary tale that does not send the family packing back to the South but, rather, requires that they seek an alternate space to call home.

Georgia Rose was not the only race film to offer a corrective to Hollywood's black-cast musicals. Themes of modern black life, including migration, performance, and intergenerational relationships, informed a number of productions, from Oscar Micheaux's early sound films, *The Exile* (1931) and *Darktown Revue* (1931), to the later Clarence Muse vehicles, *Spirit of Youth* (1938) and *Broken Strings* (1940). In particular, Micheaux's films explore the complex dynamics of black life in the country and the city and the challenges posed to the migrant in both places. *The Exile*, his first feature-length sound film, and *Darktown Revue*, a non-narrative musical film short, employ musical sequences in innovative ways. As J. Ronald Green has argued, nightclub numbers and comedic skits serve a dual purpose in these films. On the one hand, they met the expectations of an audience that enjoyed such forms of entertainment. On the other hand, these entertainment forms inserted critical commentary on post-migration black life in the modern city.[59]

Perhaps because of the folk's association with caricature, Micheaux never produced a folk musical. Like *Georgia Rose*, however, *The Exile* does complicate the material spaces of the folk musical, the country and the city, and comment on the relative merits and shortcomings of each for the black migrant. Jean Baptiste is an educated middle-class city dweller who rejects life with Edith, a "queen of the underworld," for a ranch and the love of a country girl in South Dakota. Even though Micheaux associates the cabaret dances with the underworld, he shows Baptiste enjoying them, thus demonstrating that not all of city life is detrimental. Baptiste's character is similar to Ralph's in *Georgia Rose*. They are sophisticated and educated men who enjoy the pleasures of urban life without being corrupted by the city's negative forces. Their choice to settle in the country is a comment on the potential of western farms rather than a rejection of the city as a viable locale for modern black life. In both films, their writer/directors suggest, a happy amalgamation of cultures occurs when the urbane sophisticate unites with the virtuous country girl. The folk and the modern converge and serve as a re-articulation of the country/city dichotomy promoted by Hollywood vehicles.[60]

The folk musical, as it was first developed in 1929, combined a racialized romanticism with sound technology to relocate the musical film to the rural South and effectively restrict the mobility of black people. Beginning with *Hearts in Dixie* and *Hallelujah!*, the Hollywood folk musical delineated what groups of people belong where in society. These two films negate the act of migration for African Americans by not showing it, as in the former, or by cautioning against it, as in the latter. The films were significant for their use of all-black casts and received critical assessments from black intellectuals as well as the black actors who took part in them. Commentators used these first folk musicals to negotiate the cultural politics of the folk, black representation, and black authorship on the screen. The observations with which the actors qualified their involvement reveal the extent to which the musicals were not just entertainment, but sites of cultural struggle. In the end, *Hearts in Dixie* and *Hallelujah!* sought to restrict black migration while the circumstances of their production and reception highlighted its existence.

Georgia Rose provided a corrective by traversing the same spatiotemporal axis of the earlier two films, but with significant revisions. First and foremost, *Georgia Rose* treats migration as a reality of black life directly, rather than allegorically. The film shows how migration is necessary, beginning as it does with Rose and her father on the move, but ultimately assuages audience concern with the preservation of the family structure. And finally, it negotiates rural and urban space in a nuanced fashion, depicting both positive and negative character types in each. Rose's union with Ralph effectively concludes the family's migration out of the South and Ralph's rejuvenation through an association with a traditional woman from the country.

Despite the successes of *Hearts in Dixie* and *Hallelujah!*, later black-cast musicals were few and far between.[61] The decade was instead dominated by the show musical in Hollywood, a cycle of films that featured white protagonists in backstage narratives and onstage performance sequences. Depression-weary audiences could find solace in these stories of unknowns who move up the socioeconomic ladder in American society.

In race cinema, *Georgia Rose*'s auspicious foray into black-produced sound film was a singular achievement for Aristo Films. Sound technology required a level of capital investment that most race film producers could not afford. Indeed, as many scholars have noted, the coming of sound did much to hinder independent black filmmaking in the 1930s, making the production of *Georgia Rose* all the more remarkable.[62]

3

"Not a Musical in Any
Sense of the Word"

Allá en el Rancho Grande Crosses the Border

As a successful exhibitor of Spanish-language films in Los Angeles, Francisco Fouce reported regularly on the status of Mexican film in the local press. On January 1, 1938, he proudly declared that the Mexican film industry was producing more feature films of "Class A designation than ever before in the cinema history of that country." But he saw a looming threat to the industry: "The unfortunate thing, is that Hollywood continues to swallow up the Mexican stars just as rapidly as they score successes in their native land."[1]

Hollywood's focus on Mexican talent was in large part due to the overwhelming popularity of Mexico's first musical film, *Allá en el Rancho Grande* (Over on the Big Ranch, 1936), starring the Mexican actor and singer Tito Guízar.[2] The story about a young *ranchero* (ranch hand) who grows up to become ranch foreman and marry his childhood sweetheart presented a variety of folk entertainments interwoven with symbolic imagery of *charros* (Mexican equestrians) and *rancheras* (ranch songs). It initiated the *comedia ranchera* (ranch musical comedy) genre of Mexican cinema's "golden age" and inspired dozens of imitations over subsequent decades. Nearly half of the films produced in Mexico between 1937 and 1948 followed this formula.[3]

Allá en el Rancho Grande originated as a reaction to the failure of the Mexican Revolution. Fernando de Fuentes, the film's director, was highly critical of the revolution's outcome and its limited reforms.[4] In contrast, he offered scenes of a contemporary Mexico left untouched by revolution and portrayed the feudal hacienda system as one that benefited all classes of society.

Despite its conservative message rooted in national politics, *Allá en el Rancho Grande* resonated with audiences outside of Mexico. As Ana M. López contends, "The nostalgia for an imaginary bucolic past where macho pride and true love always prevailed . . . also echoed throughout other Latin American countries where, despite different political histories, the present was burdened by the legacies of colonization and the frustrations of independence."[5] For ethnic Mexicans living and working in the United States, *Allá en el Rancho Grande* represented the home left behind.[6] It fostered feelings of nostalgia and longing for *nuestro México* (our Mexico). The success of the *comedia ranchera*, and of *Allá en el Rancho Grande* in particular, was due to its ability to attenuate the harsh effects of migration and the pressures of a transnational existence. The genre did so with a narrative that featured timeless rural settings and communities that share in the collective expression of folk song and dance.

Allá en el Rancho Grande crossed the U.S.-Mexico border with ease. The enthusiastic response of Mexican audiences in the United States reveals the extent to which the exhibition of Mexican cinema was economically viable in the mid-1930s, well before the U.S. government and the Hollywood studios actively supported and collaborated with the Mexican film industry during World War II.[7] The film's formal structure, exhibition, and reception demonstrate how *Allá en el Rancho Grande* resonated with the migrant experience in specific ways. Most importantly, the film fostered a sense of cultural pride and social membership among Mexicans living outside of Mexico through its symbolic imagery and the intimate, communal way in which musical sequences were filmed.

The film also migrated to Hollywood. Anticipating the spate of folk musicals that Hollywood produced in the 1940s and 1950s, *Allá en el Rancho Grande* introduced storylines about folkways, family, and home to the accompaniment of integrated musical numbers. Desirous of increasing box office sales in Latin America, Paramount Studios gave Guízar a contract soon after the Mexican film's release. He starred in numerous English- and Spanish-language productions for the studio in the late 1930s. These films reveal the extent to which Hollywood revised the musical genre with *Rancho Grande*'s folk sensibility in mind. In *Tropic Holiday* (1938), an

English-language production that features Guízar as a lovelorn *charro*, Paramount producers used folk qualities to amend the image of "Latins" on the screen. And in *Papa soltero* (Bachelor Father, 1939), a Spanish-language film for the studio, Guízar and his collaborators strategically placed folk sequences in the narrative in order to present a nuanced interpretation of Mexican migration. As a result of *Allá en el Rancho Grande*'s success and influence, the musical genre began to shift from one that focused on the world of American entertainment to one that celebrated the resilience of folk communities.

Allá en el Rancho Grande found a receptive and well-established audience in the United States. Approximately 1–1.5 million Mexicans entered the country between 1890 and 1929.[8] This mobile population lived transnational lives, crisscrossing the border for work and family. Most Mexican immigrants fled to the United States to escape the chaos, violence, and deprivation caused by the Mexican Revolution. Their migration, however, did not ensure freedom from harsh treatment. Discrimination in nearly all areas of life, including education, housing, and employment, made living north of the border a difficult and painful experience at times.[9]

Nor did places of amusement provide a sanctuary. Film exhibitors, responding to patrons' perceptions of Mexican uncleanliness and disease, relegated ethnic Mexicans to separate seating areas or separate screenings.[10] In his study of the Mexican population of Chicago and the Calumet region, for example, Paul Taylor found that white theater owners cited Mexicans' dress, comportment, and even body odor as excuses for continued discrimination. The operator of the Indiana State Theatre said that his Mexican patrons "are ushered to the first aisle with the colored." Although he admitted that not all Mexicans are dirty, he maintained that "many of them are not clean and we can't separate on the basis of dress, so we separate them on the basis of nationality." His strategy was so successful, he insisted, that they learned to "go by themselves to their place" in the theater or not attend at all.[11] Discriminatory practices such as these made it evident that the dominant society desired the presence of Mexicans for their labor when it was needed and not at any other time.

In addition to the personal discrimination experienced inside theaters, Mexican patrons encountered degrading images of themselves on the screen. With rare exception, Hollywood cast the Mexican male as the "greaser" or as his lawless counterpart, the "bandido."[12] These stock characters were founded in images of the Mexican Revolution. Mexican and American newsreels documented the exploits of Pancho Villa, Emiliano Zapata, and their followers. By 1917, as the newly installed administration of Venustiano Carranza de la Garza began to realize, the revolutionary, warring Mexican had become a stereotype north of the border. Carranza halted the exportation of revolutionary battle footage, but Americans' desire for lurid scenes of violent Mexicans continued.[13] These images were critical to notions of white dominance in the Southwest, as the wave of "greaser" films suggests; their titles included *The Girl and the Greaser* (1913), *Bronco Billy and the Greaser* (1914), and *Guns and Greasers* (1918).[14] In contrast to their Anglo counterparts in these films, the Mexican characters are dirty and untrustworthy. Another extreme instance of this stereotype occurs in *Martyrs of the Alamo* (1915). Directed by Christy Cabanne, a former assistant to D. W. Griffith, the film justifies the siege of the Alamo by depicting Mexicans as a threat to white womanhood and incapable of self-government.[15]

By the late teens and early 1920s, the image of the "Latin Lover" offered a relatively positive alternative for actors like Ramon Navarro. The Latin Lover was handsome and seductive, but dangerously so. His smoldering sexuality and physical prowess made him a favorite as a matinee idol; yet the stereotype tapped into white fears of the Other. An alternative to the greaser, the Latin Lover was attractive to American women, but never fully assimilated into white society.[16]

When greasers and Latin Lovers were at their height on American screens, Mexicans dwelling north of the border created and supported multiple forms of popular culture that resisted such degrading imagery. *Carpas* (traveling tent shows), *tandas de variedad* (variety shows), and solo acts entertained working- and middle-class Mexican audiences in the many Spanish-language theaters of Los Angeles. In these spaces, management did not subject audiences to prejudicial treatment or to offensive characterizations.[17]

One particularly successful entrepreneur of Mexican entertainment was Francisco Fouce. The son of Spanish immigrants who first settled in Hawaii and then in California in the early 1920s, Fouce worked in Hollywood as a child actor and later produced and directed Spanish-language films for the Columbia Studios foreign department.[18] Seeing a market for

Spanish-language entertainment in Los Angeles, he quickly became interested in exhibition. The Teatro California, where he premiered *Allá en el Rancho Grande*, was the first in a chain of four theaters that he held and operated throughout the 1930s. A shrewd businessman, he purchased his chief competitors, the Teatro Mexico and the Teatro Hidalgo, and quickly demolished them in order to redirect their patronage to his theaters. Along with the California, Fouce bought the Roosevelt, Mason, and Electric, making him the owner of the largest chain of Spanish-language theaters in California. These venues also supported his distribution company, the Spanish International Exchange, through which he successfully bargained with Columbia executives to gain distribution rights to their Spanish-language features in Los Angeles in 1933. The Exchange created a formal clearinghouse for Mexican films, replacing the individual arrangements formerly made with the Hollywood studios or Mexican film producers. By 1938, the Exchange listed nearly sixty films in its catalogue. Both the exhibition and the distribution wings of Fouce's business grew rapidly with the popularity of Mexican sound film.[19]

Mexican cultural productions found a receptive audience among English-language speakers as well. Anglo Americans sought out evidence of a primitive Mexican past that could serve as a respite from the seemingly dehumanized and materialistic state of modern society. In their neighbor to the south, many Americans believed, could be found a romantic, rural society not yet transformed by industrialization. This "vogue for things Mexican" was a response to an anti-modern impulse in white society that extended into the realms of American art, fashion, and decor, as well as forms of entertainment.[20]

The popularity of Mexican culture paralleled the era of the Good Neighbor Policy. First introduced by Franklin D. Roosevelt in his inaugural address in 1933, the policy renounced "gunboat diplomacy" toward Latin America in favor of a strategy of non-intervention and economic collaboration. The desire to restore Latin American trust in the United States was a response to the rise of fascism in Europe. The U.S. State Department initiated cultural programs that promoted "mutual understanding" among the republics. Such programs celebrated the uniqueness of Latin American culture while foregrounding commonalities with the United States.[21]

The broad interest in Mexican culture paved the way for the mainstream reception of *Allá en el Rancho Grande* on American screens. The film's emphasis on Mexican folk culture made it appealing to both Anglo and Mexican audiences, albeit for different reasons.

Allá en el Rancho Grande (Over on the Big Ranch, 1936)

With its sentimental narrative, nostalgic settings, and folkloric celebrations, *Allá en el Rancho Grande* ministered to the members of *barrios* and *colonias* in a way that no other film, American or Mexican, had ever done. The content, mode of delivery, and style of the film's multiple musical numbers contribute directly to that success. Singing the title song, José Francisco (Tito Guízar) invokes the merits of simple pleasures and celebrates the Mexican countryside and its people: "Down on the big ranch / where I lived / there was a little country girl; who used to tell me. . . ." He recalls how she would make his trousers of "wood and then of leather" for his ride around the fields.[22] Reminiscing of bygone days on the ranch, José Francisco sings the song after he has won the horse race that will allow him to marry his sweetheart, Cruz (Esther Fernández). He is a *charro* (horseman), an ideal symbol of Mexican male culture who is athletic, masculine, romantic, and chivalrous.[23] José Francisco's fellow *rancheros* request the song, pass him the guitar, and eventually join in the chorus. While Guízar sings, the film cuts to close-up shots of his friends' faces as they shout "Y luego?" ("And then?") and "Que decía, mi manito?" ("What did she say, my friend?") to anticipate the next line of the song and prompt him along. Cutting between Guízar and his audience, director Fernando de Fuentes creates a scene of communal merriment and expression. Cinematographer Gabriel Figueroa frames high-angle shots over a sea of sombreros and low-angle shots of the men's faces as they sing together. In much the same way that Yiddish and black cinema developed the folk musical structure, the makers of *Allá en el Rancho Grande* embedded musical numbers to reinforce a community and its home. The folk songs celebrate familiarity and tradition by allowing the film's characters and its audience to engage in collective performance. The Mexican film upheld the most potent aspect of the folk musical: it performed with the audience, not for it.

9. *Allá en el Rancho Grande* lobby card. Copyright 1936 by Bustamente y Fuentes. From the collections of the Margaret Herrick Library, Academy of Motion Picture Arts and Sciences.

If "Rancho Grande" elicits a cheerful way of remembering the past, other songs are more despondent. Early in the film, a *ranchero* asks Cruz to sing for him. She chooses "Canción mixteca," a traditional *ranchera* ballad that mourns the land left behind ("How far I am from the place I was born / Great sadness enters my mind").[24] This song was well known to Mexicans living in the United States, who frequently requested it from *ranchera* singers like Lydia Mendoza, the famous Tejana performer in the 1930s.[25] Like José Francisco and the other characters, Cruz commands music as a mode of self-expression. Mirroring the function that the film serves for its audience, Cruz sings for the *rancheros*, becoming their emotional conduit. Each song in the film has this spontaneous quality and communal context. The music derives its power from being integrated fully into the text so that it not only informs the narrative but also fulfills the overall project of the film, which is to invoke collectivity through the comforting images of homogeneity and social cohesion.

Musical moments such as these can also capture conflict. In the type of folk song and dance known as the *huapango*, two rivals challenge and ridicule each other in a seemingly improvised musical duel. When a fellow *ranchero* tells José Francisco that Cruz's virtue has been compromised, the *charro* challenges him at first, but then capitulates. The *huapango* easily transitions from a musical number back into the narrative. For this community, music and dance are so interwoven with their everyday reality that major problems can be worked out in both arenas. The form of the *huapango* recalls the *comedia dell'arte* theatrical tradition in that it lends an impression of spontaneity to the entertainment. As each rival picks up the verse where the other left off and further advances the musical duel, the audience becomes engaged with the number. The *huapango* was an improvisatory form that was familiar to contemporary audiences.[26] The film's use of the song enabled audiences to predict the action and even enter into the call-and-response duel on the screen.

The only choreographed dance sequence in the film is equally embedded in Mexican folk tradition. Created in the early twentieth century to celebrate the end of the Mexican Revolution, the "Jarabe tapatío" ("Mexican hat dance") carries associations of a distinctive Mexican folk culture that remained intact despite Spanish colonization. In the 1930s, it represented the persistence of Mexican culture after the political strife of the revolution and served to unite the nation through pride and heritage. Throughout the 1920s and 1930s, the Mexican state made concerted efforts to mold a national feeling of *mexicanidad* that would unite and strengthen the country's diverse population. The commissioning of public murals and the construction of monuments to revolutionary heroes were part of this initiative.[27] *Allá en el Rancho Grande* uses the dance as an example of *mexicanidad*, a symbol of what is good about Mexican life in general and Mexican ranch life in particular. The dancers Emilio Fernández and Olga Falcón perform intricate footwork as they flirt around a sombrero.[28] American reviewers praised the dance for its "leg work" and its "lavish displays of snowy belaced petticoat and other dainty lingerie."[29] In keeping with the characterizations in the film, the "Jarabe tapatío" emphasizes the strength of Mexican men and the femininity of Mexican women through its style of dance and its traditional costuming. More importantly, the number unites the world of the film with the world of the audience through a celebration of Mexican cultural life.

Allá en el Rancho Grande's musical moments were of particular interest to American critics. In its review, *Variety* applauded the film's folkloric elements. The reviewer detailed how "ranch scenes, preliminaries of a cock fight, and the trivia of daily life get careful attention from end to end, and these lend the appearance of clean workmanship and solidarity."[30] For Anglo audiences, the reviewer emphasized how *Allá en el Rancho Grande* was an "authentic" example of Mexican culture precisely because of its depiction of the "trivia of daily life." Yet, the reviewer was perplexed by the musical structure of the film. The casual and nonperformative way in which the songs enter and exit the film was a narrative strategy unfamiliar to Anglo American audiences. The reviewer noted how the "film is not a musical in any sense of the word, and the songs enter in only in the same background way as the dancing, riding, etc." With an air of disappointment, the reviewer commented that the film's "special ditties" are catchy, but "all of them should have been built up better as long as they classify special work and the proper warbler is on hand to render 'em." The producers, he wrote, "might aptly scan U.S. products for a more thorough lesson."[31]

The musicals released by Hollywood in the mid-1930s were overwhelmingly oriented toward stage and radio performances, such as Busby Berkeley's *Gold Diggers of 1935*, *Stage Struck* (1936), and *Sing, Baby, Sing* (1936). Like all show musicals, these films featured established performers playing performers on the screen. Mexican cinema, on the other hand, drew upon the folk traditions of Mexican culture to make a musical in the early years of sound. Producers Fernando de Fuentes and Alfonso Rivas Bustamente knew that the sights and sounds of ranch life resonated in ways that narratives about nightclubs and chorus girls did not. In the face of discrimination and the pressures of assimilation, scenes of an idyllic, pastoral past had deeper meaning.[32] As Los Angeles theater owner Francisco Fouce later explained to *Cinema Reporter*, Mexican audiences in the United States like films with "Mexican flavor; folkloric, vernacular, depicting their customs."[33] In this way, *Allá en el Rancho Grande* created the standard by which future successes from Mexico would be judged. Far from needing to consult American films for a "thorough lesson" in musical film production, the Mexican *comedia ranchera* gained popularity and acclaim among Spanish-speaking audiences because of its differences from the Hollywood mainstream.

Contemporary audiences of *Allá en el Rancho Grande* and its imitators recognized the film formula as one that featured traditional scenes of "our Mexico": "the Mexican countryside, the Mexican life under the Mexican sun." Film advertisements relied on the symbols of Mexican folklore to apprise audiences of the type of story—gallant horsemen, cockfights, spurs, and songs.[34] In particular, advertisements for *Allá en el Rancho Grande* identify two expressions of Mexican folk culture that resonated with migrants: the *charro* and the *música ranchera*. Both elicited pride and nostalgia among the film's audience and were a direct reaction to the stresses of the modern era. Fidel Murillo, film critic for *La Opinión*, commented on the ways in which *Allá en el Rancho Grande* portrays a Mexican identity unspoiled by the effects of modern reality: "'Alla en el Rancho Grande' is that which we would call a '*charra*' film. . . . *Charra*, because its characters all move in an environment of captivating clarity; because its men act like men in reality, with all the integrity of our youth who haven't been harmed by the influence of the city, and its women have the charm of our young girls, in whose hearts still rest all the traditional virtues of the Mexican woman, alien from the foreign influences that have so harmed them."[35] *Allá en el Rancho Grande* delivered a snapshot in time that soothed migrants weary of the stresses that urban life inflicts on otherwise stable identities and relationships. As a "master symbol of Mexican culture," the *charro* acquired transnational dimensions through various products of Mexican popular culture.[36] Tito Guízar inaugurated the singing *charro* on film, who, with his voice and music, crystallizes all that is admirable about Mexican culture for those living across the border.

Música ranchera was the musical counterpart to the *charro*. As a form, it has its roots in the nationalism spurred by the Mexican Revolution of 1910. Like the films that would give them visual expression, *música ranchera* was popular on both sides of the U.S.-Mexico border. Evoking an ideal of manliness, integrity, and patriotism, the songs solidified a connection to the positive aspects of Mexico and Mexican culture.[37] Fouce declared that in order for films to satisfy his audiences, they had to be "saturated with *ranchera* songs and typical dresses."[38] The popularity of *ranchera*s was tied to the increased movement of Mexican people to the cities.[39] Similarly, displaced migrant audiences elevated the popularity of the *comedia ranchera*, the *ranchera* song's filmic counterpart. This new film genre allowed the migrant, the immigrant, and their descendants a means of connecting to the past. As the film's publicity declared, *Allá en el Rancho Grande* portrayed "El Alma de un Pueblo que Canta cuando Ríe, que Canta cuando Llora . . ." ("The soul of a people who sing when they laugh, who sing when they cry . . .").[40] As much for its music as for its narrative content, the *comedia ranchera* quickly became and remained the most popular genre of Mexican cinema.

In his distribution contract with United Artists, Fernando de Fuentes retained the rights to *Allá en el Rancho Grande* for distribution in the United States. An indication of the film's broad appeal was de Fuentes's decision to add English subtitles, a first for a Mexican film.[41] At the time, United Artists executives were more interested in securing the distribution rights of Spanish-language cinema in Latin America; but in contracts and memoranda with Mexican producers, the studio admitted to the potential market that existed in the United States as well.[42] De Fuentes was well aware of the opportunity that existed among Spanish speakers in the United States. Theatrical venues abounded, especially in Los Angeles, to cater to the growing Mexican population's desire for entertainment. Mexican sound cinema, and the success of *Allá en el Rancho Grande* in particular, made that demand all the stronger.

After months of anticipation in the Spanish-language press, the film premiered in Los Angeles at two of Fouce's theaters simultaneously, an unprecedented move on his part. It ran continuously from noon to midnight at the Teatro California and the more modest Teatro Eléctrico, catering to the middle and working classes, respectively. Building upon an already established entertainment circuit in the United States, Fouce booked Mexican films alongside live acts. The sound film amplified the oral component of these live performances. "In some scenes in which Tito Guízar sings," one reviewer noted, "the public erupts in applause, forgetting, before a skillful reproduction, that it is mechanical." In the scene when "the guitars play dreamily under the window of the landowner's daughter, there is a religious silence." As the audience engaged in the musical numbers, filmic narrative and public performance became one.[43]

Where live entertainment was not available, exhibitors played Mexican music on a phonograph as part of the entertainment. Eusebia "Cheva" Garcia, a resident of the Arbol Verde barrio in Claremont, California, remembered an itinerant exhibitor in the 1930s, affectionately called "Circuito Roco" (the "Roco" Circuit), who would announce his arrival by playing Mexican music loudly from his truck: "There wasn't a tent or anything. He would just put benches out, you know." She added, "the whole barrio would come. . . . It was a family thing."[44]

Songs such as those in *Allá en el Rancho Grande*, especially the "Canción mixteca" and the title song, were well known to members of this community. Others were heard and learned on the radio. Tito Guízar sang on the radio throughout the 1930s. To hear those songs, audiences went to the movies more than once. Garcia recalled, "*Rancho Grande* was always popular. Some of the movies we had seen right here out in the open. We saw them in the theater over there again because they were popular movies, you know."[45] In the more remote barrio of San Benito, Texas, José D. Garcia, the son of a sharecropper, remembered that such films, which he called "*charras*," were his favorite as a young man. Garcia, who had suffered discrimination in the public school system, found solace in the films of Tito Guízar and other *charras*. For him, they were a source of pride and of hope: "*Charras* were the Bing Crosbys for us. With their beautiful costumes . . . that was an attraction." Garcia said he was drawn to such films because of the "canciónes" (songs) and because "the women were beautiful."[46]

Return engagements of *comedias rancheras* in Spanish-language movie theaters capitalized on the familiarity that audiences already had with Mexican songs from the radio. Fouce encouraged this familiarity by broadcasting a radio program from his Teatro California every morning from 6 to 9 A.M. Through this program, his listeners became acquainted and reacquainted with songs performed by the popular Mexican American group Los Madrugadores (The Early Risers), as well as local amateur acts.

According to Fouce's son, Francisco Fouce Jr., the family's chain of theaters showed *Allá en el Rancho Grande* repeatedly because "the musicals were the most popular without a doubt."[47] In this way, Fouce marketed the folk and the familiar through the exhibition of film and the showcasing of live musical acts. As part of the initial presentation of *Allá en el Rancho Grande*, Fouce booked the performance of a nostalgic "corrido de toros" (a ballad about bullfighters). After the film had received some fanfare, Fouce secured an accompanying performance of the film's music by the composer himself, Lorenzo Barcelata, who, *La Opinión* reported, would lead the *colonia* in an evening of song.[48] Such events surrounding the film created a public, performative space in which the audience strengthened its cultural and communal connections and reaffirmed its relationship to the homeland.

The scarcity of Spanish-language theaters outside of urban areas like Los Angeles made them all the more important as places where ethnic Mexicans could preserve personal dignity and cultural pride. At the Palace Theatre in San Benito, the segregation of Mexicans persisted as official policy in the late 1930s, as José D. Garcia recalls: "We could not sit on the first floor. They had signs and we all knew. We knew our place."[49]

By contrast, the Teatro Renes, the only theater on the Mexican side of San Benito, welcomed families to sit wherever they liked. Walking across the *resaca* (lake) that divided the two sections of town, Garcia would pay ten cents to see the current Mexican feature every Saturday afternoon.[50] Theaters such as these were modest in scale and decor, but they served a vital purpose in fostering pride in the face of social ostracism and discrimination.

Prior to the popularity of *Allá en el Rancho Grande*, Hollywood studios had underestimated the significance of the Mexican market in the United States. By 1938, United Artists had entered into arrangements with Spanish-speaking producers to create more musicals. As one *Los Angeles Times* reporter exclaimed, "The market in the United States is not to be sneezed at. Some sixty Spanish theaters may return a gross as high as $100,000!"[51] Fouce and his successors attempted to widen their market. Advertisements for *Allá en el Rancho Grande* encouraged Mexican patrons to "Bring your American friends too!"[52]

Tropic Holiday (1938)

The success of *Allá en el Rancho Grande* in the United States brought fame to Tito Guízar as the quintessential singing Mexican *charro*. Paramount Studios signed him in 1938, and he quickly became the latest Latin Lover whose silky voice and melodious guitar playing could melt the hearts of many a starlet. Guízar's guitar became a metonym for his characters and firmly associated him with folk music in the visual iconography of film musicals. As one Hollywood writer put it, his "guitar is as famous a Hollywood 'prop' as Jack Benny's Maxwell, Bob Burns' bazooka or Harold Lloyd's goggles."[53]

Beyond his sex appeal, however, American and Mexican industry personnel and critics recognized that Guízar's fame also signaled a shift in the representation of "Latins" on the screen. Mexican critics described Guízar as a "Latin troubadour" who had the ability to share and illuminate Mexican music, life, and culture for the American mainstream. He could therefore influence the representation of Mexicans in ways that would inspire pride in his native audience. Importing the successful formula of the *comedia ranchera*, with which Guízar was intimately connected, the Hollywood studios self-consciously attempted to revise depictions of their neighbors to the south in their version of cinematic diplomacy. Faced with the loss of European markets with the rise of fascism, American producers looked to the southern hemisphere for its international, potentially lucrative audience. They soon realized, however, that the Mexican product was on the verge of dominating that region because of its rapidly improving technical quality and, most importantly, its cultural representation. With Guízar as their star, Paramount producers believed they had a competitive edge in both American and Latin American markets.

During the production of the Paramount musical *Tropic Holiday*, producer Arthur Hornblow Jr. pointed to the damage that had been done by images of Mexicans in Hollywood. The studios had repeatedly offended their Mexican audiences by relegating Latin actors to "bandits or comedy characters." Furthermore, he argued, the loss of foreign distribution in Latin America was "largely due to Hollywood's arrogance in distribution practices and in the industry's disregard for the feelings of the foreign customers." Rejecting the practices of the past, Hornblow insisted that *Tropic Holiday* was "made with regard to Mexican pride." He touted the use of "top-rank Mexican artists" such as Guízar and composer Agustín Lara and predicted that the film "will not only retrieve the market below the Rio Grande, but will provide America with a new type of entertainment." According to Hornblow, an enlightened atmosphere reigned on the set; the Mexican talent was "not treated patronizingly, which is a common fault in the Southwest."[54]

Guízar challenged such derogatory and commonly held notions about Mexicans. His patrician manners and self-representation as a cosmopolitan interpreter of both European opera and Mexican folk tunes provided an alternative view to the public. Lighter-skinned than most Mexicans entering the United States, Guízar offered an image to American audiences that was ultimately unthreatening.[55]

Tropic Holiday attempts to bridge the cultural gap between Anglos and Mexicans. It does so by engaging with the integrative structures of the musical film, eliminating differences between insiders and outsiders through romantic relationships, song, and dance. The production team also appropriated the form and function of *Allá en el Rancho Grande* in order to offer a "new type of entertainment" where "Latins" were concerned.

The film is set in contemporary time in Tehuantepec, the southern isthmus of Mexico. Hollywood writer Ken Warren (Ray Milland) and his secretary Midge Miller (Martha Raye) have come to the Posada del Farolito (Inn of the Little Lantern) in order to write a new script for Sol Grunion Productions, Inc. Over the course of the film, both characters become involved with native Mexicans. Dorothy Lamour plays Manuela, the daughter of the innkeeper, who entices Ken to fall in love with her. Meanwhile, Midge becomes infatuated with a handsome singing *ranchero*, Ramón (Tito Guízar), but in the end decides to stay with her fiancé, Oklahoma senator Breck Jones, "The Indians' Choice" (Bob Burns). Not fazed by Midge's rejection, Ramón falls in love with Marilyn Joyce (Binnie Barnes), the Hollywood starlet who comes to Farolito in order to persuade Ken not to marry Manuela. In the end, all three couples are happily married.

Tropic Holiday hinges on the successful resolution of these three central relationships, in keeping with the conventions of the musical film.[56] In the often comical course of its development, however, the film also attempts to reconcile the differences between Anglos and Mexicans, the United States and Mexico, screen love and actual love. In order for audiences to accept these interracial/intercultural romantic relationships, the filmmakers had to place cultural understanding and exchange at the forefront of the film's message. The community-oriented, integrative musical sequences of the *comedia ranchera* were instructive here. Drawing directly from the title number of *Allá en el Rancho Grande*, the producers of *Tropic Holiday* set the scene for cultural exchange from the very beginning.

The film opens with a shot of a sign that reads "Posada del Farolito." The camera pans to an exterior shot of the inn, lit warmly from within, from which music and laughter emanate. Moving again, the camera cranes through the window to reveal a scene of merriment in which marimba players, tortilla makers, bartenders, and customers all sing together. Ramón (Guízar) soon enters, and a customer leads him to the bar and hands him a guitar. Flanking him on either side are his Mexican friends. The film cuts between Ramón's song and the responses of his adoring listeners.

From the earliest scripts for *Tropic Holiday*, writers Don Hartman and Frank Butler conceived of this opening sequence as one that would replicate the joy communicated by *Allá en el Rancho Grande*: "There is a feeling of gay improvisation as character after character are 'swung' into the number. . . . Thus we meet . . . MANUELA (Dorothy Lamour) . . . who is serving 'vino' from table to table until ensnared by the song." Referencing the earlier film, the writers referred to this number as a "Rancho Grande type of native chorale."[57]

The scene is useful for the film because it suggests an authentic view of Mexican life, as Hollywood understood it from *Allá en el Rancho Grande*. It establishes the kind of camaraderie and welcoming atmosphere that the musical film requires in order to eliminate the difference between insiders and outsiders. Successive versions of the script, with some variations, uphold the nature of this opening sequence. The writers emphasize how the characters at the Posada del Farolito are "swung into the number," foregrounding the familiarity among the people in this community and the ways in which the music itself is more atmospheric than performative.

The later scripts build on Guízar's star persona as it had been developed by *Allá en el Rancho Grande*. He is identified with the singing *charro* from his very first entrance. The script notes that the "Vaqueros . . . wear the colorful costumes of their profession" as they "leap from their horses and start towards the entrance." The camera follows Ramón, the leader of the vaqueros, as he responds to the invitation to sit on the bar. Handed a guitar, Ramón begins to sing effortlessly. The script then notes how "vivid, colorful types" listen to his song.[58]

The writers of *Tropic Holiday* appropriated Guízar's image as a singing *charro* who musically convenes the community and applied it to their project for cultural exchange. Once the opening number is in full swing, the camera pans into the upper rooms of the inn where Ken and Midge work over a typewriter. As the folk music wafts into their room, Midge becomes mesmerized by it, and her mind begins to wander to the Mexican scene outside. "Pretty soon," the script describes, "Midge, herself, is 'swinging it' out of the room into the patio, and into the number—and in all Mexico never was there so much abandon."[59]

Midge, who is much more susceptible than Ken to the allure of romance, quickly succumbs to the serenading of Ramón. As she listens, she remarks, "Gee, I'd really like to have one good fling." After her initial envelopment by the opening song and the *charro*'s serenade, Midge embarks on a process that Paramount publicity advertised as "going native." She takes part in a native celebration and dances the "Jarabe tapatío" (another sequence that mimics one in *Allá en el Rancho Grande*) on Ramón's sombrero, the traditional signal that she has chosen her suitor. Later, she dons a bullfighting costume and wrangles a bull ("El Furioso") successfully.

The notion of "going native" indicates the type of cultural exchange that occurs in *Tropic Holiday*. Unlike the characters in *Allá en el Rancho Grande*, the denizens of Posada del Farolito are not all part of the same shared community. The film shows a cultural encounter in which the Anglos partake in Mexican customs and behaviors, often to comical effect in the scenes with Midge and Breck Jones. In "going native," the film reveals, the characters learn valuable lessons from the people of Mexico.

Early in the film, Manuela explains to Ken that he knows little about Mexico and the Mexican people. Admitting to having seen some of his "Hollywood pictures," she remarks disdainfully, "Your story is the same old Mexican picture, Mexican bandits going 'boom boom.' Do I wear a rose in my hair and a dagger in my teeth like your heroines?" In this moment, the film self-consciously positions itself as a progressive and more authentic portrait of Mexican life than earlier Hollywood productions. This message is ironic, however, given that Manuela is played by Lamour, who was of Creole background.[60]

Tropic Holiday, in story and studio publicity, advances this notion of the authentic and makes the claim that Mexicans are more adept at musical expressions of feeling, human relationships, and appreciation of the pleasures of life. Repeatedly, the Mexican characters educate the American visitors. As Manuela and Ken hear the Mexicans of Farolito singing in the distance, she urges, "Listen to what they're playing, my people down there. You may write about love, but my people know about love." Manuela begins to sing the romantic ballad "Tropic Night," which Ramón then picks up and continues in Spanish. Serenading Manuela and Ken, Guízar's character aids the romantically challenged American. Later, Ken admits that he and his Hollywood bosses know nothing about true romantic feeling as it is found in Farolito. He admits, "We only make carbon copies of love." In the end, Ramón even teaches the cool American starlet how to experience true feeling. He sweeps her off her feet, and she becomes soft and womanly.

These relatively progressive examples of Mexican superiority in love also reaffirm the notion of Mexican primitiveness. The association of people of color with emotion and nature has long been a means for white society to at once admire and disdain them. The earliest of folk musicals from Hollywood, *Hearts in Dixie* (1929) and *Hallelujah!* (1929), capitalized on these associations. This impulse to value and appropriate the culture of peoples of color has much to do with the fears and anxieties of the modern era. Anglo Americans' concerns about modernity, including the rise of big cities, industrialization, and increasing alienation from nature, moved them to embrace what they perceived to be simpler, more authentic societies.[61]

The fetishization of Mexican folk was part of this broader phenomenon. While purporting to be progressive products intended to revise the Mexican image, films such as *Tropic Holiday* in fact depicted people of color as innate "creatures of feeling."[62] Ramón's sole impulse to woo and seduce the women around him positions him as a Latin Lover, a stock character predicated on the projection of a smoldering and mysterious sexual power. Driven by emotion and sexual impulse, Ramón is a product not of modern civilization but of the primitive past.

The Posada del Farolito shows no evidence of the modern day other than the presence of the Americans. Manuela and Ramón dress as simple, rural Mexican folk, and their ability to educate the Americans hinges on their ability to feel and express emotion. The one exception to this one-way learning experience, though subtly communicated by the film, is Manuela's final admission that she learned how to woo Ken from watching the love scenes in Hollywood movies. In this way, the film turns in on itself, self-reflexively suggesting the influence of Hollywood cinema.

The language of "going native" is ubiquitous in the early scripts of the film and in studio publicity. One byline for the film, "They're loose among the Latins," precisely infers the ways in which white characters like those portrayed by Ray Milland, Martha Raye, and Bob Burns lose their inhibitions when in close proximity to Mexicans. Images in the press reaffirm this transformation; they show these actors in typical Mexican dress, partaking of Mexican pastimes like bullfighting. In Mexico, the film suggests, becoming "loose" allows the stiff Americans to have fun. The country is a veritable playground for the Americans because of its beauty and simplicity; early scripts describe it as "the sort of place that Time [sic] marching on has utterly passed by." The writers frequently refer to Mexico as the "Land of Mañana," a place that exudes a "drowsy, tropical serenity."[63] Postponing everything to mañana (tomorrow), Mexicans prefer fun to work. To 1930s American society, such a theory explained the relative lack of advancement in countries like Mexico. Yet, as Tropic Holiday communicates, there is much of value to Americans in the "land of mañana," including an "anything goes" policy when it comes to having a good time. The script characterizes Bombita, Manuela's father, as one who "believes that anything anybody does is all right—just so long as they have 'fun' doing it."[64]

Like the Hollywood black-cast films that denied black modernity and migration, Tropic Holiday disavowed the migration of Mexicans northward. The film relegates its Mexican characters to a pre-modern era and therefore offers an implicit commentary on the place of Mexicans in society. As long as they remain in their primitive state and in their primitive land, the film suggests, Mexicans are benign. Indeed, given the merriment among the characters in the film, Mexicans appear happier in Mexico. The only character who migrates is Ramón, who, in the final scene, sits with starlet Marilyn Joyce in a plane bound for Los Angeles. He exclaims, "Gee, I hope I make good in Hollywood." Again, the film self-reflexively points to Guízar's actual migration from Mexico to the United States in search of stardom. Consistent with Guízar's experience in Hollywood, he presents an anomaly among Mexicans, a sophisticated troubadour whose ability to cross borders rests on his exceptional talents and privileged background. Manuela and the other residents of Farolito, by contrast, remain in Mexico.[65]

10. *Tropic Holiday* advertisement. Copyright 1938 by Paramount Pictures Inc. From the collections of the Margaret Herrick Library, Academy of Motion Picture Arts and Sciences.

Papa Soltero (Bachelor Father, 1939)

One musical film that does explore the reality of Mexican migration to the United States is *Papa soltero*. The Hollywood studios' desire to secure the Latin American market for their films prompted a renewed interest in Spanish-language production and presented new opportunities for Guízar. Paramount contracted him to two affiliated production houses, Dario Productions, a company run by Italian immigrant and former financial broker Dario Faralla, and Cobian Productions, headed by Rafael Ramos Cobian, a Puerto Rican theater operator.[66] Paramount believed that by collaborating with Mexican artists and writers, these producers would create Spanish-language features that would be better received in Latin America than their experiments in the early 1930s. In a statement to the *Los Angeles Times* in 1938, Cobian expressed his faith in these new productions. They represented a "a happy combination: American technique supervised by Latins who understand the people and the market." He asserted that, along with José Mojica, another Mexican singer and actor who starred in Spanish-language productions, Tito Guízar was a favorite among Latin American audiences, which were known for enjoying "musicals and heavy drama."[67]

To many in the Spanish-speaking film community, the moment seemed auspicious. Cobian and writers Gabriel Novarro and Miguel de Zárraga, two frequent contributors to the "Cine" section of the Los Angeles Spanish daily *La Opinión*, heralded renewed production in the face of critics from Mexico. Instead of stealing new talent from Mexican film production, Novarro and de Zárraga argued, the Hollywood studios offered exceptional training opportunities in the heart of the film industry.[68] In addition, such films promised to meld the best of both worlds. They merged the benefits of American technical knowledge with the contributions of Latin screenwriters, composers, and actors. In defending his recent work on one such film, *Verbena trágica* (1939), Miguel de Zárraga asserted that the spirit of Mexico could be captured in films from outside of that country: "The spirit is not only in the cities and the countryside of the land of the fathers, nor is it only reflected in the national monuments. . . . Outside of these countries, in countries that are technically foreign, there are enormous centers of compatriots that continue speaking our language, and continue feeling the same emotions as us . . . with our people, our customs, our letters, our songs."[69] The strong presence of "Hispanic expatriates" in the U.S. Southwest and elsewhere ensured the accurate handling of Latin subjects for the screen. In defense of his own work at Columbia Pictures and that of his compatriots, de Zárraga made a plea for accepting the reality of migration among Mexicans and other Latin Americans and appreciating their creative and artistic work produced *de afuera* (from outside).

Papa soltero is distinctive among Hollywood musicals of this period because it places migration and the struggle of the immigrant at the center of the narrative, a plot line that was rarely explored in explicit fashion. Produced by Faralla, the film employed the talents of poet/novelist Dana Wilma (Faralla's wife) and Arthur Vernon Jones for the story and script and Mexican writers Gabriel Novarro and Enrique Uthoff for the Spanish translation and dialogue. Richard Harlan, from Peru, who had produced some Spanish-language films in the early 1930s, directed. Guízar and his wife, Nenette Noriega, collaborated on the musical score. Tana, a young Mexican actress, and Paramount contract songwriters Frederick Hollander, Alec Templeton, Neville Fleeson, and Ralph Freed made contributions as well.[70]

The film has a two-part structure. The story begins in contemporary Mexico and moves to Los Angeles. It concerns a young Mexican, Carlos (Guízar), who works on a construction crew along the U.S.-Mexico border. Carlos receives word that his uncle, Don Fernandez, has died and has left the young man his estate in Los Angeles. As he says his farewells to the camp, a car accident occurs nearby, leaving a little girl, Lolita (Sarita Wooten), orphaned. Carlos decides to take Lolita with him to Los Angeles and reunite her with her sister, who works there. Once in the city, their search proves futile. Adding to their difficulties, the executor of Don Fernandez's estate, Cruz, informs Carlos that there is very little money left to him. Disappointed and poor, Carlos and Lolita rent a room in a boarding house run by the Garcia family. There they meet Tana, a "flamenco singer" in a local casino. When she injures her back, Carlos replaces her and becomes an instant hit. He also meets Marta, a cigarette girl at the casino, with whom he falls in love.

Later, it is revealed that the owner of the casino is Cruz and that the casino itself is Don Fernandez's home. Carlos realizes the deception and successfully proves that he is the true inheritor. In the end, Carlos reopens the casino as his own and employs all of his friends as partners. Through a remarkable coincidence, Lolita realizes that her older sister is indeed Marta, who had changed her name when she first migrated to Los Angeles. The film's finale shows this reunited family in song with Carlos and the patrons of his club.

The review of *Papa soltero* in the *Hollywood Reporter* noted that the film was a "surefire comedy romance [that] is expertly tailored for Guízar, and provides him with several opportunities to render musical numbers without breaking up the continuity."[71] The overall quality of the film, reviewers stated, was better than most Hollywood Spanish-language productions. Yet it was the ability of these musicals to maintain the continuity, the transitions from narrative to song and back again, that made them exceptional. Moreover, the construction of the narrative on both sides of the U.S.-Mexico border complements and contextualizes these transitions. The production team, including Guízar and Noriega, strategically placed the "folk" numbers among communities of Mexicans either in Mexico or in Los Angeles. *Papa soltero*'s "show" sequences, wherein the film asserts the divisions between audience and performer, occur in places of commercial amusement like nightclubs. Neither show nor folk musical, *Papa soltero* is a hybrid with a formal narrative structure that communicates degrees of social membership available to the migrant.

In most critical descriptions of the film, reviewers point out that Guízar plays a performer in Los Angeles clubs, a premise shared by many Hollywood show musicals. Films such as *Alexander's Ragtime Band* (1938) and *The Story of Vernon and Irene Castle* (1939) prove the inherent talent of a character who is typically played by a singer/dancer, like Alice Faye or Fred Astaire, with whom the audience is already familiar. The plot charts the character's rise to stardom, often featuring rough origins and a series of denials and failures along the way. In this respect, *Papa soltero* corresponds to a well-worn formula first established by *The Jazz Singer* (1927), in which an immigrant "makes good" on Broadway after first proving himself in bars and nightclubs. Guízar's character proves his worth when he gets the chance to substitute for the injured Tana in the casino. His reputation as a gifted singer made him appear natural to the film's audience. As he stands in front of the casino's audience with guitar in hand, he is performing his star persona in Hollywood. Such sequences replicate the actual performances Guízar gave in concert and on the radio.

The uniqueness of the film stems from its Mexican migrant narrative, its location shots on the U.S.-Mexico border and in Los Angeles, and its strategic insertion of folk numbers. This type of musical, advanced by *Allá en el Rancho Grande* three years earlier, reserved its musical sequences for celebrations of family and community life, upholding traditions and moments of sincere emotional outpouring. The filmmakers begin Carlos's story in Mexico while he is a humble worker on a road crew. This sequence establishes Carlos and his fellow workers as a familial community through the song written by Guízar and Noriega, "Yo Ya Me Voy" (I Am Going). A migrant's song, "Yo Ya Me Voy" is the first musical moment in the film, and it gives emotional expression to Carlos's decision to leave the camp for Los Angeles. His friends Tomás, Crespo, and Chicho understand why he must leave, but they are mournful.

In this farewell sequence, the men are huddled together in a tent discussing Carlos's impending departure. His friends insist that "if things don't go right," Carlos can count on them. They hand him a guitar and ask him to sing. He obliges with a song that expresses the bittersweet feelings of one who is leaving his community for a chance to "seek a fortune, never dreamed of." He sings, "It is with fond regrets that I bid my home farewell / I am going, going, going and may ne'er return." Promising that he will take the past with him to his new home, he insists, "Remembering, I will go." The men of the camp then join Carlos in the refrain as the camera cuts between medium shots of Carlos, close-ups of his hands on the guitar, and medium shots of the group singing with and responding to him. The scene ends with a long shot of the entire group around Carlos singing in unison, "Farewell!"[72]

Carlos does indeed take the memory of his friends with him. In the boarding house where he and Lolita reside, he encounters many strangers, but with the help of Tana, a fellow migrant herself, they create a displaced community. Through songs that they sing informally to each other, including "Chichen-Itza" and "Pecesitos," they overcome the alienation that besets migrants in the urban north.

It is not until the end of the film that Carlos re-creates the community that he had in Mexico. Once his rightful inheritance has been secured, Carlos, Marta, and Tana realize that they can re-establish family and community within the walls of the nightclub, a symbol of city life. They decide that in order to run the club successfully, they will need help. The orchestra members, who have proven themselves friends, agree to stay. Candido, the owner of the boarding house, volunteers to be the cook. And at Lolita's suggestion, Carlos brings his friends from the road camp to Los Angeles to serve as waiters. Marta declares, "Carlos, it would be marvelous. Just think. A partnership of all your friends working together. Why, we couldn't fail!"

On opening night, the characters emphasize their camaraderie. As Candido gives instructions to the waiters, Tomás, Chicho, and Crespo, he exclaims, "The harmony! Society without classes . . . but with respect." Having reunited and reconstructed community in the north, Carlos and his friends repeat the folk song "Chichen-Itza," but this time the audience joins in the performance. The camera encircles everyone, performers and audience, in a celebration of unity. Carlos bids them, "Now, my dear friends let's all sing together!" The camera cuts between a series of medium shots of couples seated at the tables, Carlos, Tana, and Marta in the center, Candido serving the food, Lolita dancing, and the orchestra. In this final moment, Carlos's past merges with his present. As the folk and the show musical elements come together, so do the migrant and his host society.

Guízar's character in *Papa soltero* is forced to migrate out of necessity, leaving family and friends behind. The final sequence, however, grants the migrant's desire to bring home with him. Like *The Jazz Singer, Papa soltero* reveals the extent to which success is desired, but not at the expense of home and family. The film takes a condition specific to Mexican migrants— leaving home for the big city, Los Angeles—and lends it visual and musical articulation in ways that offer comforting resolution. Unique in the Hollywood studio system, such films engage with the Mexican experience from the Mexican perspective.

Tito Guízar had moderate success with his Paramount productions, but he was ultimately dissatisfied with the limited opportunities in Hollywood. The Spanish-language films, in particular, though offering room for innovation, had small budgets and limited distribution. In 1939, he said as much to *La Opinión*: "The fact is that, although the films in which I have taken part in Hollywood have premiered with success in our countries, they don't satisfy me completely." Instead, he announced his intention to "film in Spanish in Argentina, Mexico, or in Cuba." Although he insisted

11. Carlos asserts his rightful claim to the Los Angeles casino. *Papa soltero* lobby card. Copyright 1939 by Paramount Pictures Inc. From the Hollywood Museum Collection of the Margaret Herrick Library, Academy of Motion Picture Arts and Sciences.

that he would continue to work in Hollywood, his decision to pursue roles in other national cinemas resulted in better salaries and greater authorial control.[73]

Guízar's roles in Mexican and American musicals of the 1930s demonstrate how the genre was in a moment of transition. Fears among studio executives that they were losing the Latin American market to Mexican cinema prompted them to reconsider their onscreen treatment of "Latins" in general and Mexicans in particular. For better or worse, the resonant images of *Allá en el Rancho Grande* framed Guízar's film persona for the entirety of his career. Deftly, he used the popularity of "Tito Guízar and His Guitar" to his advantage. Embracing the folk and show narrative formulas to reveal the differences between the Mexican countryside and the American city, Guízar inserted a uniquely Mexican migrant's consciousness into the Hollywood musical.

The Mexican musical's influence also extended to the mainstream. In *Tropic Holiday*, the imagery of singing *charro*s and bucolic *rancho*s recalls the setting and characters of the Mexican genre. Such depictions were progressive in comparison with the more standard images of Mexicans as untrustworthy, dirty, and lawless. As producer Arthur Hornblow Jr. asserted, films like *Tropic Holiday* were necessary in order to mend relations between Hollywood and Mexico. More than superficial imagery, however, these films also appropriated the formal structure of the *comedia ranchera*. *Tropic Holiday*'s emphasis on cultural exchange prompted the producers to show Mexicans in their "natural state" as a folksy people who sing and dance in order to express emotion and celebrate family and community. Ultimately, the film highlights cultural exchange only to the extent that it benefits the Anglo American characters and the audience.

In the years following *Allá en el Rancho Grande* and Guízar's productions for Paramount, the United States entered World War II, and neighborly relations with Latin America became all the more important to hemispheric security. The Motion Picture Producers and Distributors of America, the organizing body of the Hollywood studios, hired Latin American expert Addison Durland to oversee scripts with "Latin" themes and to advise producers of any aspects that might be deemed offensive.[74] Nelson Rockefeller's Office of the Coordinator for Inter-American Affairs, created by executive order in 1941, established a Motion Picture Division that produced features to promote cultural exchange in the Americas. Hollywood did its part with a series of show musicals featuring the Brazilian star Carmen Miranda.[75]

Beginning in the late 1930s, the increased prominence of the Hollywood folk musical revealed the saliency of migration as an important theme in the genre. Similar to the ways in which Guízar's Spanish-language Paramount features represented the folk as a condition of the pre-migratory state, Hollywood musicals increasingly bound white communities to home as well. An emphasis on home, and the tensions surrounding its perseverance in the face of change, migrated to the mainstream of American cinema in subsequent decades.

4

"Our Home Town"

The Hollywood Folk Musical

Over the course of his career at MGM in the 1940s and 1950s, producer Arthur Freed consistently praised the merits of the "period musical." This type of film, he insisted, "can capture a charm that many people long for today." Commenting to the *New York Times* in 1959, Freed explained that the period musical "lets us enjoy, for a while, a more easy and more gracious way of life than exists in our now everyday life." The lives of Americans are driven by speed, he argued. "I think many of us want to go back and see the world as it was when it took eighty days to go around it."[1]

Freed theorized that such films were beloved for their "once upon a time quality," their ability to transport audiences to a place and time before the fragmentation and uncertainties of the modern era. Such musicals as *Meet Me in St. Louis* (1944) and *The Harvey Girls* (1946) celebrated American folk life: "American folk music, plus the folk lore that goes with it, yields the most universally appealing, interesting and satisfying musical." Folk subject matter, Freed observed, "is material known by and beloved of the whole population, and its values are not transient."[2]

These films thematically explore continuity versus rupture and stasis versus change. From *The Wizard of Oz* (1939) to *Seven Brides for Seven Brothers* (1954), the Hollywood studios made a series of original musical films that privileged the collective. The characters in these films are ordinary members of the town or rural community whose bonds to each other and the place where they live are intertwined with musical evocations of folk life.

Such films defined and upheld a folk heritage at a time when change and uncertainty dominated discussions about American character and values.[3]

Despite Freed's statement to the contrary, the folk communities in these musicals are far from universal depictions. Departing from the subject matter of folk musicals of the past, those made from 1939 to 1954 were dominated by white communities. The shift to white folk was an abrupt departure that paralleled the show musical's temporary fall from dominance in Hollywood. Freed recounts this transformation: "We at MGM realized in 1940–1941 that musicals were undergoing a revolutionary change." This change was a structural one: "Gone were the gigantic production numbers, the trick camera angles, the dances and songs that stopped the plot cold until the last chorine waved her last ostrich feather in the camera's focus."[4]

The genre's integration, wherein musical sequences evoked or advanced the film's narrative, had occurred before the period that Freed identifies. Directors like Ernst Lubtisch (*One Hour with You*, 1932; *The Merry Widow*, 1934), Rouben Mamoulian (*Love Me Tonight*, 1932; *High, Wide and Handsome*, 1937), as well as the many musicals starring Fred Astaire, featured bold musical performance sequences that were relevant to the narrative subject matter. Unlike many interpretations that insist on meriting Broadway's 1943 production of *Oklahoma!* as the first integrated musical, we see from these examples and those of ethnic cinema in the 1930s that integration of the musical happened much earlier and in quite different contexts.[5]

As part of the transformation that occurred in the late 1930s, it appeared to Freed and others that a narrative shift followed as well. Producers replaced the once dominant show musical with another kind of musical story that featured ordinary people in everyday situations. Suddenly, white communities became folk subject matter. In 1939, Judy Garland ushered in a new era for the musical when, as Dorothy Gale, she sang "Over the Rainbow" in the middle of a Kansas farm.[6]

Since the beginnings of sound cinema in the late 1920s, Hollywood had cast racialized subjects as primitive and therefore inherently musical. *Cabin in the Sky* (1943), MGM's first black-cast musical since *Hallelujah!* (1929), was in keeping with this tradition, although it was an anomaly among the other folk musicals of the time. In *Cabin in the Sky*, Little Joe returns home after carousing with loose women in the city, much like Zeke in *Hallelujah!*. But like Dorothy in *The Wizard of Oz*, Little Joe wakes in his bed to realize it was all a bad dream. The return to the comfort of family and friends is more pronounced in *Cabin in the Sky* than in the earlier black-cast films. Ethel Waters's role as Petunia, Little Joe's wife, is a prominent one that invests the home space with significant moral weight. Like Dorothy, who realizes her desire to reunite with Auntie Em, Little Joe ultimately returns to Petunia. The narrative arc of *Cabin in the Sky*, produced by Arthur Freed and directed by Vincente Minnelli, indicates how racialized notions regarding blackness and primitivity coexisted side by side with new ideas about the relationship of white peoples to a folk past.

Certainly, the musicality of white folk had been evoked before 1939. Lubitsch's *One Hour with You* and *The Merry Widow* and Mamoulian's *Love Me Tonight* are romantic tales that draw upon European musical traditions. Set in fantastical kingdoms and populated by princes and princesses, feudal lords and peasants, these films justified the musicality of their subjects with their fanciful storybook locales. Such settings have prompted Rick Altman to distinguish these films as part of the "fairy tale" cycle of Hollywood musicals.[7]

Moreover, the Fred Astaire/Ginger Rogers vehicles of the 1930s, such as *The Gay Divorcee* (1934), often reveal their characters as musical beings, but as a condition of Fred Astaire's star persona as a song-and-dance man. Astaire's talents allow him to be musical both onstage and off, by himself and with his romantic interests. His films are set most often in places where performances are expected to occur (such as nightclubs, rehearsal halls, and dance floors). It is Astaire's attempt to woo Ginger Rogers's character that propels the narrative and prompts the musical consummation of the relationship via choreographed dance sequences.[8]

The Hollywood folk musical, however, developed in a different direction. It shifted both form and content to foreground ordinary, specifically American subject matter that found its musical inspiration not in European kingdoms or places of entertainment, but in the idyllic American countryside and small towns and cities of the early twentieth century. This chapter charts the development of the Hollywood folk musical from 1939 to 1954, from *The Wizard of Oz* to *Seven Brides for Seven Brothers*. In addition to these films, *Meet Me in St. Louis*, *State Fair* (1945), *The Harvey Girls*, *Centennial Summer* (1946), *Summer Holiday* (1948), and *In the Good*

Old Summertime (1949) feature musical white folk in picturesque, quintessentially American settings. To varying degrees, they privilege collectivity
on both narrative and formal levels by emphasizing communal and kin
relations via musical sequences that arise in an organic, integrated fashion
from the material context of the film. Musical numbers are atmospheric,
drawing their inspiration from nature or the natural ordering of things.
Space becomes unified as time is experienced cyclically with the celebration of the seasons, rituals, and life events.[9]

I choose to focus on original Hollywood productions in these years
(though some are adapted from novels and plays) in order to chart the ways
in which the folk musical developed in mainstream cinema. By the time of
the Hollywood adaptation of *Oklahoma!* in 1955, the studios had created a
series of original productions with their own set of themes, musical scores,
and spatial and temporal structures. Though certainly not divorced from
Broadway productions, the Hollywood folk musical of the 1940s and early
1950s was heavily influenced by the cinematic representations of folk from
the beginnings of the sound era.

Migration continued to be a reality of American life from the late
1930s to the early 1950s. Economic displacements, wartime mobilization,
and the demand for cheap, unskilled labor prompted regional and transnational migrations in this period. Mobility signaled opportunity and lib-
eration as well as fear and alienation. The folk musical functions as an
allegory of migration by emphasizing the pre- and post-migratory experiences of its characters. Moving from home to a new place necessitates a
journey. In the case of *The Wizard of Oz*, the journey is violently initiated
by the tornado that hurls Dorothy's house to the Land of Oz. In *Meet Me in
St. Louis*, the journey is a dreaded one, as the family fearfully imagines what
life in New York will be like. The act of migration is one that is rarely given
much prominence in these films. Rather, it is the effect on the home or the
migrant that is of most concern. If a character goes away, like young Richard
in *Summer Holiday*, he quickly learns the error of his ways and returns to the
comfort and constancy of his home. Therefore, migration functions figura-
tively in this cycle of films as a journey that is thwarted or taken and regret-
ted. It manifests on the level of the personal and the familial, rather than the
epic. Dorothy's tearful words are the migrant's refrain. "There's no place
like home" expresses the yearning to return to the place left behind.

The folk musical evolves in this period because of the widespread relevance of migration, but also because of the growing perception of a white folk heritage that was in danger of extinction. Folklorists succeeded in bringing the nation's folk music to the level of national interest in 1937, when the Library of Congress's Archive of American Folk Song first received government funding. What was distinctive about this effort was that it sought to collect and preserve music from all areas of the United States, including the folk music of white communities in Appalachia, Indiana, and Ohio. One year afterward, Thornton Wilder won the Pulitzer Prize for his play *Our Town*, which offered audiences a bittersweet story of life in turn-of-the-century New England. Throughout the 1930s, white Americans' desire to celebrate their past also prompted and perpetuated the success of national radio shows like "National Barn Dance" and "Grand Ole Opry." Given sanction by the nation's official and popular culture in that decade, white peoples of the United States became folk too.[10]

There was yet another reason that the white folk musical appeared in the 1940s and 1950s. Soon after the end of World War II, Freed denied that he would ever "make a picture for the purpose of delivering a message or achieving a propaganda end." Nevertheless, he felt strongly that "a good musical which has the American scene and scheme of living as its basis or background is the most successful and satisfactory ambassador of American democracy to the world-at-large."[11] World War II inspired patriotic feelings in most Americans. Demands for unity on the home front while troops fought the war abroad were codified into official Hollywood procedure through the collaborative efforts of the studios and the Bureau of Motion Pictures (BMP) of the Office of War Information (OWI). In these years, Hollywood released patriotic pictures that supported a sense of duty to and sacrifice for the country, family, and home. The coalition between Hollywood and Washington meant little interference with production and saved the studios from the wartime conversion to which the steel, auto manufacturing, and construction industries were subjected.[12]

Hollywood producers and representatives of the OWI insisted that American films were superior in both production quality and appeal, which justified export around the world. As head of the BMP, Francis S. Harmon declared that the movie industry "recognizes its responsibility to the free society of which it is both a part and a symbol."[13] In this context, the

Motion Picture Producers and Distributors of America (MPPDA), the movie industry's self-regulatory organization, became the "silent salesman" of American life. As Ruth Vasey has found, the MPPDA actively "encouraged the perception of the [film] medium as universal, capable of transcending cultural boundaries" in order to secure American cinema the broadest appeal and revenue possible.[14] To create this perception, producers had to make films that appealed widely to peoples both at home and abroad. The MPPDA's self-censoring agency, the Production Code Administration (PCA), worked closely with producers to foster textual ambiguity and multivalence in its films. From the advent of sound, the PCA and Hollywood producers labored to create levels of interpretation that enabled spectators to "read through the action on the screen to identify deliberately displaced meanings," depending on the spectator's willingness and experience. This strategy minimized potential offense and maximized each film's relevance to a diverse audience.[15]

After the Allied victory in 1945, unity at home was no less important. The spread of communism and the nuclear arms race kept Americans wary of the future. The destabilizing effects of war and its aftermath compelled middle-class Americans to develop a "domestic ideology" that bolstered their home lives. Elaine Tyler May has documented the high rates of marriage and birth at the war's end. "The family," May writes, "seemed to offer a psychological fortress that would protect them against themselves . . . and the hazards of the age."[16]

A cycle of films that evoked darkness, fear, paranoia, and alienation gave expression to the insecurities of the era. Films such as *Double Indemnity* (1944) and *Mildred Pierce* (1945), Vivian Sobchak argues, occupy the flip side of the Hollywood folk musical in this era, with "the loss of home" as a "structuring absence in film noir." "Lounge time" settings in nightclubs, bus stations, and motels in such films are far removed from the spaces dominated by family and community life that connect us to the past. And two of the most popular films of 1946, *The Best Years of Our Lives* and *It's a Wonderful Life*, turn on the fate of the small town as cold, moneyed interests threaten homey American values.[17]

The folk musical reacted against such forces by emphasizing continuity over change, collective contentment over the pursuit of wealth. "American folklore" became a conduit through which audiences would understand, as Freed asserted, the "American story of freedom." In such narratives, American essentialism drives the representation of egalitarianism, moral clarity, and dedication to family and community. Certainly, anxieties regarding the position of the United States on the world stage fed Freed's essentialist interpretations of the nation's identity and culture. By 1946, his multiple successes with *The Wizard of Oz, Meet Me in St. Louis*, and *The Harvey Girls* convinced one *Los Angeles Times* reviewer that he was a "film genius" for his ability to "search out and confine in celluloid some little piece of Americana which he can fasten in your mind with music." From the 1940s to the early 1950s, Freed's prominence as a producer of musical films was shaped by his ability to develop and situate the folk musical as a quintessentially American product.[18]

While they eschew personal advancement for any one individual, these folk musicals do not disavow or criticize capitalism. Instead, they offer an image of a capitalist society that is self-sustaining and democratic. The films position the white folk community as the embodiment of the middle-class ideal. With very few exceptions, class and ethnic diversity do not register in the world of the folk musical because they do not exist. Ultimately, the families and communities need nothing more than what they already have.[19]

The Hollywood folk musical sent its message to audiences both at home and abroad. At home, it ministered to a public weary of the changes wrought by modernity and a society that was increasingly mobile in search of work and a better way of life. Looking beyond national boundaries, producers like Freed also sought to wield the folk musical's depictions of Americanism to thwart criticism of the nation and to prove the inherent virtue of American values and ideals. The extent to which this latter effort was successful is dubious. Historically, Hollywood musicals did not fare well in the European market, especially those about specifically American subjects. *The Wizard of Oz* was an exception. British airmen found solace in singing "We're off to see the wizard," as they flew off to repel the German Blitz, associating Dorothy's journey into the unknown with their own. And the image of resilient folk communities who celebrated their land with song and dance was not uniquely American: many Soviet musicals used the same conventions to justify communist regimes.[20]

Nevertheless, this period of Hollywood filmmaking represents a moment when the folk migrated to the mainstream of American culture. The deeply embedded historical associations that connected peoples of color, natural surroundings, and music broadened to include majority white cultures. White communities keenly felt the changes occurring in society in the 1940s and 1950s and sought nostalgic, backward-looking images of an idyllic America. In a time of great uncertainty, the Hollywood folk musical featured homogeneity in its depictions of race and class and located a romanticized moment in the rural spaces of the country and its turn-of-the-century cities and towns.

Each film's narrative is structured according to the relationship between space and time. The films are set in rural locales, small towns, and small cities. These material locations create a unity of place that intertwines the characters with each other and the land. The characters' lives are ordered by cyclical time that brings about ritual events and the convening of the collective with activities that foster togetherness. In this way, the films project an image of historical continuity. Often, however, continuity is ruptured by the migrant journey of one community member who ultimately restores stasis when he/she returns home. The functioning of time and space in these films reveals the ongoing tension between romanticism and modernity in American life. Ultimately, the folk musicals reject change in favor of stasis, supporting the conservative tenor of the era. In order to achieve the utopia that they seek to project, the films must erase evidence of social difference so that the ideal of an egalitarian society of which everyone is a member can be upheld. A universalizing whiteness replaces peoples of color, plenty stands in for want, and communal contentment trumps personal desire.

Town and Country

The folk musical creates unified space by foregounding the interconnectedness of people, their community, and the land. This unity is achieved on the levels of both form and content. By the 1940s and early 1950s, most Americans lived in cities and suburbs and increasingly regarded the farm and the small town as nostalgic relics. The folk musical infuses both of these spaces with natural qualities that allow for organic and spontaneous musical expressions among their residents. Even folk musicals that re-create turn-of-the-century cities like St. Louis (*Meet Me in St. Louis*), Phil-adelphia (*Centennial Summer*), and Chicago (*In the Good Old Summertime*) purposely set their stories in a period before modernity altered the look and feel of those places. In reality, of course, the late nineteenth and twentieth centuries saw rapid industrialization, urbanization, and immi-gration, which dramatically transformed American society. As the films suggest, however, St. Louis in 1903–4, Philadelphia in 1876, and Edwardian-era Chicago are more bucolic than urban, more provincial than cosmopoli-tan. More like small towns than cities, they are places in which families have lived for generations and have adapted their daily activities to paral-lel nature's patterns. Major life events like births and weddings occur just as naturally as the change of seasons. In this way, the films infuse city life with comforting imagery that sustains a connection to nature rather than fractures it.

Of the films set in small cities, *Meet Me in St. Louis* has received the most attention. As Richard Dyer has pointed out, it is considered a "perfect musical" for its marriage of "narrative and spectacle, dialogue, and song" in the depiction of the Smith family of St. Louis. The film's imperfect quali-ties and ambiguities, Dyer asserts, such as the star persona that elevates Judy Garland above all other characters, have received less consideration. Studies by Serafina Bathrick, Gerald Kaufman, and James Naremore have instead focused on the narrative and formal integration of the themes of family, home, and modernity.[21]

The Smith family's home is central to these discussions because the majority of the film's action occurs there.[22] The home represents unified space both within and without. Director Vincente Minnelli shows us the home's exterior at the beginning of the film as a Victorian postcard of the street magically comes to life. Just as important as the location of space in this opening scene is the evocation of the season. It is summer-time in St. Louis. We see the horse-drawn ice wagon and children in light-colored clothes playing on the green lawns. Inside the house, Mrs. Smith (Mary Astor) and the family's maid, Katie (Marjorie Main), prepare catsup in the hot kitchen, and young daughter Agnes (Joan Carroll) enters after tak-ing a swim. The film's depiction of seasonally inspired activities establishes a connection between the natural and the human worlds. As in the opening scene, the seasons structure and advance the film's storyline. Summer turns to autumn, which we understand from the changing colors and falling leaves. The children celebrate Halloween by dressing in costume and erecting a massive bonfire in the middle of the street; Katie marks the occasion, as she always does, with a hickory nut cake. Winter brings snow, sleigh rides, and the annual Christmas dance. And spring returns the lawns to a vibrant green, the roses bloom, and the Smith family women shed their winter coats for frilly white dresses. The St. Louis of 1903–4 is a civilized place, but it has not lost touch with nature.

In two subsequent films about city life, *Centennial Summer* and *In the Good Old Summertime*, the seasons similarly link family space with nature. In the first, the Rogerses of Philadelphia, like the Smiths of St. Louis, go about their routine while eagerly anticipating the opening of the Centennial fairgrounds. Summertime finds members of the family lounging on the front porch swing and taking leisurely strolls in the moonlight. By day, they go about grooming their horse, feeding the chickens, churning the butter, and preparing meals. These latter activities appear as one continuous movement in the number "I Was Up with the Lark This Morning," in which the family members cheerily greet the day by emphasizing their interaction with nature: "Breezes sing to me / Sing of spring to me / Flowers bow and whisper, 'Howdy.'" Though set in the city, this sequence in particular reveals the ways in which the Rogers home is idyllic. The camera fluidly moves around their yard, an image of nature's bounty populated by budding flowers, horses, and chickens. No evidence of the city intrudes upon this space.

Much like *Meet Me in St. Louis, In the Good Old Summertime* structures its narrative around seasonal change. As indicated by the title, the film begins and ends with summer, marked by leisurely strolls, picnics, and concerts in the park. The action takes place in a music store, where the two main characters, Veronica Fisher (Judy Garland) and Andrew Larkin (Van Johnson), gradually fall in love. Otto and Nellie (S. Z. Sakall and Spring Byington), an elderly couple who work in the store, encourage the young lovers' romance. Set in Chicago, the film progresses through the seasons as summer gives way to fall and winter. The cooler weather and snowy streets drive the characters indoors, lit by warm lights and comforting fireplaces. When summer returns and the characters venture back into the city park, Veronica and Andrew carry a young child with them. Mirroring the seasons, the narratives of these musicals give meaning to the development of their characters' lives by infusing them with naturalness and order. Despite their urban settings, the films establish unified space via seasonal depictions of time.

In other folk musicals of the period, the countryside itself imparts these qualities. On the farms of Iowa (*State Fair*) and Kansas (*The Wizard of Oz*) and in the frontier spaces of New Mexico (*The Harvey Girls*) and Oregon (*Seven Brides for Seven Brothers*), the connection to the land takes the form of labor and bounty. Just like their harvest, the people are products of the earth—hardy, resourceful, and humble. Their mode of existence is simple but dignified, and they enjoy a job well done. Dorothy's farm in *The Wizard of Oz* is beset by economic hardship and the unpredictability of nature. Yet its constancy and familiarity are what Dorothy longs for once she lands in the strange world of Oz. In *State Fair*, the family happily anticipates their annual summertime journey to the fair, a frenetic and exciting place that leaves them exhausted and heartsick for the comfort of their farm.

In the latter two films of this cycle, *The Harvey Girls* and *Seven Brides for Seven Brothers*, the people on the frontier are so close to nature that they border on the primitive. In the first, unkempt and rowdy men dominate the western town of Sandrock, New Mexico, where they seek the base pleasures of the saloon. It takes the civilizing forces of the Harvey girls, waitresses for the Harvey restaurant chain, to bring order and domesticity to this place. The song "On the Atchison, Topeka and the Santa Fe" explains that they hail from all areas of the United States. As the young women become romantically involved with the local men, *The Harvey Girls* demonstrates how this frontier town stands in for the national community. Feminized civility and male rowdiness create a new social grouping that is infused with the ruggedness of the landscape, but softened with some added refinements and social graces. The film concludes with a wedding ceremony that merges frontier space and civilized space. When he acquired the rights to *The Harvey Girls*, Freed made it clear that he desired to tell the story in a reverential way. For him, the material conjured both "romance" and an "American folk quality." The folk was to be depicted not with scorn but with dignity, in keeping with the importance of this "American work."[23]

This dynamic is even more pronounced in *Seven Brides for Seven Brothers*. The frontier town where Adam Pontipee (Howard Keel) first finds Milly (Jane Powell) is a rustic, but orderly and polite collection of pristine storefronts and homes with well-appointed parlors. Adam and his six brothers, however, introduce a rowdy element. They have been raised in relative isolation from the town. Based on a story by Stephen Vincent Benét, "The Sobbin' Women," the film associates the Pontipee brothers with backwardness: "The townspeople quickly peg them as unsociable; tribe-like; independent, handsome in a wild sort of way. . . . Gradually they become a legend, being known as the wild folks who live up in the valley like bears." They are closer to nature than to civilization, and it is Milly's job, as well as that of her six female friends, to tame them. Ultimately, however, the film does not privilege civilization over the Pontipees' natural wildness. As production materials and reviews of the film insist, "teaching them city manners, dressing them up properly, teaching them to dance and to court a girl, and making gentlemen of them" works only "to a certain degree." Ultimately, it is their closeness to nature that distinguishes them from the men in the town and makes them appealing to the young women. They can "outdance anybody and outwork anybody," and "when they fall in love, all at the same time, their mass emotion durned near wrecks the Oregon Territory." As one reviewer stated of director Stanley Donen's interpretation, "it is wildly funny, but he never ridicules people and situations that are a part of the personal heritage of many Americans." Ultimately, the young women are the ones integrated into the world of the brothers rather than the other way around.[24]

Aside from their depictions of nature, the folk musicals formally construct unified space by the use of atmospheric musical numbers. Chorales, songs that are passed along and sung together, emanate from this natural environment that the films work to establish. Spontaneity in the musical number, as Jane Feuer has argued, is one of the most important qualities in the transformation of "mass art" to "folk art." The "bricolage number," a musical number that makes use of non-musical props, "attempts to cancel engineering (a characteristic of mass production) by substituting bricolage (a characteristic of folk production)." In the folk musical, these spontaneous, atmospheric numbers are less concerned with props and more invested in foregrounding relationship to place. More than any other device, the atmospheric chorales establish the community as folk and unite that folk to the land. Like the chorales and call-and-response patterns used to indicate folk communities in films like *Hallelujah!* (1929) and *Georgia Rose* (1930), *Allá en el Rancho Grande* (1936) and *Tropic Holiday* (1938), the songs in Hollywood's folk musicals of the 1940s and 1950s appear to arise naturally from the environment with which the characters are identified.[25]

The songs "Meet Me in St. Louis," "Our State Fair," "Our Home Town," and "In the Good Old Summertime" are the first to be sung in their respective films. They celebrate locality as a part of nature both by their lyrics and by their performance. "Meet Me in St. Louis" is the only original period song that is used in this way. During the opening summer sequence in *Meet Me in St. Louis*, Agnes starts the song as she enters the house from her swim: "Meet Me in St. Louis, Louis, meet me at the fair." She sings as the camera follows her up the stairs, "Don't tell me the lights are shining any place but there." The film passes the song to Grandpa (Harry Davenport) with a cut to the bathroom where he is finishing his toilet. He carries the song as the camera follows him into his bedroom. Overhearing voices coming from outside the house, Grandpa looks out the window and sees granddaughter Esther (Judy Garland) and her friends singing the song as they pull up in a horse and buggy. Celebrating St. Louis, young and old members of the family share in this chorale, which unites the domestic, interior space of the house (from kitchen, to stairway, to bathroom, and bedroom) with the natural, exterior space of the outside world.

In their first film production, Richard Rodgers and Oscar Hammerstein II use a chorale to open *State Fair*. The film begins with a shot of a billboard announcing the opening of the Iowa State Fair. The camera cranes to show farmer Dave Miller (Percy Kilbride) driving down a country road while whistling and singing, "Our state fair is a great state fair, don't miss it, don't even be late." The film cuts to show farmer Abel Frake (Charles Winninger) carrying the song as he works in the barn. His refrain is answered by the snorts of his prize pig, Blue Boy. The film cuts again to show his wife (Fay Bainter) singing the tune as she cooks in the kitchen. Like "Meet Me in St. Louis," "Our State Fair" creates an onscreen community out of shared investment in an annual event.

The chorale is an especially powerful tool for establishing community and place, even in locales that do not lend themselves to such a device. The fair to which the Frake family migrates simulates an urban space where strangers are encountered and thrills and entertainments are offered. Nevertheless, in the scene in which Wayne Frake (Dick Haymes) and Emily Edwards (Vivian Blaine) dance in the pavilion for the first time, the urban space becomes a folk space. The bandleader performs the song "It's a Grand Night for Singing," to which the members of the audience listen and dance. As he gazes into Emily's eyes, Wayne picks up the song—"maybe the reason I'm feeling this way has something to do with you"—as an illustration of his emotions. Following his lead, the couples around them continue the song. "To create the feeling that this is a popular song they all know," an early continuity script indicates, "this should be sung in unison, not harmonized." The pavilion's microphone projects the song across the fairgrounds as the camera cuts to couples on roller coasters and Ferris wheels singing along. Included in this sequence is Wayne's sister, Margy (Jeanne Crain), who joyfully rides on the Ferris wheel with her romantic partner, Pat (Dana Andrews). The purpose of this sequence is to unite the fairgoers in the experience of the fair. Sharing the song evokes a folk community that is transmitted by a form of modern technology, the fairgrounds' loudspeaker. Barriers between performers, audience members, and fairgoers are broken down as the song is passed in unison. In the process, elements of difference are erased. Significantly, an early draft of this scene included among the couples in the roller coaster "a clean-looking negro boy and girl" who carry the song as their car passes by the camera. Ultimately, this reference and one to a "Ubangi Village" at the fair were cut from the final film. In both instances, stark evidence of racial difference, however casually introduced, would have disrupted the unity of place in which such folk musicals are deeply invested.[26]

A celebration of ordinary spaces and ordinary pursuits pervades these chorales. The song "Our Home Town," which opens *Summer Holiday*, is an ode to the small community of Danneville, Connecticut. Nat Miller (Walter Huston), the local newspaperman, expresses appreciation for his home, where nothing very special occurs: "There was nothing ever done to carry off a crown, no one ever won very much renown, but it's our home town, it's our home town." This idealized turn-of-the-century New England town centers around ordinary places like a soda fountain, a public high school, and pristine homes with white picket fences. As he arrives home from work, Mr. Miller continues, "life is routine, every day is the same, and we never worry." His family members engage with the number, in song or in rhymed speech, as they go about their daily activities of cooking, playing, and enjoying one another. As one reviewer noted, "The musical numbers, tastefully chosen and skillfully staged, are not spotted arbitrarily, but stem naturally from the situations." This opening number, like those in *Meet Me in St. Louis* and *State Fair*, unites family, community, and place through the musical and formal structures of the atmospheric chorale, thus setting up the fracturing of such unity that functions as the folk musical's primary source of conflict.[27]

Continuity and Rupture

In the Good Old Summertime begins with a pan of the Chicago skyline, circa 1949. A series of dissolves move us through the modern city. The low-angle shot of a skyscraper reveals its grandeur as the camera slowly tilts down toward the street. Another dissolve leads to a high-angle shot of a busy thoroughfare with crowds, cars, buses, and taxis. Speaking over these images, Van Johnson's character Andrew Larkin reflects: "When I look at Chicago today it's hard for me to realize that it's the same city that I knew when I was a boy. All those skyscrapers. That steel and concrete. Those busy streets. And the crowds! We didn't have them. . . ." Another dissolve moves us back in time to the days of Andrew's youth. The music shifts from staccato rhythms to a waltz as we are transported to a tranquil street lined with brownstones. It is a high-angle shot, but not as panoramic as the one of the modern city. Only a few people move unhurriedly through this space, along with the occasional horse and buggy. The voiceover continues, "In my day life was more leisurely. The women didn't wear anything on their faces then. But the men made up for it. You weren't a substantial citizen unless you wore a mustache." The film then introduces us to Andrew and the charming world of Chicago at the turn of the century.

This opening sequence is emblematic of Arthur Freed's notion of what constitutes a successful musical film. Allowing us to enjoy a "more easy and more gracious way of life," films like *In the Good Old Summertime* emphasize the experience of time as different in the modern and premodern eras. Even though the Chicago of the film is encountering change, such as the growing popularity of Tin Pan Alley songs versus classical music, it is decidedly less modern than the city of 1949. The absence of skyscrapers, crowds, steel, concrete, and frenetic motion renders the Edwardian city as a place of constancy and refuge. "Life was more leisurely," Andrew remembers. Whereas the speed of the modern city implies abrupt change and a drive toward productivity, the leisureliness of Chicago's past connotes stasis and an emphasis on enjoying the natural rhythms of life. If change is to occur, it will be gentle, if not imperceptible.

The Hollywood folk musical was able to attenuate modernity and its effects by projecting historical continuity as a function of natural time. The emphasis on the seasons and their ordering of human activity contributes to this impression of cyclicality. In *Meet Me in St. Louis*, we follow a year in the Smith family's life. As a season marked by leisure, warm and languid days, and outdoor, together activities, summertime is particularly relevant to the folk musical's project. In *State Fair, Centennial Summer*, and *Summer Holiday* we witness the passing of the summer season from country to small town and city, from Iowa to Philadelphia and Danneville, Connecticut. And *Meet Me in St. Louis* and *In the Good Old Summertime* place special emphasis on the sensory feelings and experiences of summer.

Life rituals are attached to the experience of the seasons. By their very nature, rituals are repetitive activities infused with symbolic meaning for a collective. The observance of holidays establishes the characters' sense of belonging to land and nation. Musical numbers such as "Independence Day" and "While the Men Are Drinking" in *Summer Holiday* and "State Fair" and "Iowa" in *State Fair* demonstrate pride in place through the celebration of annual activities. These holidays constitute the together activities that establish the folk community.

Other together activities mark both the passing and the continuity of time. Life events such as births and weddings indicate the addition of new members to the folk community and the promise of the collective's endurance into the future. *Seven Brides for Seven Brothers* celebrates the courtship ritual and the birth of new life. The Pontipee brothers learn about courtship from Milly in the number "Goin' Co'tin'." At the summer barn raising, they fall in love with the girls in the town as communicated by a folk dance wherein they compete for, and ultimately win, the girls' affection. Believing that they will be unable to gain the parents' permission, the brothers kidnap the girls in the middle of winter and trap them in the backwoods where their families cannot retrieve them until the roads have cleared. Furious at their behavior, Milly bars the brothers, including her husband, Adam, from the house.

Over the course of the winter, the girls' feelings begin to thaw. They sing "June Bride" in anticipation of the coming spring and summer ("Oh they say when you marry in June, you're a bride all your life"). The lyrics bemoan the long winter ("February finds a drift and the storm that seems never to lift") and look forward to the possibility of spring ("April showers will come so they say, but they don't and it's May"). Just as the girls sing the last of the verse the snow stops falling ("You're about to forget the whole thing . . . all at once, one day, it's spring"). Moving through the months of the year, "June Bride" marks time as it predictably repeats itself. Embedded in this experience of time is both the feeling of stifling stasis and the excitement of liberating change.

With spring comes the reunification of the brothers and the girls. The script makes clear the effect of the season on the couples: "As we see the ice and snow melting, we show the girls' anger against the brothers melting with the coming of Spring." The number "Spring, Spring, Spring," sung by six couples as they stroll through the farm and surrounding country-side, celebrates the rejuvenation of life that the season annually brings. The script describes how this sequence "should be a poetic unfolding of Spring": "A crocus breaks through the snow. Skunk cabbage suddenly pops up beside a stream. The branches of a pussy willow turn red, and burst into silky grey buds." The emphasis on new life is made clear as the couples witness the various newborn animals, including a doe, a litter of pigs, ducklings, baby chicks, skunk, and quail. The images suggest that the romantic couples are themselves destined to bring new life into the world. We see the manifestation of spring in the subsequent scene, in which Milly holds her newborn baby and welcomes Adam home. The final sequence reveals all six couples being married at once, witnessed by Adam and Milly and the girls' parents. The mass event indicates the expansion of a family and the promise of new generations.[28]

In addition to songs that emphasize continuity of the collective and the land, folk musicals also offer songs that admit the existence of modernity and the disruption of cyclical time. Songs of longing and movement provide the anticipation of change that the folk musical so vehemently warns against. Dorothy's yearning for a new land, as expressed by "Somewhere Over the Rainbow," indicates that she is not entirely satisfied with her home environment. Her Kansas farm, in the midst of the Dust Bowl, is bleak and dry. More catastrophic for Dorothy, however, is her menacing neighbor, Miss Gulch, who threatens Dorothy's dog Toto. Faced with separation from her loved one, Dorothy longs for a land "where troubles melt like lemon drops away above the chimney tops." Such threats against the family are pronounced earlier in *The Wizard of Oz* than in the other folk musicals of this era. It is the bewildering and menacing world of Oz that makes the troubles in her Kansas home pale by comparison. Ultimately, the phrase "there's no place like home" overturns the longing for a journey in "Somewhere Over the Rainbow."[29]

More often, in the films set in towns and cities of the turn of the century, folk musicals admit the interruptions caused by modernity, but ultimately incorporate them into the cyclical, communal activities that maintain constancy in their characters' lives. Songs about new forms of transportation—"The Trolley Song," "The Stanley Steamer," and "On the Atchison, Topeka and the Santa Fe"—foreground the sensory experiences that new technologies offer. The lyrics describe the sounds of the trolley ("clang, clang, clang went the trolley / ding, ding, ding went the bell"), the Stanley Steamer automobile ("honk, honk"), and the train ("Do you hear that whistle down the line? I figure that it's engine number forty-nine"). These songs express the excitement that comes from moving through time and space; as Judy Garland sings in the latter number, "if you get a

12. The romantic couples celebrate the coming of spring on the farm. *Seven Brides for Seven Brothers* copyright 1954 by MGM.

hankerin', you wanna roam / Our advice to you is run away / On the Atchison, Topeka and the Santa Fe." Even with such a promise, the train creates community rather than disrupts it. As *The Harvey Girls* demonstrates, the girls who migrate to the frontier integrate and coalesce the community of Sandrock, New Mexico. The prologue explains that the girls are "unsung pioneers," "civilizing forces" armed with "a fried egg and a cup of coffee." Contributing to the domestication of this space, the girls create home and community for the men who live there.[30]

Even if some characteristics of modernity are incorporated into the folk musical's community-making project, others threaten home and stasis. Each rupture of the folk community involves a journey that takes a family member away from the home or displaces the home itself. The violent depiction of Dorothy's house swirling in the tornado and being dropped in Oz is an extreme example of her character's migration to another land.

Just as dramatic, if less drastic, are the sequences in *Meet Me in St. Louis* in which the Smiths grapple with their impending move to New York City. During their festive Halloween celebration, the father, Alonzo Smith (Leon Ames), announces that his law firm is transferring him to New York, where he plans to relocate the family after Christmas. This news sends the family into despair. Mrs. Smith accuses him of being calm while he packs them off "lock, stock, and barrel." Insisting that he has "the future to think about," he mentions the financial pressures of sending his children to college. When Agnes declares that she wants to take her cat, the family's maid informs her that she will have to keep her "cooped up in a tenement." "Rich people have houses," daughter Rose (Lucille Bremer) says sulkily, "people like us live in flats, hundreds of flats in one building." To this, Tootie (Margaret O'Brien) whines, "I'd rather be poor if we could only stay here! I'd rather go with the orphaluns, at the orphaluns' home!"

As this dialogue suggests, New York City in 1903 was an immigrant city. In the film, St. Louis is cast as a small town, even though it was a major urban center. As Mrs. Smith explains, "New York is a big city. Not that St. Louis isn't big, but it just doesn't seem very big out here where we live." Such a reinvention was necessary to make a stark contrast between modern New York and the home of the Smith family. The references to tenements, buck stoves, and cramped spaces reveal that the Smiths fear that theirs will be the experience of the immigrants who live and work in

13. The Smith family reacts to the news that they are moving to New York. *Meet Me in St. Louis* copyright 1944 by MGM.

New York. Not only will their living space change, but their familial bonds will be in jeopardy. Will Katie and Grandpa be able to live with them there? What will happen to the budding romantic attachments of daughters Rose and Esther? And will young Tootie be able to grow up in a safe and healthy environment? These are concerns faced by all immigrants in search of a better life. Representing the antithesis of home and belonging, New York is cast as the "villain" in the film, a place of rupture and deracination.[31]

As the family leaves the dinner table in despair, only Mr. and Mrs. Smith remain. Mrs. Smith goes to the piano, a symbol of family togetherness and the American middle class. She begins to play "You and I," a song written by Freed for the film. The lyrics reinforce the bonds between husband and wife, parents and children. She sings, "Time goes by / But we'll be together / You and I." As she sings, Mr. Smith joins her (his voice is dubbed by Freed), and one by one, the family members return to the room to listen to their parents. "You and I" is an assertion that the family will not be separated and that their love will bind them together no matter what happens.

This sequence, however, provides only momentary salve. In a subsequent scene, the terror of leaving is made real through the perspective of the youngest Smith, Tootie. On Christmas Eve, Esther comes home from the annual Christmas dance and finds Tootie still awake and waiting for Santa Claus. She is worried that he will not know where to find her after the move to New York. Esther sings "Have Yourself a Merry Little Christmas" to cheer her, but the song ultimately provides an image of the future that is tenuous at best. Written for this film by Ralph Blane and Hugh Martin, the song expresses the hope that the family might be united sometime in the future, though they may be separated for the time being.

The song's original lyrics reflect a disillusioned and even sinister vision for the family. Suggesting that this Christmas "may be your last," the song foretells how there will be "no good times like the olden days, happy golden days of yore" and that "faithful friends who were dear to us will be near to us no more." To be sure, these lines evoke the more realistic results of a family's move to a foreign environment. Thinking the song too harsh to sing to a little girl, Judy Garland asked that the lyrics be softened. The producers eventually altered the song to offer a hopeful message.[32] It wishes listeners to have a "merry little Christmas," for "next year all our troubles will be out of sight." "As in olden days," it promises, "faithful friends who were dear to us will be near to us once more." An indication of the song's original melancholy message remains, however: "Someday soon, we all will be together, if the fates allow / Until then, we'll have to muddle through somehow."[33]

The two versions of this song reflect the paradox of modernity that exists in the Freed folk musicals. The earlier version admits the shocks and jolts of migration; it is not a happy process even if it is a necessary one ("Next year we may all be living in the past"). It also suggests the impossibility of returning home ("No good times like the olden days / Happy golden days of yore"). Furthermore, the song indicates that the social integration of home is one of the key comforts that will be lost in the process of migration ("Faithful friends who were dear to us will be near to us no more").

The second version of the song provides a utopian vision of home as something that remains intact and can even accompany the migrant. The folk musical achieves this promise with its narrative, such as in the final lyrics of "Have Yourself a Merry Little Christmas" ("Some day soon we all will be together"). The film suggests that the future will be bright ("Next year all our troubles will be miles away") despite the pain, however in attenuated form, associated with having to migrate in the first place ("Until then, we'll have to muddle through somehow").

Hopeful sentiments aside, the song propels Tootie into a fitful rage. She runs into the cold, snowy night and begins to knock down snowmen. Realizing that she will not be able to take everything from home with her to New York, she screams, "I'd rather kill them if we can't take them with us!" Clearly for Tootie, the value of what is left behind far outweighs anything of merit that life in New York City promises.

Tootie's hysterical outburst prompts Mr. Smith to change his mind. As he walks through his house and observes the bare walls and packed boxes on Christmas Eve, he stops to light his pipe. The glow of the burning match illuminates his face, and suddenly, as though by divine inspiration, he realizes the importance of remaining at home. He calls the family to his side to announce that they will stay in St. Louis. In a joyous scene, they embrace around the Christmas tree and form the supreme image of familial unity. The resolution means that the family will get to see the fair, Esther and Rose may marry and perpetuate the family, and the children can go on with their familiar games. Most important of all, the family will remain together in St. Louis. As *Variety* noted, the film's theme is that "'getting ahead and going to New York' isn't everything."[34] The film confirms that an appreciation of home and its gifts is of paramount importance despite the lure of migration to a better life.

By contrast, in *Summer Holiday*, an actual journey takes place, with disastrous effects. Rouben Mamoulian directed this musical version of Eugene O'Neill's 1933 play, *Ah, Wilderness!*, which tells the story of a boy's coming of age in a turn-of-the-century New England town. Seeking to depict "typical Americana," Mamoulian conceived of the town as a Grant Wood painting, with the comforting, muted tones of nature, such as yellow, beige, and green.[35]

By contrast, the city sequence communicates strangeness initially with its dark back alleys and then with the saturated, bright colors of young Richard Miller's (Mickey Rooney) drunken hallucination. He goes to the city after being spurned by Muriel (Gloria DeHaven), his high school sweetheart. He accepts an invitation from a "Yale man" to date some "New Haven girls." In this sequence, Richard walks through an unfamiliar part of town where shadowy and dirty alleys signal an urban space. As his friend tells him, "it's not much of a neighborhood." They enter the Danneville Music Hall, where scantily clad chorus girls perform for a raucous audience. Going backstage, Richard and his friend meet the girls from New Haven. Soon, Richard finds himself alone in a bar with "Belle," his girl for the evening. Though he is underage, Belle plies him with liquor. Mamoulian gives us Richard's perspective, revealing his disoriented state with a blurry and distorted shot of Belle, whose dress turns from light pink to fiery red. Belle succeeds in seducing him, but when a wealthier man walks in, she turns her attentions toward the better prospect. Like the nightclub sequence in *Hallelujah!*, the depiction of Richard's seduction conforms to notions of the city as a space where moral decay goes hand in hand with erotic pleasures and salacious entertainments.

Drunk and dejected, Richard stumbles home from his journey into that dark world. Like Dorothy, he wants nothing more than to return to the place from whence he came. The next day, Mr. Miller has a stern talk with his son and reminds him of the evils of drinking and loose women. Richard assures his father that his night out was merely an indiscretion. He does not really want that life of compromised values. He declares that he plans to return home after college and marry his high school sweetheart. *Summer Holiday* negotiates the paradox of modernity and migration by simultaneously embracing its positive qualities (such as a ride on the Stanley Steamer) and warning against the forces that will permanently disrupt the family's bucolic existence.

The final scene of the film restores the stasis that had been ruptured by Richard's journey away from home. It is evening, and Mr. and Mrs. Miller observe the various members of their family, happy to be "surrounded by love." Uncle Sid and his sweetheart (Frank Morgan and Agnes Moorehead) sway on the porch swing. As they sip lemonade, she sighs, "I don't see how you could want anything better than this," to which Sid answers, "You're darn right, Lily." Richard walks outside to wave to Muriel across the street, and the camera cranes upward to reveal Mr. and Mrs. Miller embracing on the balcony. The parents gaze down over the tableau in blissful contentment. The scene binds the various generations, proving that their hometown is a place in which family ties are maintained and that the future is secured.

This return to stasis, symbolized by the (re)unification of the family, is repeated again and again in the folk musicals of this period. The last scene in *The Wizard of Oz* shows Dorothy waking from her slumber in her own bed, surrounded by the familiar faces of family and friends. The Smith family of St. Louis attends the fair together, an affirmation that migration to New York has been averted. In *State Fair* the Frake family returns home to resume their daily activities. And the final frame of *Centennial Summer* freezes the united Rogers family on a train platform as they happily wave goodbye to a meddlesome aunt who threatened to disrupt their lives. Even the romantic couplings that occur in *The Harvey Girls, In the Good Old Summertime*, and *Seven Brides for Seven Brothers* are in service to the creation and preservation of community in the face of change. They promise ongoing cyclical time as families perpetuate themselves against the stable backdrops of home, land, and nation.

Romanticism and Modernity

Hollywood's folk musicals of the 1940s and 1950s held modernity in check with a strong cultural current of romanticism. For contemporary audiences, these films seemed to capture a way of life that exuded charm and graciousness. Freed and his audiences romantically ascribed these qualities to the days before the wars and mass migrations of the twentieth century. With *State Fair*, Twentieth Century–Fox attempted to turn back the clock. As studio publicity and reviewers were quick to point out upon the film's release, state fairs had been closed for the previous four years, "one of the war's most deeply missed casualties." Both the carefree feelings and the material resources that the fairs commanded could not be justified in those years of sacrifice and rationing. With sumptuous Technicolor photography, *State Fair* resurrected this American institution as proof of the nation's unchanging values and its hopeful future.[36]

Released domestically just two weeks after the Japanese surrender, *State Fair* was very much a product of wartime anxieties. The Twentieth Century–Fox pressbook notes the many ways in which, despite adversity, the film was able to show "America's best-loved institution" in all its glory.

"In ordinary times," the press-book reported, "the studio would send a company to the Iowa State Fairgrounds at Des Moines and film what was necessary." During wartime, however, the studio reconstructed the fair on sound stages. Ordinary material items found at fairgrounds, such as balloons, hamburgers, and hot dogs had to be creatively and synthetically constructed for the production. Even "carnival help and performers were almost impossible to get" because their labor was needed in the war effort. The real-time difficulties made the lavish production seem all the more remarkable. Its "vivid authenticity" transported audiences to the time and place that "Americans knew before Pearl Harbor."[37]

Critics revisited the relationship between musicals and the lost innocence of American society with the reissue of *The Wizard of Oz* in 1949. The issues that surrounded that film's first release in 1939—the Depression and the start of hostilities in Europe—took on different meaning by the war's end and the beginning of the atomic era. As if to mirror the folk musical's emphasis on cyclical time, the re-release indicated to critics like Bosley Crowther of the *New York Times* that some things remain the same despite change in modern life. Crowther begins his review with the expectation that the film will entertain a new generation much as it did in 1939. He writes self-consciously, however, from the position of "one who saw it ten years ago and who looks at it now with vagrant memories of much that was happening then and has happened since." *The Wizard of Oz*, he maintains, "is still a delightful experience," despite the "painfully realistic thoughts, called up by the mere association." In a time when studio reissues were rare, it was striking to have the same movie-going experience after ten years' time: "the entertainment value of the attraction is actually enhanced for those who saw it previously by the wistful nostalgia it stirs." Justifying both the feelings of escape and the domestic tranquility that the film conjures, Crowther foregrounds the ways in which the film lends solace: "this picture can rouse pleasure out of pain." In advance of the 1949 opening the *New York Times* emphasized the film's continued relevance by featuring a picture of Dorothy and her companions with the caption, "Old Friends Return."[38]

The Hollywood folk musical projected images of white communities in solidarity during the war years and into the 1950s. Its makers, Arthur Freed foremost among them, harnessed the growing interest in American folk culture in order to make musical films that were enduring and "not transient." The idyllic countryside and small towns provided the settings for folk songs and traditions to be exploited. More significantly, however, these settings were structuring devices for delivering the most salient messages of these films. The folk musicals project social membership via the family and the community that are intertwined with the space they inhabit. Close to nature's rhythms, life in these settings draws its purpose from rootedness in and duty to homeland. Holding romantic space and modern space in precarious balance, the folk musical offers allegories of migration that ultimately reaffirm the collective at home.

Unlike earlier folk musicals, such as *Hallelujah!* and *Tropic Holiday*, the white-cast films focused not on restricting mobility but on resurrecting and preserving a set of values that were in danger of being lost. In this respect, Hollywood's output of the 1940s and 1950s had more in common with the musicals of Yiddish, black, and Mexican cinema that ministered to communities of migrants for whom home and homeland were contested locations. Presenting images of unified spaces and cyclical time, the narratives and songs of Hollywood's folk musicals were defensive products for a society in transition. They offered social membership for the displaced at home while they presented a fiction of social unity to the world at large. During the social and political strife of the 1960s, the folk musical's departure from contemporary realities became all the more pronounced. In that decade, a growing conservative element in American society used folk musicals like *The Music Man* (1962) and *The Sound of Music* (1965) to voice concerns about the state of the nation's cities, families, and position on the world stage.

5

"Tahiti, Rome, and
Mason City, Iowa"

Musical Migrants in the Postwar Era

After moviegoing audiences reached a peak in 1946, the Hollywood studios experienced serious challenges. The Paramount Decree of 1948, the result of a Supreme Court antitrust case, dismantled the vertical integration of the studios and separated them from their exhibition units. Three years later, Louis B. Mayer, the long-time head of MGM, was fired and replaced by Dore Schary. As described by Lela Simone, the former music coordinator for the Arthur Freed unit at MGM, the change was significant: "Louis B. Mayer was an intimate friend of Arthur Freed's. Intimate friend. And therefore, the whole operation manner at MGM could be very different than what it was afterwards." For the most part, according to Simone, Freed and his team retained creative and artistic freedom during Schary's control; but the "whole trend in motion pictures came down," and the excitement that had surrounded musical production during the previous decade greatly diminished.[1]

Other challenges to the musical film came with the age of television. Gene Kelly described the shift: "In the late 50s, everyone would come home at night, turn on the tube and watch singers and dancers. So why go out to a movie?"[2] Variety shows made up a significant portion of early television programming and competed with the movie musical by featuring many of the same stars. The studios countered with the production of show musicals such as *White Christmas* (1954), *Anything Goes* (1956), and *Pal Joey* (1957), which featured stars like Bing Crosby, Danny Kaye, Donald O'Connor, and Frank Sinatra performing specialty acts much like their stints on television.

Faced with the possibility that musical films might become obsolete, Kelly became an outspoken advocate of the genre through the 1960s and 1970s. Although he recognized the work opportunity offered by television variety shows, he nevertheless lamented their negative effect on the genre. "If I do a one-hour [television] special," he asked, "why go to see me on film? For doing the same things, we get paid well in each medium." Threats to the originality of musical film production came from within the industry as well. "If I were to go to any studio with an adult, original musical," he claimed, "I doubt very much if any of them would be interested—at least, it would be very hard going. It is very hard to get a musical off the ground if it has not been brought from Broadway."[3]

Of the five movie musical successes in the early 1960s—*West Side Story* (1961), *The Music Man* (1962), *Mary Poppins* (1964), *My Fair Lady* (1964), and *The Sound of Music* (1965)—*Mary Poppins* was the only original production. Critical observers of this trend saw it as the death knell of the genre. Arthur Freed, who had produced thirty-nine original musical vehicles at MGM, disapproved: "Hollywood should stop being afraid of making its own musicals. . . . It should remember that so many of the biggest musical hits in films were made for the movies and not borrowed from Broadway." Unwilling to take risks, the studios desired only tested material from the stage. "Nothing is 'proven,'" Freed argued. "Nothing is sure except that the surest way to make something mediocre is to copy someone else."[4]

Film and television producer John Cutts concurred with Freed. In an article entitled "Bye Bye Musicals," he warned against the creative paralysis that had taken hold in musical film production: "The real danger of this present 'go for broke' [big-budget musicals] policy is that it leaves little or no room for development of any kind." Declaring that "musical cinema" was not "healthy," he regretfully predicted its demise: "A cinema which neglects the development of its own resources carries the seed of its own destruction with it."[5]

Despite such warnings, the studios proceeded with plans to adapt Broadway successes for the screen and were rewarded in some of their earliest attempts.[6] Twentieth Century–Fox's *The Sound of Music* had the most spectacular success. By 1969, four years after it first premiered, the film's box office revenues of $135 million had far exceeded its $8 million production budget.[7] Derided by critics as "The Sound of Money," the film seemed to restore faith not only in the marketability of the musical but also in the studio system of old.[8] As producer and writer Ernest Lehman declared in 1968, "After seeing the grosses on 'The Sound of Music' everyone has jumped on the bandwagon."[9] At the time, Lehman was working on *Hello, Dolly!* (1969) for Twentieth Century–Fox, and Warner Bros. had just released *Finian's Rainbow* (1968), starring Fred Astaire and Petula Clark. The musical seemed alive and well in the 1960s, notwithstanding the dire projections by Freed and Cutts. Musicals that followed *The Sound of Music* included *Camelot* (1967), with Richard Harris and Vanessa Redgrave; *Thoroughly Modern Millie* (1967) and *Star!* (1968), featuring Julie Andrews; *Funny Girl* (1968), with Barbra Streisand; and *Doctor Dolittle* (1967), with Rex Harrison.

The fact that the studios ultimately lost money on most of these films had more to do with their inflated budgets than with their inherent appeal to audiences. Producer Cy Feuer said as much in an interview about his production of *Cabaret* (1972): "[The musicals] grossed many, many millions of dollars. . . . The people who got to see those pictures do not know the cost of them. If you are to examine these grosses, putting aside the budgets, there's a lot of business out there for musicals. There's an audience for them." He disparaged the studios' "runaway budgets" and declared, "Had those pictures been brought in at sensible levels there would have been a hell of a margin of profit. I think they've all done over $10 million, and some of them a hell of a lot more, 'Dolly' included."[10]

Film scholars have called for a revised look at the status of the musical in the 1960s. Rather than a decade of "marked decline," recent scholarship has suggested that the desire for musicals was quite strong in this period of great social strife and dramatic shifts in audience demographics. Considering the box office numbers and putting aside studio profits, the musicals of the 1960s remained quite popular. The appeal of *The Sound of Music* and *The Music Man*, in particular, rested in their ability to speak to and assuage the concerns of their time.[11]

As folk musicals, these two films address issues of social ordering and belonging through projections of bucolic communities that are held together in the face of change. Unlike the folk musicals of the 1940s and 1950s, however, *The Music Man* and *The Sound of Music* create folk communities where there are none to begin with. Fractious, joyless, and disillusioned, the societies in River City, Iowa, and Salzburg, Austria, require the rejuvenating powers of musical migrants to minister to them and make them whole. Harold Hill and Maria bring with them the power to invoke community. As musical beings, they reinforce the relationship between a community's members and the land in which they live.

It is no coincidence that *The Music Man* and *The Sound of Music* appeared at a time of unsettling change. In postwar American society, family-oriented amusement parks such as Disneyland and Knotts Berry Farm treated fairgoers to an experience steeped in nostalgia for a simpler, idealized era. Such amusements ministered to a desire for tradition and morality that seemed threatened by liberal reforms in society and a cold war that careened from one international crisis to another. In her history of the origins of the new American Right in the postwar era, Lisa McGirr points to the "effervescent liberalism" in the early 1960s that "promised change on the horizon" and the simultaneous sense of ineffectiveness felt in political and social circles on the Right. Conservatives were fearful that the nation was headed for "collectivism," in which a welfare state and civil rights reforms compromised individual liberties and a traditional American way of life. These "suburban warriors" became active in their local schools, churches, and politics, aiming to preserve the American nuclear family and the moral guardianship of children. The introduction of liberal curricula in schools, the menace of desegregation, and the increasing sexuality and violence on film and television screens prompted concerned parents to become vocal in their championing of American traditions and "clean" entertainment for the entire family.[12] *The Music Man* and *The Sound of Music* met the desires of Hollywood's conservative audience but also resonated with more than just that niche of society. Most demonstrative in their commendation of these films were the Americans who, in letters to the filmmakers and in box office receipts, made their preferences known.

A critical consideration of these two films not only suggests the sustained saliency of the folk musical in the 1960s but also reveals the ways in which a growing conservative segment of society met the challenges of the age. Relatively little attention has been paid to *The Music Man*, perhaps because it was overshadowed by the enormous box office success of *The Sound of Music* three years later. The earlier film's reception, however, is indicative of the growing popular support for wholesome, family-friendly entertainment that would make *The Sound of Music*'s success possible.

The reception of both *The Music Man* and *The Sound of Music* illuminates the widening cultural divide between the conservative, mass-produced "folk" of Hollywood and the socially conscious "folk" of the counterculture. Artists Joan Baez and Bob Dylan performed their politically inflected songs at venues like the Newport Folk Festival in the early 1960s. Identifying inequalities and calling for change in American society, these songwriters were mobilizing the folk for progressive reform. Many people who made up Hollywood's family audience believed such music to be more damaging than helpful to the nation. The folk musical's treatment and attenuation of modernity made it particularly useful as a reactionary force. Critical reviews and distribution and exhibition records convey that audiences considered the act of viewing *The Music Man* and *The Sound of Music* as a form of resistance to the moral and social decay that they witnessed around them. Seen from this perspective, the musical became a weapon in the fight to save an imperiled America.

The Music Man (1962)

Meredith Willson's *The Music Man* opened on Broadway in 1957 and subsequently won the Tony Award for Best Musical. Along with Willson, director Morton DaCosta adapted the show for the screen in 1962. The story follows Harold Hill (Robert Preston), a traveling salesman, as he arrives in River City, Iowa, on the Fourth of July weekend in 1912. He intends to con the town's residents into buying instruments and uniforms for the purpose of creating a boys' band, which will never materialize. During his stay, Harold becomes romantically attached to the town's unmarried librarian and piano teacher, Marian Paroo (Shirley Jones), who falls in love with him despite his duplicity. Over the course of Hill's visit to River City, he wins the trust of the initially dubious townsfolk, brings harmony, both socially and musically, to the town's opposing groups, and instills excitement and romance into Marian's lovelorn heart. In the process, Hill realizes that he too has been transformed. No longer satisfied to run from town to town swindling people, he settles in River City and creates what he had falsely promised at the start: a boys' band.

At the beginning of DaCosta's film adaptation, Hill rallies the folk of River City in the town square with the musical admonition "Ya Got Trouble." Framed by the statue of the town's founder, Henry Madison, Harold points to the new pool table in the billiard parlor as an ominous sign of things to come. He successfully manipulates the townsfolk's fear of change and their narrow-mindedness regarding all things different. In the process, the film's audience discerns the fundamental differences between the salesman and his latest victims. Harold arrives in River City with a wealth of information about the "tell-tale signs" of sin and corruption. He has seen the damning effects of pool tables: "next thing ya know / Yer son is playing for money / In a pinch-back suit. / And listenin' to some big outta town Jasper / Hearin' him tell about horse-race gamblin'." Playing on his audience's puritanical sensibilities, Harold invokes gambling, the presence of strangers in town, and horse racing to get their attention. He knows that they are concerned with the processes and signs of change in their community and, especially, with the corruption of their children. From the pool hall, Harold warns, the children will head "for the dance at the Arm'ry, / Libertine men and Scarlet women / And Rag-time, shameless music / That will grab your son and your daughter, / With the arms of a jungle animal instinct, / Mass 'teria! / Friends, the idle brain is the devil's playground, trouble!"

Harold's knowledge of these dangers stems from his sexually sophisticated, metropolitan background. His invocation of ragtime, in particular, is a reference to the spread of African American music out of the South and into northern cities, where it became woven into the mainstream. The song references race mixing through the suggestion that a "jungle animal instinct" will "grab" the sons and daughters of the town. Harold's song produces a frenzy among the townspeople and ultimately primes them for accepting his proposal of a boys' band.

In "Ya Got Trouble," Harold positions himself as a refugee from the sinful city, but one who has the townspeople's welfare at heart. He is precisely the "outta town Jasper" of whom he warns in the song, but in transposing the town's fears onto the pool table, he deflects attention away from himself. Furthermore, his description of the degrading effects of ragtime on town youth belies his own appropriation of the jazz idiom in order to persuade and manipulate. Willson uses horns and syncopated rhythms for

14. Harold Hill delivers a warning to the townsfolk in "Ya Got Trouble." *The Music Man* copyright 1962 by Warner Bros. Pictures.

the majority of Harold's numbers. From the gospel-like "Ya Got Trouble," to the jazzy horns of "Seventy-Six Trombones," to the sensual burlesque stylings of "Sadder But Wiser Girl," Willson suggests Harold's urban sophistication in counterpoint to the choral, string-based score that undergirds the scenes for the townsfolk and Marian.

Critic Bosley Crowther described Harold as a "migrant music man."[13] That status stems from his knowledge of other places and behaviors, acquired as a traveling salesman. As we are made aware in the film's first number, "Rock Island," the day of the traveling salesman is nearing its end. The scene begins with a train car of salesmen talk-singing about the changing state of their profession: "Why it's the Model T Ford made the trouble made the people wanna go, wanna git, wanna git, wanna git up and go, . . . who's gonna patronize a little bitty two by four kinda store anymore?" In addition to the automobile, chain stores such as Woolworth's and mail-order businesses that deliver goods (of which the "Wells Fargo Wagon" number is illustrative) place the traveling salesman at a further disadvantage. The salesmen in "Rock Island" point to the products that had been theirs to sell but are now archaic with the advent of mass production and the introduction of disposable packaging, such as "the hogshead cask and demijohn, gone with the sugar barrel, pickle barrel, milk pan, gone with the tub and the pail and the tierce."[14] A keen observer of the folk vernacular in his hometown of Mason City, Iowa, Willson inserted the names of these outdated storage and measuring items in order to lend an aura of authenticity to the story.[15]

Like other salesmen, Harold is a self-made man, a paragon of the entrepreneurial, individualist American character. Unlike Willy Loman in Arthur Miller's *Death of a Salesman*, penned eight years before the stage version of *The Music Man*, or the real-life characters in Albert and David Maysles's documentary *Salesman* (1968), Harold is not a tragic character precisely because he refuses to allow himself to become obsolete. Rather than watch the American dream die around him, he lives by his wits.

The townsfolk are wary of Harold from the beginning. His status as an outsider, foreign to the ways of River City life, makes him not only different but ultimately suspect. Though they are a fractious bunch, the small community is made up of families who have known one another for generations. Harold is a "migrant music man," a "dubious drifter" who has come from unknown origins and presumably has no accountability to home, family, or community.[16] Highly mobile, he is without roots or stable identity, able to pass himself off as anyone or anything. Similar to the "confidence men" of the nineteenth-century city who lied to unsuspecting, respectable women to get what they wanted, Harold is a trickster whom the townspeople instinctively distrust.[17]

In contrast to the protagonists of most folk musicals, this musical migrant does not journey from the country to the city but vice versa. Harold is the realization of the fears of the Smith family in *Meet Me in St. Louis* (1944): having absorbed the city's corruption, he represents rootlessness, privileging of the individual over the collective, and lack of respect for the virtues of small-town life. He has been altered by his mobility and now, fortified by his cunning, stands to infect a community like the one from which he presumably came.[18]

Harold's urbane and worldly character has a parallel in the parochial and backward community he attempts to swindle. To establish the locale of River City and the character of its people, DaCosta uses the opening number, "Iowa Stubborn," sung by the townspeople to Harold as he first steps off of the train. Scriptwriter Marion Hargrove demonstrated his understanding of the cinematic language of the folk musical when, in an early treatment, he described the sequence as one that should appear as an effortless and natural passing along of a song that culminates in the participation of a full chorus. Various townspeople, from the grocer to the banker, carry a line of the song as Hill passes from the depot through the streets.

Hargrove emphasized that a highly mobile camera that singled out each of the town's characters would indicate that Harold has entered an insular community.[19]

As in the opening scenes of *Allá en el Rancho Grande* (1936), *Tropic Holiday* (1938), *Meet Me in St. Louis*, and *Summer Holiday* (1948), the mobile camera introduces the world of a small, insular community to the film's audience. Like the chorales in earlier folk musicals, "Iowa Stubborn" is rooted in place and atmospheric in inspiration. It is the spontaneous evocation of a community and its relationship to the land. In contrast to the earlier films, however, this chorale is performed for an outsider who does not take part in it. As a migrant from the outside world, Harold is at once welcomed by the town ("But what the heck, / You're welcome, / Glad to have ya with us") at the same time that he is made aware of his outsider status ("Join us at the picnic / You can eat your fill of all the food you bring yourself"). Rather than an expression of open-mindedness, this chorale emphasizes the intractable and unfriendly qualities of the community. As one townsperson forcefully explains, "We're so by God stubborn we can stand touchin' noses for a week at a time and never see eye to eye." Far from the communities in which brotherhood and affection abound, River City lacks the folk spirit.

In his script, Hargrove positions the River City "natives" in counterpoint to Harold's sophistication. Not only are they native to the area, they are also "native" in terms of their insularity and backwardness. In early story treatments, Hargrove used the terms "indigenous" and "aborigines" to describe the people of River City. One scene has Harold telling Tommy Djilas (Timmy Everett), a local youth, that he is wasting his time among such backward people when civilization is just steps away.[20] Although this dialogue was dropped from the final version of the film, it is instructive that Hargrove and his team used such terms. Allusions to hibernation, aborigines, and uncivilized man indicate the likening of River City folk to Third World peoples who are out of step with the modern era.

Willson insisted that *The Music Man* was written "not as a cartoon, but as a valentine to my native state of Iowa, sent with love."[21] Nonetheless, he inserted a great deal of parody and criticism of its people's narrow-mindedness. Despite appearing as a unified whole, the townspeople gradually reveal the social fissures among them. For example, Marian's mother,

Mrs. Paroo (Pert Kelton), signifies her outsider status with her Irish accent, referred to as an "Irish brogue" in the original playscript.[22] Not a member of the mayor's wife's inner circle, Mrs. Paroo is widowed with two children and keeps to herself. Although Marian is assimilated to the point that she does not have an accent, she nevertheless exists as an outsider due to her unmarried status and her advanced education. Her younger brother, Winthrop (Ron Howard), fears society because of his own mark of "difference," a speech impediment that effectively renders him silent. The Paroo family lives on the community's margins and, as a result, becomes the special focus of Harold's attentions.

The town's intolerance is more glaring in the portrayal of the local juvenile delinquent, Tommy Djilas. In the original script for the Broadway show, Tommy's origins are more clearly defined than they are in the film. Willson conceived of Djilas not just as a delinquent, but as an ethnicized immigrant.[23] Mayor George Shinn describes Tommy's class and ethnic background by highlighting his father's occupation as a day laborer and noting his inability to speak English.[24] Revealing Mayor Shinn's bigoted nature, Willson has him alternate between calling Tommy a "wild foreign kid" and using the ethnic slurs "hon-yock" and "bohunk." The mayor's malapropisms, as opposed to Harold's mastery of verbal persuasion techniques, reveal him to be a hypocrite with no more claim to River City than Tommy. The slurs were not used in the film, but Tommy's non-American origins are specified as Lithuanian— "Nithilanians," as the mayor calls them. Taking Tommy under his wing, as he does the Paroo family, Harold protects him from the town's hostile forces, encourages his courtship of the mayor's daughter, and gives him a leading role in the band.

Despite Harold's lies and manipulation, he ultimately creates a folk community where there was none, bringing social harmony to the town through efforts that are facilitated by and channeled through music. He unifies the space by fostering romantic attachments and musical collaborations between the otherwise disparate townsfolk. We see such instances of literal harmony begetting social harmony when the members of the school board sing "Sincere" and when the ladies of the town join in "Pick-a-Little, Talk-a-Little/Good Night Ladies."

To distract from his grand ploy, Harold facilitates gatherings in River City's public places. Routine activities such as going to the town hall

meeting or ice cream social, enjoying a drink at the soda fountain, reading at the library, or waiting for the Wells Fargo wagon result in a new
social ordering because of Harold's efforts. He conjures romance at the
soda fountain and the library, coaxes musical harmony out of discord in
the park and on the sidewalks, and unites the townsfolk in musical play
at the town hall. These spaces represent continuity in the town, which
Harold marshals for the purposes of rejuvenating its people and curing
them of their social ills. Cyclical events like town hall meetings and the
arrival of the Wells Fargo wagon become all the more joyous and meaningful as a result.

The musical score for *The Music Man* supports this project of social
integration. Willson abhorred "interruption" and "jerkiness" between
musical numbers and the dialogue. "I want to have an underlying unsus-
pected rhythm underneath the dialogue when I'm ready for a song," he
explained, "like a cable running along underneath Powell Street—then
I can hook on to it any time I wish without the audience realizing it."[25]
The process of transitioning into and out of a musical number had always
been considered to be a "problem" in Hollywood. In his memoir, Willson
recounts how studio executive Darryl F. Zanuck "did not want any music
in any musical picture from his studio that was not justified." Accompaniment coming from an "unexplained orchestra" was less effective than
music emanating from a "justified source."[26]

The bifurcated structure of the musical, its division into "real" narrative space and "unreal" musical space, posed structural dilemmas that
have been addressed differently by the makers of show and folk musicals.
While the show musical cast its characters as performers on a stage, the
folk musical had more potential for unjustified musical sources as songs
grew out of the natural environment. In *The Music Man*, Willson eliminated
the division between dialogue and song altogether. He composed the dialogue with a musical and rhythmic foundation. His desire, he wrote, was
"to make the whole show like one song lyric. . . . All in one piece."[27]

The unified formal structure of *The Music Man* was innovative for its
time. Rhythmic speaking is what enables Harold to woo the townspeople
in "Ya Got Trouble," flirt with Marian in "Marian the Librarian," and call
forth the fantastical creation of a marching band in "Seventy-six Trombones." *The Music Man* eliminates difference and intolerance through the

relationship of the central male and female characters, each representing opposite values, who resolve their ideological conflicts through music and a romantic union at the end of the film.[28] Willson's rhythmic speaking enables this seamless transition near the end of the film, when, on the cusp of being caught in his lie, Harold sings a duet with Marian. Their respective songs, "Seventy-six Trombones" and "Goodnight, My Someone," dovetail, and eventually they trade parts. With just this integration in mind, Willson wrote both songs as two versions of the same melody.

The finale of the film represents Harold's integration into the community, but it also illustrates the transformation of the community itself. Amid cries to tar and feather Harold for his scheme, Marian defends him by asking the people of River City to remember the time before he came. She implores them to appreciate how Harold has changed their community: "After he came, suddenly there were things to do and things to be proud of, and people to go out of your way for. Surely some of you can be grateful for what this man has brought to us." The happiness of her own family and Winthrop's confidence to speak again are a direct result of Harold's presence. Tommy Djilas, who has flourished in the band and found romance with the mayor's daughter, quickly organizes the boys' band to play in Harold's defense. They play out of time and out of tune, but the boys' parents are so pleased with their effort that they offer Harold their forgiveness. The small band of boys instantly transforms into a professional marching band of 150 musicians.

As this scene makes clear, the migrant music man has been reformed to recognize and appreciate the small town, but only after the intolerance of River City has been reformed. Harold has traded his wayward quest for self-advancement for love and rootedness. River City has abandoned its fear of outsiders and embraced social integration. For its willingness to forgo idealization and explore the flaws of small communities, *The Music Man* is unique among folk musicals.

Ya Got Trouble: Selling *The Music Man*

Both Warner Bros. and the film's audiences willfully ignored *The Music Man*'s inherent criticism of towns like River City and instead regarded the film as a paean to the nation. This interpretation had much to do with the social and cultural context in which the film premiered. Hollywood executives and the American public perceived a crisis in the early 1960s that stemmed from the growing cultural clash between moviegoing generations. To lure audiences back into theaters, adult-oriented dramas such as *The Long Hot Summer* (1958), *Psycho* (1960), and *Butterfield 8* (1960) promised titillating subject matter, while cautionary films like *Where the Boys Are* (1960) featured the sexual exploits of coeds on spring break. European imports like Michelangelo Antonioni's *L'Avventura* (1960), Jean-Luc Godard's *À bout de souffle* (1960), and the string of vehicles featuring the French bombshell Brigitte Bardot represented a trend toward strong sexual and violent content and received positive critical attention in art houses and on college campuses. Spectators looking for family-friendly options felt increasingly betrayed by Hollywood and looked instead to the Disney Studios for entertainment.[29]

For Hollywood, the musical film had been a popular genre for family audiences because of its wholesome qualities: an emphasis on romance rather than sex, no profanity or overt social criticism, and the supreme importance of popular forms of song and dance to produce joy and happiness. Although *Gigi* (1958) proved that traditional musicals could still attract audiences, the production of "social problem" musicals like *South Pacific* (1958) and *West Side Story* (1961) and the exploitation-driven "rock musicals" starring Elvis Presley showed how even this safest of genres was not impervious to the times. The beginnings of the civil rights movement, the unpopular escalation of American involvement in Vietnam, and the growing unrest among American youth made the conservative sector of Hollywood's domestic audience highly critical of any film that challenged the American way of life. For this reason, *West Side Story*, though a popular and critical success, did not receive the sanction of the family audience. It used a folk musical structure to expose rather than eliminate social difference, setting its story of racial intolerance and prejudice in the unclean streets of New York City slums and ridiculing traditional authority figures. In many ways, *West Side Story* was an exception to the development and the appeal of the folk musical in the 1960s and foreshadowed the ethnic revival musicals of the 1970s and 1980s.

The folk musical's project of social ordering took on significance beyond *The Music Man*'s fictive world. In 1962, the River City of 1912 represented what had been lost and what should be regained in American life. In this way, *The Music Man* completed the project that had been begun by the Hollywood folk musicals *Meet Me in St. Louis* and *Summer Holiday*. The incorporation of the folk musical into the mainstream necessitated the separation of the genre from its roots in racialized, culturally specific groups. Although the folk musical had always proved a reactive force against unsettling change, especially change as a result of migration, Hollywood's productions employed the genre's language for a fundamentally conservative purpose, namely, preservation of the status quo in American life. In the hands of immigrants and migrants, the folk musical assisted in the often painful process of cultural adjustment. In Hollywood, however, the genre reacted against the progressive forces for change in the postwar era. With the assistance of the Warner Bros. publicity department, audiences ignored the more critical and innovative aspects of Willson's film in favor of upholding an ideal of social insularity free of strife from racial minorities, angry youth, and censure on the world stage.

Early in the plan for distributing *The Music Man*, Warner Bros. recognized the opportunity for capitalizing on the film's setting. Rather than booking the film in standard fashion, the distribution department settled on an "advanced roadshow campaign" with special engagements in small towns. Usually, these places had to wait until first-run attractions had been introduced in the more lucrative urban markets. Small-town exhibitors and audiences had lamented this practice since the early days of Hollywood and were especially sensitive to film fare that privileged big cities and urbane, sophisticated situations in its content.[30] When Warner Bros. distributing agents encountered resistance in marketing *The Music Man* because it was a musical, they assured theater owners that the film would appeal to small towns because of its subject matter and that the marketing campaign would focus on small towns before the big cities.[31]

Theater owners' predictions about the musical's lack of appeal can be traced back to the earliest days of the genre, when the show musical, which often featured the struggles of young members of the chorus trying to attain Broadway stardom, held little interest for small-town audiences who lived far from the New York stage.[32] *The Music Man* presented the perfect opportunity to bridge the divide between the small town and the musical film because of its setting and its concerns with family and community life instead of show business. To prove the difference between *The Music Man* and other musical films, distributors traveled with large color photographs of the film and a phonograph on which they played the soundtrack.[33] The images and score proved that this musical did not offend or discount, but rather favorably featured small-town life.

Furthermore, *The Music Man*'s distribution offered the rare instance in which small towns would receive a highly anticipated attraction first. One distributing agent in New England remarked that small-town exhibitors were taking favorable notice of the attention that the studio was giving them.[34] Warner Bros. agents were very aware that this unique campaign flattered those exhibitors with whom the major studios did not have an especially strong relationship. Their successful selling point in this instance was that *The Music Man* not only showcased small-town scenes and values, but also gave the small town preference in its distribution.

The investment in community was an integral part of *The Music Man*'s campaign and positioned Warner Bros. as a studio that not only produced quality, family-friendly entertainment, but also gave back to the communities that made up its audience. The studio reached out to local fraternal organizations, but paid special attention to women's groups, such as the PTA and the Junior League.[35] Their support, the studio calculated, also ensured the attendance of children.[36] Gaining the patronage of married women had long been a strategy for lending respectability to the motion picture theater. In the postwar period, the shifting demographics of Hollywood audiences made the married, female patron all the more valuable, for with her came the family back into the theaters.[37]

The Warners publicity department also integrated the small-town setting of the film into its campaign. The studio system had long ago established a well-honed publicity machine, featuring pressbooks that suggested various tie-ins with local and national businesses, but the campaign for *The Music Man* was unique in its attempt to make life imitate art. The first effort was a publicity tour that sent traveling salesmen across the country in Chevrolet station wagons. The studio announced that "Warner Bros. 'Music Men' Are Everywhere!" and touted the "hand-planting" campaign that had salesmen traveling to all regions of the country in order to place publicity material directly into the hands of local newspapers and radio stations.[38]

Second, the publicity department organized a world press premiere and a two-day "Music Man Marching Band Competition Festival" in Mason City, Iowa, the town on which Meredith Willson based River City. The event elevated the annual Iowa Band Festival, which had been held in Mason City for twenty-three years, to a national competition. Thirty high school bands from as many states as well as ninety "host" bands from Iowa and Minnesota were invited to participate in the four-hour parade on June 19, 1962. The city's population of 30,000 swelled to 120,000 that day, with many families in the Mason City community hosting the visiting band members in their homes. Stars Robert Preston and Shirley Jones presided over the event along with Meredith Willson and Morton DaCosta; television host Arthur Godfrey served as the master of ceremonies. Sponsored by Warner Bros., the Mason City Chamber of Commerce, and the Richards Music and Webcor Sales Company, the event effectively reproduced the film's finale and reaffirmed Harold Hill's message that a boys' band was the solution to society's woes. Willson communicated as much to Jack Warner in a telegram sent that day, declaring that the event was a contribution to the improvement of the country.[39]

15. Meredith Willson leads a band in Mason City, Iowa, for the world press premiere of *The Music Man*. From the author's personal collection.

The Music Man could not have been released at a better time for Jack Warner. Several high-profile scandals in the early 1960s revived accusations that Hollywood promoted decadence, immorality, and depravity. At Twentieth Century–Fox, *Cleopatra* (1963), which had begun production three years earlier, was quickly becoming the most expensive film ever made. Even more damaging to the studio's image was Elizabeth Taylor's very public affair with Richard Burton while filming in Rome. Another major production, MGM's *Mutiny on the Bounty* (1962), received bad press for the behavior of its star, Marlon Brando, on the set in Tahiti. Three days before *The Music Man*'s release, the *Saturday Evening Post* devoted its front page to "Marlon Brando: How He Wasted $6 Million by Sulking on the Set." The article charged Brando with demanding changes to the script that resulted in the hiring and firing of numerous screenwriters while on location and holding up production by insisting on improvising many of his lines.[40] Brando came off as self-indulgent while Hollywood appeared wasteful.

Neither scandal reflected directly upon Warner Bros., but Jack Warner knew that such incidents perpetuated negative impressions of the industry as a whole. As a preemptive strike, he placed a full-page ad in the *New York Times,* the *Los Angeles Herald Examiner*, and the *Wall Street Journal* on the morning of *The Music Man* premiere. Entitled "Tahiti, Rome, and Mason City, Iowa," the statement attempted to divert attention away from Hollywood scandals and toward *The Music Man*'s release:

> In recent weeks the motion picture industry, to which I have devoted my life, has been getting more than its share of what is politely termed "unfavorable publicity." Lots of sensational headlines and editorial disapproval. Scandal in Rome. Waste in Tahiti. Fiasco in Hollywood. I personally would like to show you the other side of the coin. The many conscientious, devoted and talented people in our industry, who for half a century, consistently have provided the world with what is still its greatest single form of entertainment, should not be pulled down to the level of the few misguided in our midst. So instead of Rome or Tahiti or Hollywood, for the moment let's talk about Mason City, Iowa, in the heart of America.[41]

As one of the founders of Warner Bros. studio in 1918, Jack had witnessed the beginnings of the industry. He was part of the immigrant generation of film exhibitors turned producers who were wary of attacks on their industry and its leaders, the majority of whom were Jews. The Motion Picture Production Code, created in 1930, was Hollywood's attempt at self-censorship in order to deflect both domestic and international criticism against the movie industry. The heads of the studios proudly professed their patriotism and staunchly defended their industry as an ambassador of American values and ways of life. In many ways, Jack Warner's statement was in keeping with this impulse. He reminds his readers that the film industry has "provided the world with what is still its greatest single form of entertainment." Specifically, with "its over-all theme, its great and rousing spirit and all the things it sings and says," *The Music Man* is "gratifying evidence of how healthy and vigorous and triumphant our industry—and our country—can be."[42] Warner obscured the commercial intention of the film by likening its "rousing spirit" to that of the industry and that of the country. He implored his readers to see *The Music Man* and be reminded that American ideals and values would persevere despite indications to the contrary.

The ad's prominent placement garnered attention from industry leaders and audiences alike and revealed the deep-seated concerns harbored by both. It inspired an immense outpouring of support for Warner Bros. and *The Music Man*, an indication of the extent to which anxieties about the film industry and the nation had spread. Within days, Warner received numerous handwritten letters applauding him for his message and for his new film.[43] The authors admired Warner's courage in speaking out against the wayward direction of the film industry and simultaneously credited *The Music Man* for bringing quality and morality back to entertainment.[44]

For many, *The Music Man* represented an antidote to recent films that prominently featured sex and violence. The film seemed to recognize a forgotten family audience that was wholesome, clean, and concerned about the image of the nation that circulated abroad. Both exhibitors and concerned moviegoers mentioned the ill health of the movie industry, as indicated by the "filthy" products it was increasingly releasing. *The Music*

Man, one moviegoer wrote, was evidence that the industry was returning to a healthful state.[45] This sentiment was echoed by the many fan letters written to Warner over the course of *The Music Man*'s initial release. One woman wrote that she was tired of movies about degraded, drug-addicted characters. Another commended Warner for steering away from films about the "cesspool of human experience." Maria Gyarmathy of Los Angeles wrote a separate letter to DaCosta, which applauded him and Warner for making films with "no urgent or depressing social problems, no rape, no cliff hanging, no morbid sexual undercurrents, or narcotic addiction." She and the other letter writers concurred that more family-friendly movies would surely bring people back into the theaters.[46]

These filmgoers found *The Music Man* to be remarkable for its simplicity and lack of overt social criticism. The letters to Warner reveal the growing divide between a critical element of American society that sought social reforms and the audiences who appreciated films like *The Music Man* because they affirmed a certain vision of American life. Some critics of the film were quick to expose the "corn" of the story, which DaCosta adamantly defended. *Time*, for example, referred to it as "overcute, overloud, and overlong." In response, the director stood up for the charm and sentimentality of his film: "I maintain that streets were once clean and the fact that people are going to the picture in droves might indicate, among other things, that maybe they want to get a look at clean streets again."[47]

It is evident from the letters to Warner that audiences were affected by the simple sentimentality of a film that transported them to a place they longed to experience. As Gyarmathy explained, "The simplicity of the problems in the story, the romance of summer evenings, the crickets and other backgrounds, not forgetting the music, were put together in such a manner that by some mysterious gift of the Director, everyone went along with the whole so completely it was obvious we all remembered being part of that scene or piece of life, even though we couldn't possibly have been there." Despite the film's inherent criticism of small-town life, audiences who needed celebratory images and wholesomeness found them in *The Music Man*. While the typical Hollywood narrative film fosters audience identification in general, with its sympathetic protagonist and its cause-and-effect narrative structure, the folk musical provides a level of absorption that prompts the perception of certain films as lacking in ideology.[48] In other words, films like *The Music Man* appear to depict a way of life that seems natural in its separateness from any commercial or ideological mediation on the part of Hollywood or society in general. The musical numbers, as Richard Dyer has argued, "present themselves as pure realms of feeling" that are profoundly effective in communicating cultural values.[49] When encountering films like *The Music Man*, audiences believed themselves to be experiencing something authentic that offered a reprieve from modernity.[50]

Calling attention to these qualities of the film, audiences felt compelled to express their desire for more. Frequently, audience members confessed that they had seen *The Music Man* several times because it inspired such happiness in them. One moviegoer admitted that she was in the theater for the fifth time when she witnessed the singing and stomping of feet of those around her.[51] The film's structure as a folk musical encouraged audience participation just as the nonmusical Harold Hill is able to create music and harmony everywhere he goes.

Audience members' support of the film was echoed by the awards it garnered. *Scholastic Magazine* named it an "outstanding recommendation to the nation's junior and senior high school students."[52] *Boxoffice Magazine*, an industry publication for theater owners, gave it the Blue Ribbon Award for "fine family entertainment," stating that "it shows there is still a public which wants wholesome motion picture entertainment the family can enjoy together."[53] And the Catholic Legion of Decency concurred with a special recommendation of the film for being "superior, wholesome entertainment for the entire family."[54]

Although the musical film had always been generally popular among audiences of all ages, it was not until the postwar period that the musical, and the folk musical in particular, became the paragon of family entertainment in Hollywood. It was clear to industry observers that the demographic element that made up *The Music Man*'s audience and the viewers who felt compelled to write to Jack Warner were troubled by the stress of changing times. Americans with these concerns had found their voice with *The Music Man* and went on to propel another folk musical, *The Sound of Music*, to the position of most profitable film made to date.[55]

The Sound of Music (1965)

Made three years after *The Music Man*, *The Sound of Music* replicates that film's basic narrative arc and formal structure. Both films feature a protagonist who takes a journey, enters a fractured community, and uses his/her musical talents to create social harmony. Set in pre-Anschluss Austria, during the "golden days of the Thirties," *The Sound of Music* follows the experiences of a young novitiate who leaves a Salzburg convent to work as a governess for a retired navy officer. Into the cold and sober household of Captain Von Trapp (Christopher Plummer), Maria (Julie Andrews) brings warmth and happiness through the "sound of music" that she carries with her.

Like Harold Hill, Maria is a troubadour. We first encounter her alone in a mountain-top meadow singing an ode to music and nature—"the hills are alive, with the sound of music"—and when she undertakes her journey from the convent, she packs her guitar and proceeds to teach the Von Trapp children how to reintroduce music into their lives. As in all musicals, the place of music as entertainment is firmly established; yet *The Sound of Music* asserts more, namely, that music is central to human existence. Music, the film demonstrates, is part of the natural world around us ("My heart wants to beat like the wings of the birds / That rise from the lake to the trees"), and it ministers to the soul ("I go to the hills / When my heart is lonely / I know I will hear / What I've heard before").

As Richard Dyer argues, Maria is seemingly "of the land," as communicated by her early identification with the hills of Salzburg. An orphan, she has no family other than nature itself and no worldly possessions other than her guitar. Of a presumably peasant class, she was adopted by the nuns and reared with the values of piousness, humility, and poverty. The film explains her ability to produce music instantaneously, whether in nature or in the Von Trapp family home, by positioning her with an "uncomplicated closeness to the sources of music, nature and herself."[56]

This is the talent she brings to the broken home of the Von Trapps. In her journey from the convent, she girds herself with "I Have Confidence," a song that imagines what her new home will be like. Assuring herself that "everything will turn out fine," Maria likens her sureness in her own abilities to the constancy of the sunshine, rain, and the coming of spring. In a series of jump cuts, director Robert Wise moves Maria through time and space in order to convey her migration from the town to Von Trapp's pastoral estate. Because of the continuous soundtrack, these edits are not jarring, as they are meant to be in films like *Á bout de souffle*, but rather add to the momentum of the sequence. Maria's voice fluidly overlaps with the various places she encounters on her journey, including city thoroughfares, the bus, and a country road.

The Von Trapp household is joyless and deviod of music. Maria brings her musicality into this space in order to unite it and restore the social harmony that will render it impervious to outside threats. In each of the musical sequences with the children, Maria invokes the natural world. "My Favorite Things," "Do Re Mi," "The Lonely Goatherd," and "Edelweiss" either take place in nature or praise its glories. Through these musical moments, Maria is able to strengthen the bonds between family, home, and homeland. In the process, she becomes integrated into the family's structure as well. Like Harold Hill's migratory character, Maria finds a new home in the one she makes for herself.

The Sound of Music conveys rituals and cyclical events in keeping with the folk musical tradition. The ritual begins with a comment on the passing of the day. The nuns observe vespers, the fifth of six services that mark the daily routine of life in the convent. At the same moment, Maria observes her own ritualistic activity: going to the hills and communing with nature. After her departure from the convent, Maria maintains her religious devotion by saying prayers at meal times and before bed. Later in the film, the

16. Maria sings of her confidence as she leaves the convent for a new life with the Von Trapp family. *The Sound of Music* copyright 1965 by Twentieth Century–Fox Film Corporation.

grandiose wedding between Maria and the captain is a ritualistic, solemn activity followed by the family's performance at the Salzburg Folk Festival, an annual event for the city.

When there is a break in the ritual cycle, the film uses the musical reprise to give meaning and to provide constancy to changes in the characters' lives. The repeated occurrence of songs like "How Do You Solve a Problem Like Maria," "Edelweiss," "The Sound of Music," and "So Long, Farewell" create their own cyclicality by putting the past in service to the needs of the present. The first of these numbers, "How Do You Solve a Problem Like Maria," expresses the nuns' exasperation with Maria's wild nature; it recurs as a celebration of her taming through marriage. "So Long, Farewell" begins as a performance by the children for their father's party guests. It symbolizes the return of music to the Von Trapp household as well as the division between children and adults. When the song returns as part of the Von Trapp family's performance at the folk festival, it has taken on different meaning. Foreshadowed by the call-and-response at the end of the song's first appearance, when the party guests sing "goodbye" in unison, the song's second iteration represents a permanent separation of the family from their homeland. "Edelweiss," presented in the film as the Austrian national anthem, at first appears as a charming song shared by father and daughter, then becomes an expression of political protest. In its reprisal at the end of the festival, the captain begins the song. Maria, the children, and the Austrian audience gradually join him. "Edelweiss" becomes an expression of national autonomy and resistance to occupation by the Nazis. Shots of the Nazis' faces reveal their discomfort as the Austrian people musically communicate their shared identity. Such cyclical patterns established by the reprise foster the feelings of unity and continuity in the film.

In *The Music Man* new technologies and amusements represent the unsettling encroachment of modernity in River City; in *The Sound of Music* it is the division of the fatherland that threatens change. Not only is the family in peril, but the entire nation faces takeover by a foreign, hostile power. Maria's refreshing introduction of music into the lives of the Von Trapps fortifies the family and the nation against sinister forces. The nuclear family, which Maria restores through song and through marriage, is a symbol for the nation in *The Sound of Music*. Both are threatened simultaneously and find their resilient strength in music and in nature. The film ends as it began, with Maria going to the hills for sustenance and protection, but this time she brings her family. The final aerial shot of the Von Trapps hiking over the mountains echoes Maria's earlier journey in the film. They must leave their home in search of a place where they can remain together in freedom. The endurance of the family, as a symbol of the strength of the nation, was central to the film's strong appeal to domestic and international audiences in the mid-1960s.

The enormous response generated by *The Sound of Music* surprised everyone. It had been a success on the Broadway stage, but the general consensus was that the material was too "schmaltzy" for a film version. As screenwriter Ernest Lehman told the *New York Times Magazine* in 1966, "I remember 'The Sound of Music' had a certain—well, stink is not quite the right word about it. I saw Burt Lancaster, who was doing 'The Leopard,' in the cafeteria one day, and he looked at me and said, 'Jesus, you must need the money.'"[57] Robert Wise agreed to direct the film with a "visually clean and spare" approach to the material. In advance of the film's premiere, Wise told the *Los Angeles Times* that "the sentimentality and *gemütlichkeit* (excessive niceness) that worked fine on stage could easily become heavy-handed on the screen."[58] He explicitly ruled out "cute Tyrolean outfits."[59]

Such efforts notwithstanding, critics Bosley Crowther, Judith Crist, and Pauline Kael panned the film, causing doubts about its future. Kael, in particular, wrote a scathing critique in which she referred to the film as "the sugar-coated lie that people seem to want to eat" and castigated the "self-indulgent" and "cheap and ready-made" responses that it conjures. Stuck between her critical sensibilities and the will of the people, she asked: "Why not just send the director, Robert Wise, a wire: 'You win. I give up'?"[60]

The *gemütlichkeit* against which Wise had warned prevailed onscreen despite the makers' efforts. As Lehman observed, "the very things we were on guard against are the things that appeal to so many people." The film's emphasis on family and the expression of joy through song were elements that inspired the most criticism and the most applause. Lehman explained, "In a world which has changed enormously in the last few years, the movie is a kind of fantasy about a world which no longer exists, where everything comes out right. . . . Our astronauts have succeeded in getting out of this world, but those who haven't go to see 'The Sound of Music' one more time."[61]

The astounding box office numbers for the film made news on its own. Industry observers noted that the film, booked on an advance basis in urban centers, attracted repeat viewings that exceeded the number of the immediate area's population. For example, in Salt Lake City, admissions amounted to 309,000 in a city of 199,300. *Variety* reported that a woman from Los Angeles saw the film 58 times, a resident of Nottingham, England, 102 times, and a sailor in Puerto Rico, 77 times. A man from Florida, who had seen the film 10 times, made news when he wrote out the dialogue from memory and sent it to Wise, an astounding feat in the age before home theater equipment.[62] Such repeat viewings prompted exhibitors to encourage more with "anniversary cakes, 'favorite scene' contests, on-stage quiz shows and Gargantuan postcards addressed to Miss Andrews."[63] The film's long run, four years in some instances, also gained attention. Notably, college students in Moorhead, Minnesota, protested outside of the local theater after the film had been running for a continuous forty-nine weeks.[64]

The film's longevity in theaters can be explained by its appeal to the family audience. As Wise noted, much of the fan mail that he received was from families who had seen the film together multiple times.[65] Like *The Music Man*, the film facilitates a journey to a simpler time, "where everything comes out right," as Lehman asserted. *Boxoffice Magazine* bestowed its Blue Ribbon Award on *The Sound of Music* for being "ideal family entertainment" and reported the comments from its board, many of which echoed the letters sent to Jack Warner. Mrs. Irvin J. Haus of the Federation of Motion Picture Councils in Milwaukee remarked, "This simple, unaffected story was a joy to behold after some of the more questionable themes of recent months." Mrs. Henry F. McGill of the La Canada, California, PTA called it "family life at its best." And Judge J. May of the *Florida Times-Union* in Jacksonville wrote, "'The Sound of Music' is the only film of any consequence on the list, for the entire family."[66] Beyond the industry, conservative religious organizations embraced the film as well. The Catholic Legion of Decency lent its endorsement, as did the Church of Latter-day Saints. Mormon leaders were so inspired by the film that they created a body to administer an annual award for the "Best Family Picture of the Year."[67]

The Sound of Music also achieved an international success that eluded *The Music Man*. Its focus on the parent-child relationship in a non-American setting made it especially marketable overseas. One anonymous fan in Japan made headlines when he left 40,000 yen with a letter at the box office: "I am very impressed with this picture at a time when sex and rough pictures all over the city. If I had children, I would want to be sure that they see this film. However, I am not blessed with any, so would you please arrange to let some orphans see it with this money, although it is not as much as I would like to contribute."[68] *Variety* reported similar concerns among parents in Mexico: "This 'family' film is the perfect answer to troubled Mexican parents seeking surcease from films of sudden death, sex, violence, alcoholism and other pathological problems, and provides something for all ages."[69]

Not surprisingly, however, the film did not find a receptive audience in Germany and was the subject of some controversy. Responding to poor box office returns in Munich, the branch manager of that city's Twentieth Century–Fox distribution office requested that the "anti-Nazi" sections of the film be cut. As *Variety* reported, the edited version ended abruptly: "Various viewers of the print unreeled here first on May 20 who had seen it before were astounded when 'The End' flashed right after the wedding of Baron von Trapp and Maria. The rest of the story was not shown." The trade magazine also noted that a "local Deutsche paper" had recently printed an article entitled "Will Hollywood's Hate of German [*sic*] Never End?" Robert Wise and the studio protested, and the scenes were eventually restored in order to uphold "ethnic and artistic considerations" despite risking any loss in revenue. The studio removed the branch officer from his position as a result of the scandal.[70]

Its reception in Germany notwithstanding, *The Sound of Music* provided audiences with a rallying point for the advocacy of family films much as *The Music Man* had done three years earlier. The activity at the domestic and international box office, the awards given to the film, and the film's staying power attest to its family appeal. Pulled from theaters in 1969, *The Sound of Music* was released again in 1973 and made Nielsen records when it was broadcast by ABC in 1976 and again by NBC in 1979.[71]

The sensation caused by *The Sound of Music* was anticipated by the fervor surrounding *The Music Man*. Although made by different studios and with drastically different settings, both films used the folk musical to counter the forces of modernity in the early 1960s. As projected by the Warner Bros. marketing campaign to the small towns of America, *The Music Man* presented the return of family entertainment to conservative audiences who demanded an idyllic vision of the nation. The film provided an opportunity for audiences who feared the loss of conservative values to voice their concerns. Their written support of the film foreshadowed the enthusiastic reception of *The Sound of Music*, which quickly became the most lucrative film to date and sent producers scrambling to produce similar vehicles.

Both films signified the importance of the folk musical in the early 1960s, a time in which conservative audiences felt under attack. They offered hopeful depictions of resilient families and communities that withstand the ominous forces of change, and they also provided the opportunity for families to enjoy clean and safe entertainment together. The folk musical's integrated structure of song and narrative fortified the family onscreen and off. In the early 1960s, this function of the genre was called into bold relief. The musical migrant no longer assuaged the processes of cultural adjustment for people of color, as in the earlier folk musicals, but comforted the dominant culture in the face of threats from marginal segments of society.

The polarization of Hollywood's audience that began in the postwar era only increased throughout the 1960s and beyond. The rise of the counterculture and political unrest realized conservatives' fears. The studios' initial attempts to capitalize on the success of *The Sound of Music* with other family-friendly musicals failed largely because of inflated budgets. Looking elsewhere for profits, Hollywood returned to films that featured immigrant communities and peoples of color in the 1970s and 1980s.

6

"Ease on Down the Road"

Folk Musicals of the Ethnic Revival

When Edward R. Murrow assumed the role of chief of the United States Information Agency (USIA) in 1961, he took the opportunity to speak to Hollywood moviemakers about the depiction of the nation in American film. Since the early 1950s, the USIA had worked to bolster public diplomacy through various media outlets, including radio, print, and film. A well-respected journalist, Murrow implored moviemakers to stop making films that gave a negative impression of the United States to foreign powers. Rather, he insisted, the movies should depict a "healthy image" of American life.[1]

At the height of the cold war, Murrow's message resonated with many members of the public, who feared for America's loss of prominence on the world stage. One recently released and highly regarded musical film, *West Side Story* (1961), about interethnic gang violence in contemporary New York City, seemed to exemplify exactly what Murrow warned against. Michael H. Cardozo, then a visiting professor of law at Northwestern University, responded favorably to Murrow's message in a letter to the *New York Times*. He called for films that portrayed a "truer picture of this country": "Uninformed viewers simply assume that all of American life is colored by violence, gun slinging, drink, dope, and family discord." Looking for solutions, Cardozo suggested that the USIA subsidize a few minutes of additional footage to be attached to the beginning of exported American films to show "a little of the typical scene in this country in contrast to the picture's theme." For Cardozo, appropriate scenes would be "views of an American small town" with "typical American youths."[2]

Even though *West Side Story* was a popular and critical success at home and abroad, its subject matter sparked a debate about the responsibility of American movies in depicting the nation. In this instance, the criticisms of society came from an unlikely source, the musical film. Although subsequent 1960s musicals, like *The Music Man* (1962) and *The Sound of Music* (1965), provided pro-family, palliative visions, *West Side Story* exposed the nation's dirty laundry, one of the first musicals to do so.[3] Ethnic and racial difference, discrimination, poverty, and the decay of the nation's cities were themes that *West Side Story* introduced to the musical screen, ones that would be more characteristic of the musical films of the post–civil rights era of ethnic revival in the 1970s and early 1980s.

Not surprisingly, folk musicals predominated in this period, with stories that focused on ethnic groups and their musical forms of expression. Films like *Fiddler on the Roof* (1971), *The Wiz* (1978), and *Zoot Suit* (1981) indicated a return to the beginning, as the folk musical moved away from white American communities and closer to its culturally specific origins. Nevertheless, Hollywood's continued mediation of these images and the material realities of Jewish, African American, and Mexican American audiences rendered the ethnic revival musicals substantially different from their predecessors.

The cinemas to emerge out of the civil rights struggle of the 1960s were works of rebellion. The complete rejection of Hollywood stereotypes and modes of production and of mainstream (white) society's norms characterized works of independent cinema, such as *I Am Joaquin* (Valdez, 1969) and *Sweet Sweetback's Baadasssss Song* (Van Peebles, 1971), and the films of the "LA School," such as Charles Burnett's *Killer of Sheep* (1979) and Haile Gerima's *Bush Mama* (1979). Studies of ethnic filmmaking in this era often focus on these works and their cultural politics. Rather than advancing a counter-hegemonic position, however, the makers of the ethnic revival musicals were more integrationist in their politics and desired to be embraced by rather than exist outside of Hollywood. Unlike the earlier folk musicals of ethnic cinema, *Fiddler on the Roof, The Wiz,* and *Zoot Suit* were geared toward mainstream audiences, most of whom were outsiders to the culturally specific communities that the films depicted. What united these films and their audiences was not a common experience but a belief in the redemption offered to mainstream white society by the ethnic margins. Overarching their storylines is the pluralist assertion that the immigrant experience is a fundamental part of the American narrative.

The social and cultural anxieties that so troubled the audiences of *The Music Man* and *The Sound of Music* had heightened by the 1970s. The escalating loss of American lives in the Vietnam War, political assassinations, inner-city riots, and the Watergate scandal produced a generation that harbored significant resentment and distrust toward the state. Moreover, the cutbacks in social services during the administrations of Richard Nixon and Ronald Reagan, deindustrialization, and high unemployment drastically affected the nation's minority populations. During the 1970s, major urban areas, once the symbol of American progress, descended into decay. The problem of the city was racialized for most television viewers as news outlets called attention to rising poverty and state-facilitated dependence on public welfare systems, implying that the liberal reforms of previous administrations had gone awry.[4]

Ironically, cultural pluralism enjoyed a new vogue in this period. David A. Hollinger dates the resurrection of a pluralist discourse to the early 1970s, when the failure of an integrationist-oriented black civil rights struggle fueled a strong cultural nationalist element, white ethnics embraced and celebrated their own immigrant roots, and the new immigration law of 1965 prompted a steady influx of Asian and Latino immigrants who bolstered the ethnic identity of immigrants already here.[5] This renewed consciousness about the nation's pluralism, eventually to be called multiculturalism, caught the attention of Hollywood filmmakers, many of whom, like Norman Jewison (*Fiddler on the Roof*) and Sidney Lumet (*The Wiz*), were white liberals who sought to make progressive statements about social tolerance with their films. Consistent with the historical pattern, times of economic and social crisis prompted a search for solace and redemption at the margins of society. During the 1970s, as Hollinger writes, "the periphery presented itself as a source of potentially countervailing cultural power."[6] The Hollywood studios, led by Universal, made significant efforts to reach these ethnically specific, niche markets with their films.

For most of the studios, the late 1960s and early 1970s were years of great distress, as the aftermath of the Paramount Decree, new technologies, and changing public tastes pushed the Hollywood studio system into fragmentation and decline. Despite the success of family-friendly films like *The Music Man* and *The Sound of Music*, the studios found it increasingly difficult to reach the burgeoning demographic of countercultural youth. To meet this challenge, the studios invested in a number of young, relatively inexperienced directors with edgy subject matter and an innovative approach to cinematic language. Ultimately, the crisis in Hollywood led to films that reflected the new atmosphere, such as *Bonnie and Clyde* (1967), *Easy Rider* (1969), and *M*A*S*H* (1970). By the mid-1970s, as Thomas Schatz demonstrates, the "blockbuster syndrome" had set in, resulting in fewer productions with larger budgets. Such an approach indicated that the studios were finally acclimating to "an increasingly fragmented entertainment industry—with its demographics and target audiences, its diversified 'multi-media' conglomerates, its global(ized) markets and new delivery systems." For example, in making *The Wiz*, Universal Studios partnered with Motown Productions in order to tap the popularity of major recording stars like Diana Ross and Michael Jackson and to reach the lucrative audiences made up of youth and minorities.[7]

With changes in the industry also came the revision of traditional generic forms. *West Side Story* foreshadowed musical films that would find their subjects in Jewish American heritage and the place of African Americans and Latinos in contemporary society. In this way, the folk musical returned to its roots in the depiction of marginalized communities and offered its familiar themes of historical and cultural continuity in the face of social and geographical mobility. Hoping at once to capitalize on the niche ethnic markets and to appeal to the mainstream moviegoing public, which was predominantly white and suburban during this period, the makers of *Fiddler on the Roof, The Wiz,* and *Zoot Suit* sought to explore culturally specific subjects (Jews, African Americans, and Mexican Americans, respectively) within a pluralist framework. The films cast the ethnic, migrant experience as being both specific and universal. In other words, they show the unique experiences of the ethnic margins at the same time that they portray those experiences as ones that all Americans can share. Presenting a color-blind philosophy before it had been advanced by conservatives in the 1980s, the folk musical of the ethnic revival returned to its roots, but recast its message to redeem and incorporate Hollywood's white mainstream audience.

Fiddler on the Roof (1971)

On location for much of 1970 in small villages of what was then Yugoslavia, Norman Jewison and his international cast and crew for the film version of *Fiddler on the Roof* educated themselves in rural life. While Jewison complained of shooting setbacks due to uncooperative weather, sickness, and the demands of the production company, Mirisch Productions, he was firmly convinced of the film's fundamental importance. Writing to his good friend and fellow director Hal Ashby, Jewison confided, "Whether it's the effort to remain totally honest and simple or my deep desire to understand the Jewish religion and culture—or my need to deal with truly basic emotions, for a change,—whatever—I've been involved with the damn thing night and day for months—."[8] A film based on the iconic 1894 story by the celebrated Yiddish author Sholom Aleichem had been produced by Maurice Schwartz for a Yiddish-speaking audience in 1939. Jewison's *Fiddler* was based on the 1964 Broadway production by Joseph Stein and Jerome Robbins, with music by Jerry Bock and Sheldon Harnick. Like other highly successful stage musicals in the postwar era, it seemed to have all the ingredients for substantial box office returns as well, including a powerful score and impressive choreography. But it was nostalgia that made the work particularly resonant with the era. The story about Tevye the milkman and his five daughters set amid *shtetl* life in eastern Europe conjured sentimental, familial feelings and satisfied a growing curiosity about the immigrant generation among white ethnics. As Matthew Frye Jacobson has argued, a "powerful current of antimodernism" flowed through the ethnic revival of the 1970s, and the enthusiastic reception of *Fiddler on the Roof* was among its first signifiers.[9] Looking for respite from modernity's detrimental effects on individual expression and community belonging, white ethnic audiences in the 1970s embraced their ethnic roots and found in them a "haven of authenticity." White ethnics, third- and fourth-generation Jews included, romanticized the journeys and struggles of their immigrant forefathers and recast them not as Jewish or Irish or Italian narratives, but as American ones. The notion that the immigrant story was America's story became increasingly entrenched in the popular consciousness with films like *The Godfather* (1972) and the dedication of the Ellis Island Immigration Museum in 1990. *Fiddler on the*

Roof was the earliest film musical example of this growing trend, and it was a highly influential one.[10]

Jewison's letter reveals the director to be mobilized by an anti-modern sensibility rooted in his quest for an authentic Jewishness. His desire to remain "honest and simple" and to deal with "truly basic emotions" informed his approach to the re-creation of an eastern European *shtetl.* Jewison saw in the *shtetl* a return to the values of community solidarity, familial cohesion, and closeness to the land. Escaping the realities of Ronald Reagan's governorship of California, Jewison wrote, "I love the country—the simplicity and peace of peasant life, the warmth and honesty of everyone. Refreshingly distant from Reagan land."[11]

Jewison's film goes to great lengths to transport audiences back in time. The typical Hollywood musical based on a stage production in this era attempted to "open up" the show and make it as realistic as possible in grand, panoramic form. Film critic Vincent Canby expressed his distaste for this impulse: "[The studios] want to show us everything, to give us our money's worth. In so doing, they've not just opened up the play, they've let most of the life out of it."[12] Bringing a sentimental past to life, one that resonates with symbolic memory and deep-rooted tradition, was the folk musical's purview. With depictions of folkways and folk life, it obscured the very modern, technological developments of which it was a part. Canby's criticisms to the contrary, "opening up" was precisely what audiences desired because it enabled their identification with the "true and simple" story being told. Canby's critical review provoked a response from the president of United Artists, David V. Picker: "How sad that [Canby] cannot take a chance and let himself feel, or touch, or see because he might be moved, or touched or even cry."[13] One filmgoer felt compelled to write that he found the film "thrilling, sweeping, touching, a memorable synthesis of music, story, and human relationships."[14] Another insisted that he and the audience members around him felt something genuine in the theater: "No matter how pre-conditioned I was by Canby's review, I laughed a little, applauded three times and had to use my handkerchief to wipe away my reaction to the sentimentality. Almost everyone around me seemed to be enjoying themselves."[15]

The filmmaker took pains to foster this reaction. For the bucolic *shtetl* scenes in the first half of the film, Jewison used a silk stocking to create an effect that was "warm and yellow."[16] He also chose to depict Tevye (played by Topol) as a man rooted in folk life, as expressed by the first song, "Tradition." Much like the opening numbers in other folk musicals ("Meet Me in St. Louis" and "Our Home Town," for example), "Tradition" unifies space and time. Using a mobile camera, Jewison weaves together scenes of daily life in the village of Anatevka. The community is cohesive and bound by tradition, without which, as Tevye says, "our lives would be as shaky as a fiddler on the roof!" Emphasizing the activities of their daily routine, such as delivering milk, cooking, and praying, the film privileges continuity in its characters' lives.

Sholom Aleichem's Tevye was a man caught between tradition and modernity. Ken Frieden has pointed out that in the original text, Tevye's "rebellious daughters act out the dilemmas of modernity, which he himself recognizes and debates privately."[17] This original Tevye grew out of Aleichem's perception that, in 1894, the traditional patriarchy of the *shtetl* Jew was already in flux; his Tevye was the product of a changing world. The Tevye in *Fiddler*, by contrast, represents an old order that is fixed and highly romanticized. Such an interpretation was necessary for Jewison if he was going to contrast Tevye's world with modernity as represented by pogroms, the loss of children, and emigration. The pains associated with change are felt more keenly after we have seen the simplicity and beauty of Tevye's life in the *shtetl*.

One critical way in which *Fiddler* departs from earlier folk musicals is in the harsh depiction of change. In musicals like *Meet Me in St. Louis* (1944), the change that threatened a family was ultimately thwarted. In *The Music Man* and *The Sound of Music*, change occurred, but families and communities proved to be resilient and became stronger as a result. By contrast, in *Fiddler on the Roof* a series of events precipitated by outside forces inflicts substantial pain on Tevye's family and the villagers of Anatevka. We witness a pogrom during his eldest daughter's wedding that is only alluded to in the stage production. We sit at a train station with Tevye and his second eldest as she leaves to join her revolutionary boyfriend, perhaps never to see her father again. And we watch as Gentiles evict the Jews from their village, forcing them to emigrate to a foreign land. In each of these scenes, the film communicates the pathos of change narratively with the depiction of violence, formally with the use of "gray and cold" lighting effects, and emotionally with music.[18] Like *West Side Story, Fiddler on the Roof* showed film audiences a different type of musical, one that was not shy about presenting society in conflict.

Another way in which *Fiddler* departs from earlier folk musicals is its self-reflexive admission that its audience is not primarily Jewish. The first half of the film shows us an insular, ethnocentric world that requires definition and translation. The song "Tradition" establishes this insider/ outsider dynamic between the film and its viewers. It begins with Tevye's direct address to the audience, explaining the presence of a fiddler on the roof: "You may ask, 'Why do we stay up there if it's so dangerous?' Well, we stay because Anatevka is our home. And how do we keep our balance? That I can tell you in one word: Tradition!"

Earlier folk musicals took for granted the identification of their audiences with the narrative. *Fiddler*, however, demands exposition from its main character in order to educate and, ultimately, integrate its audience into the world of the film. Rouben Mamoulian used a similar strategy in the opening of *Summer Holiday* (1948) with the number "Our Home Town." In that instance, however, audiences would have easily recognized turn-of-the-century Danbury, Connecticut, with its main street and soda fountain, as a part of the nation's heritage. *Fiddler* makes the case for the eastern European *shtetl* as a significant site of the nation's past, but such an argument necessitates explanation.

Tevye speaks directly to the audience and gives a series of introductions and explanations about *shtetl* life at the turn of the century, mirroring the process that Jewison himself underwent in order to make the film. "Tradition" cuts between Tevye's explanations ("Here in Anatevka, we have traditions for everything. How to sleep, how to eat, how to work, how to wear clothes. For instance, we always keep our heads covered and always wear little prayer shawls. This shows our constant devotion to God.") and the chorus singing about the roles of the papas, mamas, sons, and daughters. Tevye also introduces us to the village rabbi, the matchmaker, and the beggar. Ominously, he refers briefly and through voiceover to the Christians who reside in the village ("So far, they don't bother us."). A rapid montage of shots punctuates this sequence and presents the material symbols of Jewish life, such as the Torah and the Menorah. At first calling attention to cultural difference, Tevye's direct address quickly assimilates

17. Tevye explains the significance of tradition. *Fiddler on the Roof* copyright 1971 by The Mirisch Corporation and Cartier Productions.

the audience into the ways of his people. *Fiddler* invites us into this unfamiliar world and ultimately, through the powers of cinematic narrative, builds empathy for the plight of Tevye's family.

The film purports to tell a story that is at once specific and universal. It begins with an ethnographic introduction and then suggests that the story of the immigrant is one that everyone can share. *Fiddler* ends where the American narrative begins, with Tevye's family joining the exodus of Jews to the United States in the "great wave" of immigration at the turn of the century. In effect, it functions as an origins story for what many white ethnics saw as the birth of America, its foundational immigrant past come to life. Ethnic revival musicals like *Fiddler on the Roof* appealed to Jews and non-Jews alike, who wished to see a celebration of America's multiethnic origins and longed for redemption therein. Significantly, the success of this film communicated to Hollywood producers that musicals about specific cultural groups had the potential to reach a mass audience.

The Wiz (1978)

Fiddler on the Roof hearkened back to a nostalgic time and place that satisfied audiences' curiosities about and longing for an authentic homeland. In contrast, Universal's production of *The Wiz*, a reinterpretation of *The Wonderful Wizard of Oz* with an all-black cast, did not look back to the past but rather engaged directly with the present. During the 1970s, Hollywood increasingly embraced the possibilities of catering to niche markets. The surprising popularity of *Sweet Sweetback's Baadasssss Song* and its successors directed the attention of the studios toward a young, black audience with box office influence. Concurrently, however, that audience identified with and demanded a cinematic image that more honestly reflected their contemporary urban existence. The assassinations of civil rights leaders, the race riots in the late 1960s, and the decline in social services for the urban poor drove young African Americans in particular to adopt a cultural and political position that rejected the possibility of social integration and harmony in the United States.[19] Such conditions produced the themes and cinematic language of blaxploitation, a genre that was angry in tone and gritty and confrontational in its depiction of racial violence. Musical scores in such films, as Richard Dyer has pointed out, engage more directly with the world of the characters, adding to African Americans' claim to physical and cultural space in the genre.[20]

Although blaxploitation had an obvious saliency, such films were too edgy for Hollywood to reproduce for a mass, interracial market. Instead, Universal Studios chose to attract a different black audience, one that was more moderate in its demands and integrationist in its politics. Six years before the "Cosby moment" that Herman Gray has identified, *The Wiz* presented an opportunity to feature contemporary black life in a way that appealed to black moviegoers and did not offend the sensibilities of white audiences.

The Wiz opened on Broadway in 1975. Recognizing its potential, executives at Twentieth Century–Fox had invested in the production in order to gain the movie rights. When the studio changed hands during the stage run, Warren N. Lieberfarb, formerly an executive at Fox, wrote a memo to his new employer, Warner Bros., detailing the many reasons why the property should still be filmed. He insisted that Fox's mistake in abandoning the film "lies in perceiving the motion picture as inherently limited to the Black audience." He cited the "nature of the material" and the interracial audiences who saw it on Broadway as evidence that the film could be "a mass audience movie." Lieberfarb pointed out that non-Jewish audiences accounted for a significant part of the $35 million domestic film rental for *Fiddler on the Roof.* A new version of *The Wizard of Oz* promised to achieve the same success. In his words, "*The Wiz* is as black as *Fiddler on the Roof* was Jewish!" His memo reveals the growing perception among Hollywood executives that films about non-white, ethnically specific groups could resonate with a broad audience. In other words, *The Wiz* had the potential to transcend its blackness just as *Fiddler* had transcended its Jewishness.[21]

Producer Ken Harper emphasized the show's "cross-over appeal" in a promotional booklet aimed to attract potential investors: "Pssst! . . . Updated to carry a new Dorothy from a farm in the South through all kinds of adventures in the fabulous City, all the way home again." Likening it to other successful ethnic adaptations of classic works, the pitch continues: "Wow! It's like making *Black Orpheus* out of an old legend . . . and like making . . . like making *West Side Story* out of a play by Shakespeare and like making . . . The United States of America . . . We just said . . . Pssst!"[22] For Harper, an African American, the migration theme was crucial. Rather than a journey from Kansas to Oz and back, Harper's Dorothy replicates the migration of African Americans out of the South to the cities of the North. The story is both historically specific and broadly illustrative of migration in American life, a theme that enjoyed increased popularity during the era of ethnic revival. The migration story to which the 1939 film version indirectly alludes became literal in the 1970s, when cultural producers advanced the idea of "immigrants all."

Harper was not disappointed in his belief that such a retelling would bring substantial profits. The first major Broadway show produced by an African American, *The Wiz* set a new box office record and attracted a significant number of African Americans, many of whom had never been to the Great White Way.[23] Many critics attributed the show's popularity to its presentation of a "different kind" of black theater. As Harper commented to the *Houston Chronicle*, "*The Wiz* does not capitalize on Blackness. It capitalizes on entertainment."[24] Veering away from political black protest theater advanced by the Black Arts Repertory Theatre, the Negro Ensemble Company ("The River Niger"), and Melvin Van Peebles ("Ain't Supposed to Die a Natural Death") in the 1960s and early 1970s, *The Wiz* stayed in the realm of make-believe, favoring fantasy over dramas of racial oppression.[25] Barbara Ann Teer, founder of the National Black Theater in Harlem, supported Harper's project, pointing to the need for subjects other than oppression and poverty. She declared, "*The Wiz* works. It's what Black audiences want. And the fact that a Black man produced it is even more reason why it should be applauded."[26]

Harper's production aligned perfectly with the kind of work that Hollywood hoped to exploit. In his memo, Lieberfarb concurred that *The Wiz* "offers a new approach to Black Theatre; a visual fantasy done with irreverent contemporary urban humor." Rather than being confrontational, Lieberfarb argued, the show was primarily about self-actualization, "namely that anyone can be or do anything if only they believe in themselves."[27]

Sidney Lumet's *The Wiz* opens not on a farm in Kansas or in the South but on 125th Street in Harlem. The first shot pans from a mural on a brick wall to a street lined with brick apartment houses. Inside one apartment, Dorothy (Diana Ross) and her Aunt Em (Theresa Merritt) prepare to welcome the extended family for dinner to celebrate a newborn child. The scene is warm with familial feeling as Aunt Em, the matriarch, sings "The Feeling That We Have" and the men, women, and children enjoy one another's company. Dorothy, however, does not partake in the merriment. She quickly reveals herself to be a shy and emotionally closed person, an elementary school teacher who has "never been below 125th Street." Aunt Em encourages her to apply for a better job that would help her to gain some independence, but Dorothy is adamant to stay at home and depend on her aunt and uncle.

When her dog Toto escapes into the wintry night, Dorothy runs after him. A violent blizzard develops and deposits her in the land of Oz, a surreal version of New York City. This Dorothy does not have the wanderlust of the character in L. Frank Baum's book or in the 1939 film, so her desire to return home does not indicate that she has come to appreciate its gifts. Instead, her trip through Oz becomes a lesson in self-realization as she meets the Scarecrow (Michael Jackson), the Tin Man (Nipsey Russell), and the Cowardly Lion (Ted Ross), who also learn about their own inherent talents. The musical score emphasizes this theme, from Dorothy's first introspective lines, "What am I afraid of?" in "The Feeling That We Have," to the Scarecrow's defeatist anthem, "You Can't Win," to "Ease on Down the Road." At the end, Glinda the Good Witch (Lena Horne) sums up the story's message with the directive, "Believe in Yourself." By the time Dorothy hears the lyrics from that song, "If you believe, within your heart you'll know, that no one can change, the path that you must go," she has learned that she can be a confident, independent individual. It is only after she has believed in herself that she can go home. To the Scarecrow, the Tin Man, and the Cowardly Lion, she admits that she is ready to change. The final scene of the film shows Dorothy holding Toto on 125th Street, heading for home.

Director Sidney Lumet insisted that *The Wiz* departed from previous interpretations of the classic story because it was based more closely on the original book. In an interview for *Film Comment*, Lumet highlighted Baum's theme of self-knowledge and the ways in which the Lion, Scarecrow, and Tin Man realize that the qualities they desire are ones they already possess. Lumet observed, "Now, as soon as that becomes clear, the rest is simple. It doesn't really matter how old Dorothy is; it doesn't have to be on a farm."[28]

When one considers the historical and material realities of the 1970s, however, it becomes clear that the changes to the story, including casting an older woman as Dorothy, jettisoning the rural setting, and, most significantly, foregrounding the theme of "self-knowledge," were the result of turning *The Wonderful Wizard of Oz* into a black-cast production. In his study of 1970s genres, George Lipsitz argues that Hollywood's increased willingness to foreground race "did more than desegregate previously all-white genres." Rather, he asserts, "the prominence of race called the generic form itself into question, leaving filmmakers and audiences with no consistent guide to resolving familiar dilemmas."[29] In a similar fashion, musicals in that decade referenced social problems and realities in ways they had never done before. While Lumet, a liberal filmmaker working in the Hollywood system, believed himself to be making a positive statement about individual potential, he could not divorce the film from its contemporary context and the historical relationship between African Americans and geographic and socioeconomic mobility. In privileging internal over external conflict, Lumet redirected the struggles in contemporary black life from the historical and material realities of racial oppression to an individualized, psychological fight for self-determination. For this reason, *The Wiz* is an early indication of neoconservative values that would mature during the 1980s, namely, the backlash against group rights won by the civil rights movement and the privileging of "individualism, market-based opportunity, and the curtailment of excessive state interventionism."[30] *The Wiz* effectively renders Dorothy a "model minority" because, in the end, she asserts her independence without reliance on anybody or anything.

Though not Lumet's intention, the making of a black version of *The Wizard of Oz* carried these weighted associations.

Bringing *The Wiz* to the screen was a joint effort of the show's original producer, Ken Harper, Motown Productions, and Universal Pictures. Harper created the Broadway show that first introduced the marriage of the black experience with the Baum story. In this original stage version, Dorothy, played by the young Stephanie Mills, undertakes the familiar journey from a farm to Oz, replicating the country to city migration that had made the story resonate with audiences in the past. The decision to cast an older Dorothy and relocate the setting to Harlem resulted from the collaboration of Motown Productions, the new film and television branch of the record label, and director Sidney Lumet and producer Ned Tanen at Universal.

Motown's involvement with the film was a natural progression from its previous cinematic efforts, among them *Lady Sings the Blues* (1972), starring Diana Ross. The record label moved to Los Angeles in 1972 to extend its activities into film and television production. Motown Industries president Berry Gordy placed Rob Cohen, a young filmmaker, as head of the new branch. Cohen pointed out that while Motown had no "physical studio overhead," there were advantages to spinning off a movie production company from a hit record label. The company's success would be based on the fact that "the record artists of Motown have built great public identification which is almost exactly like old Hollywood 'star quality.'"[31]

Casting Motown artists Diana Ross and Michael Jackson in *The Wiz* ensured a sizeable audience for the movie and the soundtrack. Both musical artists had achieved stardom based on their popularity with a mass audience, something that Motown had always prided itself on. As Suzanne de Passe, Motown Industries vice president, told one reporter, "I'm proud of the fact that we are a Black-owned company, but that doesn't mean we are a Black company. . . . Motown has always made music for the masses of people. You don't get millions of dollars just from Blacks." De Passe believed that Motown should not restrict itself to the black market, but should "grow and make money." She put forward Motown's pursuit of profit frankly in an interview for *Black Enterprise*: "I want my 40 acres and a mule."[32]

While Motown's productions often featured African Americans, its films and television specials were always geared toward an interracial audience in order to maximize profit. Motown's stable of stars was its strength. In his early memo to Warners, Warren N. Lieberfarb had suggested precisely this strategy of casting "known stars in principal roles and cameos" that would "lower the possibility that it would be perceived as a Black picture."[33] Rob Cohen at Motown and Ned Tanen at Universal would later echo this opinion when they ultimately agreed to Ross's request to star in the film.[34] Along with co-star Michael Jackson, Ross had already proven her ability to transcend the black audience with her music. In the reception for *The Wiz*, the producers hoped, stardom would trump race.

The film's producers were self-conscious about making an all-black picture and attempted to avert that perception not only by casting popular stars but also by altering the narrative. Hollywood and Motown aimed for the mass market, but one that was increasingly oriented toward the black experience and black music. Lumet aimed to satisfy both white and black audiences by updating the film to take place in contemporary New York City, effectively eliminating the country-to-city migration because it was "no longer relevant." Rather, he argued, it was the "urban experience that is relevant to most of us today."[35]

By 1978, the association of the black experience with the city had a long and fraught cinematic heritage. In contrast to the bucolic "antebellum idyll" shown in black-cast musicals like *Hallelujah!* (1929) and *Hearts in Dixie* (1929), the city in *The Wiz* is the home of black families. Hollywood's first black-cast musicals restricted the mobility of their subjects in an effort to deny the actual migration of African Americans to the cities and the profound social and cultural transformations that occurred as a result. In *The Wiz*, Lumet argues that migration is so far in the past that it is no longer significant. And yet, the story itself has the act of migration as its foundation, so that Dorothy's movement within the city is less effective.[36]

Trying to make a black-cast musical that was both specific to black life and universally accessible prompted Lumet not only to discard the country-to-city migration of the African American past, but also to refigure the contemporary black urban experience. A pristine, middle-class life was possible for African Americans in New York, to be sure, but it was by far the exception. For Lumet, the task was to evoke a positive image of black life, which out of necessity had to be devoid of very real socioeconomic problems: "Dorothy is, after all, from the middle class. There's a Black element in the U.S. that lives that way—no severe problems on an external level, in terms of making a living, unemployment, no dope—none of the usual things associated with ghetto life." Focusing on black people who have no "external" problems, Lumet conveniently sidesteps the need to reference the contemporary context. "If you're going for self-knowledge," he explained, "you'll want to eliminate any external social problems that could have caused the behavior and would have to be solved along the body of the picture. That's just going to muddy it."[37] In his efforts to make a positive film about the black experience, Lumet upheld growing conservative notions regarding the relationship between minorities and the state. As the director explained, "The characters of the film are oppressed, but they are willing victims in the sense that they blame their deficiencies for their predicament." In other words, they have only themselves to blame for their present condition, a realization that each of the characters makes by the end of the film. Arguing that the civil rights legislation in the 1960s had succeeded in rectifying inequalities in American society, neoconservatives in the 1970s and 1980s argued that no further special assistance was necessary. The dismantling of social reforms would characterize the Reagan era and create a nurturing environment for such popular television programs as *The Cosby Show* (1984–1992), which demonstrated how a hard-working African American family could enjoy middle-class status by "possessing the requisite moral character, individual responsibility, and personal determination to succeed in spite of residual social impediments."[38] *The Wiz* is an earlier example of such model minorities in action.

The Wiz admits to the black presence in the city, departing from previous black-cast musicals, but, in keeping with those films, it presents a skewed vision of black mobility or lack thereof. In the film, Dorothy restricts herself from movement. Though a mature woman, she will not go "south of 125th Street" because she is scared. Not only does her self-imposed confinement contrast with the women's movement then in full swing, but it also mitigates the historical forces behind the social, economic, and geographic restrictions on African Americans. An independent black film released one year after *The Wiz* provides a visual corrective. Haile Gerima's *Bush Mama* introduces a protagonist, also named Dorothy, who experiences oppression first socioeconomically from the state and society and then physically from imprisonment. As in blaxploitation films, the conflict in Gerima's film is externalized to critique institutionalized forms of oppression. Offering an interpretation radically different from Lumet's, Gerima insisted that "being Black in America" meant being stopped from "going where you want to go."[39] In *The Wiz*, no outside force keeps Dorothy from going where she wants to go. As the song "Ease on Down the Road" suggests, moving around is easy: "Come on now, ease on down the road, don't you carry nothin' that might be a load." Delivering the message of the film, "Ease on Down the Road" erases the very real sociohistorical circumstances behind African Americans' lack of mobility by negating the causal links between oppression and the movement and containment of black bodies.[40]

The quest for self-knowledge and self-advancement further strains the folk musical's form. Traditionally, the generic pattern held the solidarity of the group and the rites of collectivity, such as community gatherings and family celebrations, at its core. Directed toward an audience of insiders who shared in those rites, such films functioned as an affirmation of community and a bulwark against any change that might threaten it. The 1939 *Wizard of Oz* links the positive qualities of home, with its familiarity and family affection, with the camaraderie that Dorothy finds with the Scarecrow, the Tin Man, and the Cowardly Lion. She

18. The Scarecrow encourages Dorothy to "ease on down the road." *The Wiz* copyright 1978 by Universal Pictures and Motown Productions.

realizes that she is stronger because of these associations. Some of the folk musical's original function is retained in *The Wiz* in the opening number, "The Feeling That We Have," and in the community that Dorothy and her friends create in Oz. Nevertheless, fissures in the genre emerge from the theme of individual betterment that quickly materializes. Dorothy's inward focus produces a tension in the purpose of the film. Does it celebrate collectivity and continuity or foster individuality and mobility? In his analysis of the film *Car Wash* (1976), Richard Dyer demonstrates how black musicals emphasize "spatial and temporal stasis" through an active and recurrent use of music. Unlike white musicals, which privilege a "utopia of transformation," black musicals use spaces like the ghetto to emphasize social containment, but also the ways that people develop (musical) coping mechanisms with which to resist containment's stifling effects. Despite its black cast, *The Wiz* is more aligned with the white musical tradition that is concerned with easing down a road to self-advancement rather than the material circumstances and cultural ingenuity of black life.[41]

Ultimately, the film tries to have it both ways. It demonstrates Dorothy's solidarity with her friends over the course of their journey through Oz, which she eventually leaves behind so that she can self-actualize as an independent individual.[42] This ambiguity in the narrative makes for a discontinuous final scene: Dorothy returns home, the place that she longs for but also the place that, we have learned, she is supposed to outgrow and move beyond. Such discontinuity is one of the consequences of Lumet's interpretation.

The Wiz did not achieve the wide appeal its producers had anticipated. Made for $23 million, a sizeable sum for a black picture in Hollywood, but a modest one for a musical, *The Wiz* grossed only $21 million in domestic returns. Although the studio tried to sell it as "an event film, not a Black or white picture," its audiences were far less integrated than those at the Broadway production.[43] *Variety* reported on the film's successful preview in early October 1978 at the Loews State II in New York: "Once inside, the audience greeted the film with audible enthusiasm, and a second running of the entire film was called for (and received)." The reviewer added the qualification, however, that the audience was "predominantly Black." "Not that [Universal] officials (nor officials of any other film company for that matter) find heavy Black patronage cause for concern," he explained. "It's just that in marketing terms, 'The Wiz' must draw whites in at least equal numbers in order for the tuner to realize big rentals. It all boils down to economics rather than sociology."[44] The reporter's discounting of race as an issue in the film's exhibition was in keeping with the ways in which the studio and Lumet himself had attempted to lift *The Wiz* out of its blackness. All involved, including Motown Productions and Universal, believed that the film would bring in sizeable returns from black audiences (estimated by Motown executives to be around $20 million alone) while attracting a substantial white audience.[45]

The film's release in Chicago was illustrative of the interrelated dynamics of race and film exhibition. As *Variety* reporter Steven Ginsberg noted, most Chicago film theaters were divided racially: downtown theaters had least 75 percent black patronage for evening showings, while the first-run suburban theaters were primarily patronized by white audiences.[46] *The Wiz*'s release placed in harsh relief the sharp racial divide that had occurred as a result of "white flight" to the suburbs. While the makers of *The Wiz* hoped that the film would be the first "black picture" to achieve crossover success, it ultimately failed to do so.[47]

As the product of a black-owned company and a major Hollywood studio, *The Wiz* was unique for its time. It attempted to capitalize on the growing black market that had been developed by blaxploitation films and to attract a large enough white audience to be successful. The growing racial divide between urban and suburban theaters, however, revealed the complexities involved in making a musical film both black and universal in the 1970s.

Zoot Suit (1981)

Zoot Suit was the only one of the ethnic revival musicals to be made under the full control of a person of color. Though Universal Pictures produced and distributed *Zoot Suit*, the studio ceded the final cut to Luis Valdez, a condition that the first-time director demanded. As a result, the film reflects Valdez's vision for what he called "a new kind of American play" for a "New American Audience." Like the makers of *Fiddler* and *The Wiz*, Valdez aimed to reach a mainstream, interethnic, and interracial audience.

While those big-budget Hollywood vehicles were commercial first and foremost, Valdez sought to make a social and cultural statement with *Zoot Suit*. He desired to redraw the boundaries of what constituted American subject matter by placing the historical and material struggles of Mexican immigrants and their descendants at the center of *Zoot Suit*'s narrative. The Sleepy Lagoon murder trial of 1942 and the Zoot Suit Riot in the summer of 1943 are seminal moments in the history of Mexican Americans and, for Valdez, illustrated the racism that was endemic to the American experience. Harnessing the politics of the Chicano generation of Mexican Americans, Valdez's "New American Play" insisted on using these historical events to educate a "New American Audience" that was both ethnically and racially integrated.

The original play was a collaboration between Valdez and the Teatro Campesino, the itinerant theater troupe that he had founded to support the United Farm Workers (UFW) movement in 1965. The son of migrant farmworkers himself, Valdez grew up in Delano, which he called "a California version of Mississippi," where he experienced segregation in movie theaters: "If you were Mexican you were asked to move and that happened to me once, you know, just once. I was a kid and my brother and I were sitting in the wrong section."[48]

After college, Valdez joined the San Francisco Mime Troupe, which performed outdoor political protest theater, and eventually returned to Delano to join Cesar Chavez and the UFW in the fight for farmworker rights. Valdez's Teatro Campesino was composed of farmworkers/actors who performed on flatbed trucks in the fields and on picket lines. Their work was largely improvisatory, bilingual, and musical, "telling [the people] their history, performing for them."[49] In the first two years of the Teatro, Valdez and his troupe rallied support for the UFW and built a base audience that made up the union's core of support, an interethnic and multilingual group of volunteers. As Valdez explains, Delano at that time was "like a town in the South, I mean, it was like a Mississippi summer. . . . Outsiders from Berkeley, from Los Angeles and from UCLA and different places came to essentially integrate Delano."[50] As Valdez recalled, this "mixed audience" included Mexicans, Filipinos, Berkeley students, and black farmworkers from Bakersfield. Thriving on the challenges that such diversity posed, Valdez felt "a dynamism and electricity that helps each performance. We have found that playing just for Chicanos evokes certain things, just as playing for Anglos . . . neither is correct." His concept of a "New American Audience" grew out of the Teatro's early experiences in the fields and on the picket lines. Valdez believed that in order to succeed, his plays had to "respond to the whole audience, the whole country."[51]

In 1977 the Mark Taper Forum, the highly esteemed nonprofit theater in Los Angeles, commissioned Valdez to write and direct *Zoot Suit*, a play based on historical events of the 1940s. A number of Chicano scholars have pointed to this play as the beginning of the end for the Teatro Campesino and Valdez's involvement with that group. Arguing that Valdez went "mainstream" with this show, first to Broadway and then to Hollywood, a trend that Valdez pursued with *La Bamba* (1987), scholars such as Yvonne Yarbro-Bejarano, Tomás Ybarra-Frausto, and Yolanda Broyles-González contend that the price of catering to a mass "New American Audience" was the loss of a connection with *la raza* (the Chicano people) and the insertion of "audience-pleasing" devices like a sentimental love story, white savior characters, and musical numbers. Broyles-González has insisted that such devices dilute the strength of the sociohistorical critique inherent in the original play. Equally of concern to these scholars was Valdez's use of stereotypes both for his female characters and for the main character himself, El Pachuco, in his attempts to appeal to a mass audience.[52]

If we put aside the politics of Valdez's mainstream foray, *Zoot Suit* remains significant as a film made by and about Chicanos within Hollywood and, more specifically, as a musical of the ethnic revival. *Zoot Suit* provides a unique example of generic revision through its innovative form and content. Rosa Linda Fregoso has pointed out the ways in which the dance sequences disrupt the narrative, in keeping with the conventions of the show musical genre, and how they also demonstrate the expression of cultural identity.[53] Indeed, the film's hyper-reflexive form as a filmed play for a diegetic audience exaggerates the self-reflexivity of the show musical, in which a show is always performed for an audience within the film. On the other hand, *Zoot Suit*'s form integrates the qualities of the folk musical, with its themes of generational strife and the struggle for social inclusion and the musical numbers that express them. In this way, *Zoot Suit* more closely resembles a hybrid musical like *The Jazz Singer* (1927) in that it expresses the insider/outsider dynamic overtly as an ethnic and racialized one, a dynamic that would be submerged and displaced in most Hollywood musicals of the 1930s to the 1960s. Broyles-González misses this point when she refers to the film's "overly prominent and often gratuitous use of music, singing, and spectacular exhibitionist dancing."[54] To the contrary, the musical sequences in *Zoot Suit* are central to the film's project of grappling with the place of Chicanos in American life. In his innovative application of musical film conventions, Valdez brings the genre's exploration of the limits of social belonging back to the surface.

In part, the film's contributions to the genre stem from the material circumstances of its creation by a Hollywood outsider who struggled to gain acceptance. The film and Valdez's experience in making it reveal the split self of the ethnic outsider attempting to bridge the gap between the margins and the mainstream, ethnic heritage and assimilation. Like Tito Guízar before him, Valdez endeavored to create stories that included the experiences of ethnic outsiders through the integration of the show and folk musical forms. He searched for a way to retain cultural identity in spite of this integration. More than any other musical during the ethnic revival, *Zoot Suit* directly engages with issues of belonging and cultural adjustment.

In keeping with Hollywood's earlier attempts to capitalize on ethnic markets, studio executives turned to creators like Valdez only after their own efforts to appeal to Chicanos had failed. By the late 1970s, Hollywood had done much to alienate its "Hispanic audience."[55] The high profile of Cesar Chavez and the successes of the UFW, along with the growing significance of the Chicano movement, had produced a new cultural awareness of racial stereotypes in the media and of the historical absence of Chicano experiences on film and television. One study often cited by the Chicano press was "How Advertisers Promote Racism," by Tomás Martinez, which documents how contemporary ad campaigns, such as Frito-Lay's notorious "Frito Bandito" ads, projected demeaning and offensive imagery.[56]

The media-oriented activism of Chicanos, coupled with the cultural appeal of the ethnic revival, commanded Hollywood's attention. Convinced of a growing and largely untapped Hispanic market, Ned Tanen of Universal Studios purchased Valdez's play. He disregarded the production's poor critical reception in New York and focused instead on its popular success in Los Angeles: "I see it as a possible breakthrough for reaching Hispanic audiences in this country. We'll market it in Hispanic centers, but we're not going to eliminate other outlets." He had high hopes for the film's success, noting its "color," "energy," "style," and "music," and rejected the impulse to put out exploitation films, "Spanish 'Blaculas,'" for limited, niche audiences. The broader audience, he believed, was waiting to be tapped. *Zoot Suit*, he argued, "will help us find it."[57]

Studio executives sought to secure and exploit the Hispanic box office. The 1980 federal census estimated that the Hispanic population ranged between 18 and 23 million. Divided by geography, language, and cultural experience, however, the market had always proven difficult to reach. As Carlos Penichet, chairperson of the Chicano Media Association, stated, "The potential of the Hispanic audience is extraordinary. 'Zoot Suit' will be the proof." When Universal announced "new marketing strategies" for reaching this audience, it aggressively refuted criticisms that the film was an exploitation picture and insisted on its broader relevance.[58] Universal believed that, like *The Wiz*, this film about a specific racial group could be cathartic for Anglos seeking to understand the experiences of racial minorities. Unlike *The Wiz*, however, *Zoot Suit* engaged with the topics of racism and social injustice directly and did so by altering the Hollywood musical's form and structure.

Universal allotted $2.5 million for production and a fourteen-day shooting schedule at the Aquarius Theatre in Hollywood. With such a small budget, "opening up" the stage-bound original to location sets, as the production teams had done for *Fiddler on the Roof* and *The Wiz*, was not an option. Working within these parameters, Valdez chose to shoot the film as a hybridized stage and cinematic experience. He used two separate lighting crews, one to design the play's lighting and the other for cinematic effects. He also employed two cameras, one highly mobile and another locked on the static physical perspective of the play's audience. Rather than restricting the action to the stage, he shot several scenes outside of the theater and among the theater's audience and in the lobby.[59]

The film opens with a night shot of the illuminated "Hollywoodland" sign. The camera pans down as the exterior of the Earl Carroll Theatre comes into view. It is a still, black-and-white archival image that soon dissolves and comes alive with "Zoot Suit" on the marquee and the fig- ure of El Pachuco looming large above it. A vintage automobile drives up to the theater, and the film cuts to a close-up of the license plate: "1938

California-ZOOTER-Chevrolet." A young Chicano (Robert Beltrán), wearing a black leather jacket and a hat, steps out of the car and assists his mother and father, who are more traditionally dressed. The film cuts to an establishing shot of the theater exterior and pans upward to the silhouetted figure of El Pachuco (Edward James Olmos). The shot dissolves into the profile of the actual character, and he turns toward the camera as the spotlight hits him. We see him move slowly and purposefully down a staircase to center stage as he keeps his eye on the camera. The film cuts to show the Mexican American parents and their Chicano son take their seats amid an audience that is a racial cross-section of the nation and further diversified by age and gender. They watch El Pachuco weave in and out among dancers who are frozen in space and time. Suddenly, he turns, snaps his fingers, and points at the camera. The lights flash and the film cuts to a long shot of the stage as El Pachuco starts to sing, "Put on your zoot suit / makes ya feel real root," and the dancers erupt with life. El Pachuco weaves between the dancers, commanding the musical number and the film's narrative at once. At the end of the number, El Pachuco raises his pocketknife toward the camera and the shot dissolves to a close-up of a page from the *Los Angeles Daily Express* from 1942: "Grand Jury to Act in Zoot Suit War." The film cuts to a close-up of the image of a bomber plane on the first page. From behind, a knife cuts a long slit down the page, and El Pachuco enters through it onto the stage. We see an image of the audience, including the Mexican American family, who are clapping wildly for this first number. El Pachuco stares back intensely at them and we see a close-up of the Mexican American father and his Chicano son look at one another and smile. El Pachuco addresses them, "Ladies and gentlemen, the play you are about to see is a construct of fact and fantasy. . . ." He snaps his fingers and the story begins. We learn how a group of Mexican American youth fell victim to the racism of 1940s American society, were falsely accused of murder in an unfair and biased court, and spent several years in prison separated from their loved ones.

Throughout the film, Valdez cuts frequently to the diegetic audience in order to show their reaction to the events on the stage. The editing proves the entertainment value of the musical sequences and the dynamism of El Pachuco, but it also highlights the ethnic and racial make-up of the audience itself. Such an audience, with the intergenerational Mexican

American family at its center, is the physical incarnation of Valdez's "New American Audience," who had followed the Teatro Campesino from the beginning in Delano. By cutting back and forth between the play's action and the audience's response, Valdez demonstrates that the "New American Play" in which the experiences of racialized minorities are central and the "New American Audience" that supports such a nuanced cultural production are mutually constitutive. One naturally begets the other to produce a form of popular culture that is more inclusive in its message and accessibility.[60]

It would be easy, however, to mistake the direct address of El Pachuco and the use of the diegetic audience as proof that *Zoot Suit* is merely a late twentieth-century version of a show musical. The film also makes use of folk musical conventions. Its basic story structure, in which a community is torn apart and struggles to make itself whole again, firmly aligns the film with the folk tradition in the genre. After the jitterbugging scene, the film explores the contradiction between the desires of the main character, Henry Reyna (Daniel Valdez), for success in the Navy and a life beyond the barrio, and the sting of social injustice he faces in Los Angeles. In flashback, the film explores Henry's family life. He stands in front of his dresser mirror preparing to go out for the night as he and his brother listen to the Andrews Sisters on the radio. They are American kids with American tastes and aspirations. As the film reveals when Henry's mother calls him to the table, he is the son of Mexican immigrant parents who fled the Mexican Revolution and who have struggled to give their children the relative comfort of life in the United States. Nevertheless, they fear the ways in which American culture will pull their children from them and their values. In particular, their children flaunt the zoot suit, a flamboyant style of clothing embraced by black and ethnic youth in the 1940s; this form of teenage rebellion negates the parents' efforts to be accepted as Americans and instead calls attention to their children's social difference.

Although American courts and society stigmatize Henry and his friends because of their race and their dress, the family bonds remain strong. After he is released from prison, Henry reunites with his girlfriend and his family in a final scene that reprises the first dance hall sequence; this time, in separate spaces off to the side of the dancing, his friends and family proudly claim Henry as war hero and tragic victim, father and husband, son and brother. The embodiment of the Chicano, Henry has all of these identities within him. As the dancers assume the stance of the Pachuco, heads and shoulders tilted back, hips and one leg jutting forward, the film cuts to the audience once more as they leap to their feet in applause. The camera focuses on the Mexican American man and his son as they nod and smile at one another. The film suggests that whatever their differences, they, like Henry's family onstage, can overcome them by witnessing the history that binds them together. They entered the theater as different generations; at the conclusion of the play, they are unified by the proud heritage that has been demonstrated for them. As co-producer Kenneth Brecher observed, *Zoot Suit* represented the first time onstage and on film that "[t]he concept of the *familia* [family], a renewal of values and a rediscovery of relationships," was explored by a member of the Chicano community.[61]

In keeping with folk musical conventions, the musical numbers invoke and reaffirm community. From the very first jitterbugging scene, the film establishes the world of the interethnic, interracial leisure spaces of Los Angeles youth in the 1940s. Dance halls were places that youth claimed as their own. Within those walls, they were free to express themselves through dress, behavior, and movement. Those same outward expressions of identity were severely limited in the schools, places of work, and streets of Los Angeles.[62] On the dance floor, young people proudly pose for one another, compete for dancing partners, and engage in the camaraderie of insiders, forgetting for a time their status as outsiders in Los Angeles society. The film's camera emphasizes the interactivity of the space by moving around and above the dancers.

The jitterbugging sequences occur three times. The first one opens the film, the second one, "Vamos a bailar el swing," takes place on the night of the murder, and the last one, "Chuco Suave," concludes the film. These numbers are vibrant and dynamic because Valdez manages to integrate the audience into these sequences, suggesting that the diverse theatergoers are affected by the events and emotions onstage. He does so by using the mobile camera to communicate the dynamism of the number, much as Busby Berkeley did when directing musical numbers for Warner Bros. in the early 1930s. The camera initially establishes the divide between audience and performer only to break it down. Like Berkeley, Valdez takes the film audience where the theater audience cannot go, into the diegesis of the film. Unlike Berkeley, however, Valdez was not seeking to stage visual spectacle, but rather to bond the audience and the performer in such a way as to integrate the worlds of both, lending the audience the sensation of being immersed in the action. Greatly influenced by the meta-theatrical devices of Thornton Wilder's play *Our Town*, in which the stage manager recounts the history of a town while functioning as a character within the story, Valdez moves across the boundary between stage and audience with ease.[63] In this way, the direct address of El Pachuco, like that of *Our Town*'s stage manager, serves to invite the audience into the story, imbricating them in the action rather than keeping them out.

Valdez departs from the folk-oriented musical numbers selectively. In particular, "Marijuana Boogie" demands special attention for the ways in which it negotiates issues of identity and performance. It occurs during the courtroom sequence that follows the proceedings that will ultimately convict Henry and his friends of murder. Defense Attorney George Shearer (Charles Aidman) objects to the district attorney's order that the boys cannot wash, cut their hair, or change clothes during the trial. The judge explains, "They didn't go to jail looking like marines, Mr. Shearer." Adding to the insult, the prosecution reads aloud studies that link Mexicans to violence and ritualistic murder: "All [the Mexican] knows and feels is a desire to use a knife to kill or to at least let blood. This inborn characteristic comes down from the bloodthirsty Aztecs. And when added to the use of liquor or marijuana, then we certainly have crimes of violence." To this, El Pachuco snidely remarks to Henry, "Mmm, pues . . . put on your feathers, ese. Ya te chingaron." ("Well, put on your feathers, man. They have already fucked you.")

The film cuts to a close-up of Henry's face as a slow and suggestive piano and trumpet cue begins. The next shot is a close-up of El Pachuco's hands playing the piano keys. A sordid red light illuminates the shot, and wafts of smoke glide through the air. The film cuts out to reveal El Pachuco seated with two chorus girls flanking him on either side and one reclining on top of a neon-lit piano. The girls are dressed seductively in fitted red dresses and black fishnet stockings. El Pachuco smokes a joint and stares at the camera through the mirrored reflection on the piano as he plays and sings: "Marijuana, mari, marijuana boogie / marijuana, mari, marijuana boogie / mari, marijuana, that's my baby's name." In his stupor, El Pachuco moves his arms like a puppet's as he stiffly plays the keys and sings the song set to a cabaret style of music. In this way, Valdez calls attention to the theatricality of the trial's proceedings, in which the boys must perform for the jury. He also offers a realization of the stereotype with El Pachuco's performance as a doped and seedy Mexican. The mirrored reflection of the stereotype only highlights the artificiality of the image.

The number then segues back to the courtroom scene. The judge insists that each boy must stand whenever his name is called in order to allow the jury to distinguish among them. What ensues is a circus-like performance as the boys pop up one after another and sometimes together. El Pachuco accompanies their movements on the piano, playing maniacally and laughing and hollering. Embodying the stereotype of the drug-addicted Mexican, El Pachuco derides the trial for what it is: a farce. More profoundly, however, Valdez and El Pachuco demonstrate with "Marijuana Boogie" the superficiality of racialized stereotypes that can be easily assumed and just as easily cast off. In effect, the number reveals the extent to which the boys are feared and despised outsiders in the United States.

Far from being mere "audience-pleasing devices," these musical numbers are essential to communicating the deep cleavages between the margins and the center. Valdez distinguishes between the jitterbugging

19. El Pachuco performs the stereotype of the lascivious and dangerous Mexican. *Zoot Suit* copyright 1981 by Universal Pictures.

sequences and "Marijuana Boogie" and thereby demonstrates an understanding of the musical film's form and function. He reveals the dance halls to be spaces of social inclusion and the courtroom as one of exclusion. Musically, the numbers switch from the buoyant excitement of big band rhythms and movement to the jangling and seedy sounds of a cabaret piano. El Pachuco and the boys freely express themselves in the former and must perform an imposed identity in the latter. As with most folk musical numbers, the audience is intertwined in the action through a mobile camera in the jitterbugging scenes. Mirroring the experience of being an outsider, "Marijuana Boogie" subscribes to the show musical tradition in which a performer must act in service to what the audience desires to see. In this case, El Pachuco delivers the stereotype expected by the host society. Confronting this "national problem of a national stereotype" head on, Valdez insisted, was critical to overcoming it.[64]

Much like Tito Guízar's Spanish-language Hollywood films in the 1930s, Zoot Suit effectively demonstrates the margin-center dynamic that is inherent in the folk musical genre. But whereas Guízar's Paramount musicals focused on the differences between enjoying social belonging in the countryside and managing social alienation in the American city, Valdez introduced contemporary urban realities. The child of migrant farmworkers, Valdez recognized the differences between his parents' generation and his own and asserted that the "Pachuco is an urban expression" first and foremost "that may have seemed shocking and ugly to an older generation, but to the young people it represented everything that they needed to have in order to survive in the city."[65] Zoot Suit resonated with the contemporary Chicano experience by calling attention to the history of urban survival strategies crafted by marginalized peoples. In this way, the film is in keeping with other ethnic revival musicals like The Wiz, which observed that the experience of racialized peoples could no longer be rooted in a rural ideal. The altered behaviors, manipulated language, and new forms of dress that pachucos developed were tools for negotiating American life. The city could be a frightening and hostile place wherein the migrant must develop an aggressive character in order to survive. Concurrently, however, the city could offer the migrant a break with the past that was liberating and suggested new possibilities for one's identity. As

Valdez observed, "I saw [the pachuco] as an actor in life, and much of city life involves that sort of acting in life."[66]

Like Dorothy in *The Wiz*, Henry Reyna struggles to come to terms with his true self and the identity that society affixes to him. Unlike *The Wiz*, however, *Zoot Suit* maintains the balance between external and internal forces in the lives of Mexican American youth. Valdez exposes the systemic issues of racism and injustice in society, the courts, and the press as the cause of Henry's inner, psychological struggle. The character of El Pachuco, a musical being who is the product of Chicanos' coping mechanisms in a hostile place, reveals how *Zoot Suit* is concerned with highlighting discrimination rather than insisting that it does not exist. This structural foundation of *Zoot Suit*'s narrative is what makes the film unique as a Hollywood musical in the post–civil rights era.

But it was *Zoot Suit*'s determined exploration, musically and dramatically, of social issues that made the film a difficult one to sell. "As we approach the eighties," Valdez commented after the premiere of the play, "I think we're going to see the resurgence of the whole concept of integration again, but a qualified integration. Everyone won't have to sacrifice their sense of cultural identity, and their sense of cultural being in order to belong to the mass." Rather than desiring cultural separatism, as did some of his counterparts in the Chicano movement, Valdez envisioned the possibility of Chicano integration into mainstream society by way of retaining cultural identity, not sacrificing it. This "qualified integration" resonated with the moment of the ethnic revival in the 1970s, when the search for and preservation of one's roots became popular for the descendants of immigrant ethnics who had achieved whiteness over the course of the twentieth century. Valdez wove the Chicano narrative into this broader quest for roots, arguing that "the cultures of the world bring a vitality in their 'original state,' let's say like the original state of the immigrant, that this country cannot afford to lose." He insisted that the nation was at a turning point in the late 1970s that would have grave implications for the future. "We've come up against a stone wall, and that wall is racial and cultural differences between white people and non-white people. . . . The idea of the multiplicity of cultural expression; the ability of the country as a whole to express itself, it's what's at stake."[67]

Striking a balance between advocating "qualified integration" and appealing to the sensibilities of a cross-section of society proved difficult. On the one hand, El Pachuco is an intriguing guide who, like Tevye, invites the audience into an exciting world that is likely unfamiliar. On the other hand, El Pachuco has certain characteristics that obscure the translation of cultural behaviors, language, and values that made *Fiddler on the Roof* so accessible to non-Jewish audiences. Chief among these characteristics are El Pachuco's use of *caló*, a hybridized form of English and Spanish crafted by Chicano youth, and his often hostile and cagey demeanor. A far cry from the loveable and approachable Tevye, El Pachuco demonstrates, for better or for worse, the limits of qualified integration in Hollywood film.

Despite a grand premiere at Hollywood's Cinerama Dome, a star-studded event that took in a respectable $56,085 at the box office over the weekend, *Zoot Suit* did not make back its meager investment from Universal Studios in its theatrical run. In his article on "The Hispanic Movie Market" for *Caminos* magazine in 1982, Luis Reyes baldly asked: "What happened to the multi-million dollar Hispanic-American market everyone was convinced was there? Why didn't audiences come as expected?" The answer seemed to rest in both the ways in which Universal marketed the film and the realities of the elusive "Hispanic market" in the 1980s. As one preliminary marketing report advised, there was no single audience for *Zoot Suit*. Much like the audience for *The Wiz*, it was segmented along racial lines. Adding to the complexity, however, was the diversity of Spanish speakers in the United States, with their different national loyalties, dialects, and attitudes toward Anglos and the nation. The report ultimately called for a separate campaign tailored to each group, an ambitious undertaking that the studio was not willing to implement.[68]

Universal did make efforts to sell the film in Los Angeles and San Francisco, but it paid little attention to the larger Hispanic communities in the Southwest and along the East Coast. Latino reporters for the *Arizona Republic* were perplexed. Anticipating the film's opening in Phoenix on October 16, Michael Maza pointed out that the local press had conducted promotional contests for the film's premiere and that actor Daniel Valdez had visited the area to publicize the film—"and then . . . nothing." When questioned, a Universal spokesperson responded that the studio was having difficulty getting the picture into "good theaters in Phoenix and San

Diego"; "it looks like we're throwing the picture away, but we're not."[69] Whatever the excuses, *Zoot Suit* was a "hard sell" for Universal, as indicated by the multiple promotional campaigns and release dates set for the film and then changed again and again.[70]

The three Hollywood musicals discussed here, *Fiddler on the Roof, The Wiz*, and *Zoot Suit*, offered stories about specific cultural groups for a mass audience. Rather than presenting an image of white America as "universal" to all, as did Hollywood's previous folk musicals, these later films revised the genre by embracing the experiences of racialized and ethnic others, peoples who had been historically excluded from Hollywood's mainstream narratives. Not since the earliest folk musicals had the studios attempted to illustrate the community and family structures of peoples of color for a general audience. With the advent of the ethnic revival, the beginnings of cultural pluralism, and the introduction of racially and culturally specific musicals on the stage, Hollywood producers took notice of the potential to reach new audiences. The success of the earliest adaptation, *Fiddler on the Roof*, promised a new era in which the social issues of prejudice and discrimination could be explored alongside the musical rituals of a specific community.

The form and function of *The Wiz* and *Zoot Suit*, however, discouraged the same audience response. *The Wiz* was much more of a conventional Hollywood musical in terms of scale and budget. Its established director and star-driven cast gave the film a higher profile than *Zoot Suit*. Nevertheless, both films met with barriers at the box office that exposed the cracks in the notion that racial integration would occur in the theaters with the right kind of product. The rhetoric of cultural pluralism overlooked the very real racial divisions that remained in American society.

As musical films, *The Wiz* and *Zoot Suit* brought innovations to the conventions of the folk musical. They repositioned the notion of a universal perspective from white communities to the experiences of persons of color. In doing so, they placed an emphasis on the modern, urban realities of these groups rather than associating them with primitive, rural spaces. And, in keeping with the vogue of the ethnic revival, they geared their musical narratives toward all groups, facilitating the move between margins and center that was desired by African Americans, Latinos, and white Americans in the 1970s and early 1980s.

Offering an alternative to the culturally nationalist products coming from blaxploitation and Chicano cinema, such musicals were relatively conservative. *The Wiz* purposefully shied away from making a social statement and missed a chance to engage with the realities of African Americans in the post–civil rights era. As an analysis of *Zoot Suit* reveals, however, Hollywood's production of these ethnic revival musicals did not necessarily require the banishment of social criticism. *Zoot Suit* built on the historical discrimination of Mexican Americans in order to reassess the process of racial and ethnic integration in contemporary society. Where *The Wiz* uses its musical numbers to remove black life from social reality, *Zoot Suit* revises musical film conventions to explore the dimensions of oppression and resistance. These films provide a window onto an era that was rich in integrationist rhetoric but persistently thwarted by entrenched racial and ethnic prejudice. Their production and release demonstrate the extent to which the musical film was a site of cultural debate and identity formation in the era of the ethnic revival.

7

Home Is Where
the Audience Is

The Sing-Along

The musical film has proven to be a durable genre that continues to entertain audiences today. Recent film adaptations of Broadway shows that feature young casts, contemporary music, and fast-paced editing have been successful with younger moviegoers. As Jane Feuer has argued, however, films like *Chicago* (2002) and *Hairspray* (2007) offer little innovation in assessing the place of song and dance in our lives. By contrast, some filmmakers and exhibitors are using older musicals as inspiration for redefining the role of entertainment. We see this trend in two areas of production and exhibition. The first is the international art house film, such as *Strictly Ballroom* (Australia, 1992) and *Little Voice* (UK, 1998), in which ordinary characters "take up the position of spectators of old Hollywood musicals in a world where it is no longer possible to be Fred Astaire."[1]

The second trend is the growing practice of spectators who convene to watch and sing along with musical films on the screen. Rather than meeting these films with appreciative absorption, as in art house settings, sing-along audiences become an extension of the musical film's community. They are not satisfied to be mere spectators. Instead, they embody the film's characters, dressing and singing like them and directly engaging with their world. If genres are indeed ritualistic practices, as Thomas Schatz and others have asserted, then the sing-along is perhaps the most obvious indication of audiences making their desires and interpretations of the text known. Audiences do not merely recall and identify with Hollywood musicals of yore, they ritualistically bring them to life.[2]

185

This activism became clear when, on a typically overcast June day in San Francisco, I stood in a long line of people that extended down Castro Street. Amid leather-clad Danny Zukos and Pink Ladies of all ages, I waited for the doors of the Castro Theatre to open for the annual *Grease* sing-along. Ticket holders took pictures of the line outside the theater and admired one another's costumes. Of particular note was a family of women, including children, mother, aunts, and grandmother, dressed as Pink Ladies. The youngest, a five-year-old, proudly wore a pink poodle skirt and jacket, had her hair held in a high ponytail, and skipped around the others in line, impatiently waiting for the show to start.

As the audience entered the theater, costumed attendants handed out goodie bags filled with props, which included pom-poms, bubbles, a comb, a glow stick, and a "popper." The evening's program began with a series of live entertainments. An organist played the overture from the film. Two women who were dressed as the Rydell High School principal and the T-Bird leader, Kenickie, hosted a costume contest, which was followed by a vocal warm-up accompanied by the organist. After giving instructions on when and how to use the props, the Principal and Kenickie left the stage, the lights dimmed, and the film started to much cheering from the audience.

That same year, *Grease* (1978) found an equally receptive audience, if smaller in scale, at my ten-year-old daughter's slumber party. In the private space of our living room, five little girls anxiously anticipated the beginning of the film. At the first strains of Frankie Valli's "Grease Is the Word," they jumped off of the couch and began to dance. All seemed to be enjoying themselves until the first musical number of the film, "Summer Nights." It quickly became apparent that four of them knew the lyrics but one did not. Upset at being left out of the ensuing reenactments, she asked her friends if they would please be quiet so that she could watch the movie. Surprised and conciliatory, the others dutifully sat next to her and observed the remainder in silence.

Both of these encounters point to the ways in which the musical has become a participatory experience. The sing-along version of *Grease* was first released by Paramount Pictures in 2010, but as the slumber party (and my own memories of parties of an earlier era) indicates, *Grease* has been a sing-along for decades. Enjoying the film with friends in private or with like-minded strangers at a commercial theater has become a ritualistic activity. The audience for these events is preconstituted as one that is familiar with the film's storyline and its songs and dances. Upon arrival, audience members participate from a position of shared referents. The young girl at the slumber party felt alienated because she did not have the cultural knowledge that would allow her to join in her friends' interactivity with the film. The presence of an "outsider" in this cultural space prevented the *Grease* experience from happening that night.

Sing-alongs can be private affairs, but they are also receiving sanction as community events intended to promote pride in place or in cultural expression. The town of Mason City organized its first sing-along to celebrate one of its own, Meredith Willson, but also to commemorate the fiftieth anniversary of *The Music Man*'s premiere there in 1962. That occasion and the mass parade of school bands drew thousands of spectators and produced a great deal of goodwill. In the midst of the cold war, the day's activities indicated that small-town American values remained strong.

Fifty years later, Mason City organizers believed that a sing-along event could recapture some of those feelings of goodwill. The Music Man Square, a multi-million-dollar complex built adjacent to Willson's childhood home, re-creates the setting of the film, the streets and shops of Mason City circa 1912. Attendees could appreciate the life-sized statue of Willson in the square and visit a museum dedicated to preserving the town's history. The $30 ticket for the event included admission to the ice cream social and a screening of the 1962 band festival parade. Participants were encouraged to arrive in costume as "barbershoppers, singers, actors, maybe even dueling Marians." The local community theater provided costumes for anyone who did not have their own.[3]

As a film fostering ethnic pride and cultural heritage, *Fiddler on the Roof* (1971) has been another popular candidate for sing-alongs. Over the years, schools, synagogues, and various Jewish organizations have revived the film in order to convene the community and to share in the history that it represents. The Laemmle Theatre chain in Los Angeles began hosting sing-alongs for the film in 2008, when a distributor delayed the opening of a film in the days leading up to Christmas. Faced with the possibility of a dark screen at the Laemmle Royal in West Los Angeles, president Gregg Laemmle decided to show *Fiddler on the Roof* and to provide audience members with lyrics. He offered a pre-show entertainment that quizzed the audience on trivia from the film and asked anyone who had taken part in a production of the musical to share their experience. The event was such a success that Laemmle booked the sing-along on Christmas Eve for the next several years and in multiple theaters, including the Music Hall in Beverly Hills. Reviewer Kenneth Turan declared the sing-along his "film pick" in 2011, commenting on the continued relevance of singing "If I Were a Rich Man" after the financial collapse of 2008. Audience members told one interviewer that they found in the sing-along the chance to connect with their personal histories, specifically, the experiences of their parents and grandparents. With "nothing else to do" during the Christian holiday, moviegoers felt that singing along with *Fiddler on the Roof* was the perfect way to spend Christmas Eve.[4]

By far, the most successful and enduring sing-along has been associated with *The Sound of Music* (1965), followed closely by *Grease*. The former was born as a one-off event at the 1999 London Gay and Lesbian Film Festival. It quickly sold out, and the organizers were persuaded to schedule more screenings.[5] The following year, producer David Johnson and exhibitor Ben Freedman arranged for the film to screen at London's Prince Charles Cinema, where it consistently drew costumed audiences in large numbers. As Freedman describes, "We had initially targeted the show at the gay market and what we call the early adopters—people who go to the latest Soho bars and clubs, the latest anything in fact." The audience that materialized was a surprise: "a chunk . . . was middle-of-the-road, pretty middle-aged and female." Such wide appeal conveyed the possibilities of the sing-along format beyond niche markets and film festivals. "I realized at that point," Freedman recalls, "that it was not going to be an alternative form of entertainment but something pretty mainstream." By the turn of the millennium, "Sing-Along-a-Sound-of-Music" (as it was newly titled) had extended to New York, Los Angeles, Chicago, Australia, and Glasgow. The screenings at the Prince Charles have continued to the present.[6]

The largest *The Sound of Music* sing-along occurs at the Hollywood Bowl, where it has been running annually since 2001. The screenings fill the venue's capacity of more than 17,000 seats. The event includes a costume contest hosted by a celebrity and Charmian Carr ("Liesl"). Audiences are encouraged to bring a picnic and bottles of wine to enjoy before and during the film. They receive a bag of props that includes a sprig of edelweiss (to be waved during the song "Edelweiss"), a piece of cloth (to represent the clothes that Maria makes for the children), a ticket to Captain Von Trapp's ball, and a party popper to celebrate the first kiss between the Captain and Maria.[7] The popper is supposed to be used only at this moment, but inevitably, audience members pop when they are so moved. The enormous success of this event prompted Hollywood Bowl programmers to add the *Grease* sing-along to their annual lineup as well.

Like *The Music Man* and *Fiddler on the Roof, The Sound of Music* and *Grease* lend themselves to sing-along treatment because of their generic and subgeneric qualities. As folk musicals, they are concerned with the cohesion of a group, rooted in cyclical time, and unified in idyllic space. The collective celebrated in each, whether an Austrian family or a high school senior class, is deeply entrenched in a place that determines the rhythms of life. The places include such diverse locales as Maria's convent, the Austrian hills, and the Von Trapp family home in *The Sound of Music* and the school cafeteria and gym and the diner in *Grease.* These spaces order and give meaning to the lives of the characters who inhabit them. Effectively, they provide a material connection to place and demonstrate where these characters belong. In some cases, the place is literally home; in others, it is a figurative home, such as Rydell High School. In each instance, the

20. Audiences begin to arrive for *The Sound of Music* sing-along at the Hollywood Bowl, September 2012. From the author's personal collection.

gathering place demonstrates the interconnectedness of its occupants by showing them freely expressing themselves with song and dance.

By contrast, another subgenre, the show musical, has been notably absent from sing-along events. Some of these missing musicals are among the most critically acclaimed films of the genre, featuring stars closely associated with its formation, such as Fred Astaire and Ginger Rogers in *Top Hat* (1935) and Gene Kelly in *Singin' in the Rain* (1952). As two examples of many, these films unite two ideologically opposed characters in both narrative and musical sequences.[8] Folk musicals often have romance as a central component of their narratives, but the romance is in service to the strength of the collective, either the family or the community group or both. Their situation in a material place that defines the parameters of the collective allows for the joy of everyday activities to be expressed in a ritualistic and musical way. It is this connection to place that makes the folk musical the preferred vehicle for sing-along events. Audiences extend that community-making project into the material space that they occupy, temporarily rendering venues like the Castro Theatre or the Hollywood Bowl as places of comfort and collectivity, places of home.

Certainly, the sing-along in its most recent form owes much to cult cinema, the midnight movie, and, in particular, the fervor that surrounds *The Rocky Horror Picture Show* (1975). Exhibitors at the Prince Charles Cinema in London and the famed Waverly Cinema in New York, where *The Rocky Horror Picture Show* has had regular midnight screenings for years, were the earliest adopters of *The Sound of Music* sing-along. A number of reviewers, including *The New Yorker*'s Anthony Lane, noted how the audience's devotion, prior knowledge of the film, and participation were reminiscent of *The Rocky Horror Picture Show* experience. He observed that audiences greeted *The Sound of Music*'s new presentation at the Prince Charles in 2000 with an "apostolic level of dedication."[9]

The cult film has long fascinated scholars precisely because of its elusiveness as an object of study. It "transgresses even the boundaries we usually associate with the very notion of genre," as J. P. Telotte has pointed out. *The Rocky Horror Picture Show* is a self-conscious amalgam of genres and quickly achieved cult status after its first midnight run in 1976. It is ironic and irreverent in tone and criticizes such mainstream institutions as heterosexual relationships and the middle-class family. By sharp contrast, *The Sound of Music* is an earnest, family-oriented Hollywood musical that upholds mainstream values in every way. Audience adoration and intervention make these very different films comparable. Cult films, as Telotte explains, are determined by extra-textual elements, such as their mode of exhibition and audience engagement. Whereas some films lend themselves to such treatment, like *The Rocky Horror Picture Show*, with its ironic addresses to the audience and instructional musical numbers ("Time Warp"), others require the audience to work a bit harder. Moreover, *The Rocky Horror Picture Show* actively solicits a camp interpretation, while *The Sound of Music* does not. That is not to say, however, that *The Sound of Music* does not have camp qualities submerged in the text. Since the sing-along's premiere at the London Gay and Lesbian Film Festival, queer audiences have pulled to the forefront the campiness of the nuns, the hyper-masculinity of Christopher Plummer's Captain Von Trapp, and the closeted sexuality of Uncle Max.[10]

Cult status is not limited to the realm of the provocative and the ironic film. Certain films from Hollywood's classical period, like *Casablanca* (1942), have also achieved cult status. The films are classical in the sense that they hearken back to a mode of filmmaking perfected by the Hollywood studios that emphasized romance and glamour. Absorbing these films long after they were made produces a longing for a perceived utopia. Umberto Eco has argued that the popularity of classical cult films rests in an "archetypal appeal" that "produces in the addressee a sort of intense emotion accompanied by the vague feeling of a *dejà vu* that everybody yearns to see again." It is not necessarily the camp quality of a film but its element of nostalgia that produces both identification and yearning in the spectator. In the case of *The Sound of Music*, the nostalgia is twofold. The text re-creates Salzburg in "the golden days of the Thirties," before the impending takeover by the Nazis. For today's audiences, however, the film also represents a nostalgic return to the days before the ratings system. *The Sound of Music* is an exemplar of the type of classical, family-friendly moviemaking that was imperiled by changing audience demographics and tastes in the 1960s.[11]

Whether a midnight movie or a classical film, Telotte explains, cult cinema offers spectators the opportunity to cross boundaries, to adopt an alternate identity; but at the same time, it produces a supportive community. These films expose difference and then, in the creation of community solidarity, they normalize that sense of difference. In a *Sound of Music* sing-along, one man dressed as a nun might feel conspicuous on his way to the screening; but once there, he will meet dozens of others dressed in similar fashion.[12]

Folk musicals have embedded within them a commitment to ritualistic activities, cycles, and the creation of places of belonging. The interconnectedness of a people and the material space they inhabit is a virtue that folk musicals have consistently established and reinforced. In sing-along audiences' revivification of older musicals, they connect with "time sunk deeply into the earth," as M. M. Bakhtin has described. They experience the satisfaction of activities enjoyed collectively and cyclically. This rootedness between time and space has associations with a folk past in which communities engaged in collective pursuits and life's events were predictably ordered. Critical to this time was the absence of class stratification, a marker of social difference that is a prominent characteristic of the modern era.[13]

Cyclical time and idyllic spaces exert particularly strong influence in both the texts of the films chosen for sing-alongs and the ways in which they are consumed. Making the old new again, the sing-alongs revive decades-old musical films because the joys of collectivity still resonate. Their audiences identify with the groups on the screen (the members of the Von Trapp family, the senior class) and bring them into the place of exhibition, dressing and behaving like them and re-creating the camaraderie on the screen in the material place of the movie theater. The success of the sing-alongs reveals the ways in which these films are being repurposed to maintain their relevance long after they were first released.

In *Grease*, the community is the class of high school seniors, especially the groups of Pink Ladies and T-Birds, who gather at the school cafeteria and gym and the Frosty Freeze diner. Parents are absent from the film, although they are occasionally mentioned. The students have their distinctive forms of dress (pink and leather jackets, respectively) and behavior (such as eating lunch in the same place every day) that identify them as a collective. Sandy's identity as an immigrant outsider makes her integration into the world of Rydell High the focus of the film. In the end, she adopts a new form of dress and new behaviors in order to be one of them. From a feminist perspective, this transformation is troubling; yet, in the film, it is a necessary process if the group is to be united as a whole. The film's musical numbers repeatedly reinforce the integration of this community, from the parallel scenes in "Summer Nights" to the ultimate sequence, "We Go Together." In keeping with the folk musical, the conflict stems from the potential breakup of the collective, a prospect that threatens to come true when Frenchy drops out and the school year comes to a close. "We Go Together" is an affirmation that the students "will always be like one" no matter what the future brings. The final bell indicates the end of one year and the beginning of another.

The last number captures the experience of being part of a collective in which emotions, body movements, and even language are shared. When Jan expresses concern that the group might "never see each other again," Danny quickly dismisses her worry. How does he know? He strikes a pose and sings, "A wop bom a loo bop," and the kids quickly respond, "a wop bam boo!" Most of the song that ensues is gibberish ("we go together / like rama lama lama / ka dinga da dinga dong"), words and expressions understood only by the kids. In the face of impending separation, the kids invoke this special language to reinforce their shared identity and interconnectedness. In the sing-along, audiences joyously rattle off these nonsensical lyrics in unison.

"We Go Together" is a buoyant number that takes place against the backdrop of the colorful thrill rides of the school fair. It's a dynamic space that the kids fully occupy. The camera moves the spectator through this space energetically, communicating the dynamism of the fairground rides and even including some of the adults in the festive spirit. Always filling the frame, the kids dance in and out of the center and around the main characters. In many of the shots, however, Danny and Sandy are positioned as merely part of the larger group. They are often so far in the background that they are difficult to distinguish amid the kids who dance in front of them. The camera dollies toward and away from the action in constant motion. In one shot the camera repeatedly pans away from the main characters to reveal the other fairgoers, effectively emphasizing the group dynamic over any one individual. Toward the end of the number, the camera quickly dollies forward, showing a close-up of the kids' clasped hands. As they separate, the camera locates Danny and Sandy settled in the car that will take them into the clouds. Sing-along audiences replicate the spirit of this number by dancing in the aisles and interacting more with each other than with the characters on the screen. The audience employs "We Go Together" in the service of their real-world community.

The final credit sequence returns the kids to high school with a series of close-ups from the pages of the yearbook. Still images from the film reappear in these close-ups to remind the audience of the past, but also as a means of preserving them in the present. Just like high school, the film ends, but the memories live on. The credit sequence is the wish fulfillment of the kids when they sing "We'll always be together." Likewise, each instance of watching *Grease* transports the sing-along audience through the cyclical experience of the senior year. In numbers like "We Go Together," we see how the folk musical has the ability to extend musicality, as a state of being socially connected and rooted in place, to the audience as well.[14]

As the most popular film of 1978, *Grease* arrived at the end of a period marked by a "confidence in criticism." Michael Ryan and Douglas Kellner describe the early to mid-1970s as a period in which "the liberal and radical critique of American society" prevailed in genre films like *Cabaret* (1972) and *New York, New York* (1977). These films are pessimistic iterations of the musical's utopian project. They criticize rather than reaffirm American society and institutions, morality and ideology. By contrast, Ryan and Kellner assert, films like *Grease* are "mindless musicals" that participated in the restoration of the conservative ideology that would dominate the 1980s. More than a film about "ritualized romance" and "dates," however, *Grease* conveys the inclusive social ordering that is at the foundation of all folk musicals. Ministering to the fracturing of society, folk musicals project integrated communities in space and time. Far from "mindless," musicals like *Grease* skillfully and effectively soothe the concerns in contemporary American life.[15]

For this reason, the film is similar to the "nostalgia films" of the 1970s that Fredric Jameson has identified. Films such as *The Godfather* (1972), he argues, are a product of Americans' disillusionment with modernism, a desire for *gemeinschaft* rather than *gesellschaft* in the ordering of contemporary society. Francis Ford Coppola's film is "designed to place us in that 'nostalgic' frame of mind in which we are most receptive to the inspection of old photos and the aesthetically distant contemplation of bygone fashions and scenes from the past."[16] The simulation of historical, material spaces plays a significant role in these films. The public high school, the primary gathering space in which the action of *Grease* plays out, had been transformed by the late 1970s. After debilitating race riots in many cities during the 1960s, white flight contributed to the abandonment and decay of public institutions, including schools. Rydell High School, by contrast, is a pristine place with well-manicured lawns, clean hallways, and functioning facilities.[17] And yet, evidence of social fracturing appears overtly in the irreverent behaviors of the student body and covertly in the subtle representation of their multiethnic backgrounds.[18]

As explored in chapter 5, *The Sound of Music* also depicts a collective rooted in a specific time and space. In this film, the family maintains a strong connection to the land that has nurtured it. The material spaces from which the collective takes its identity include the Von Trapp home and the streets and hills of Salzburg, Austria. Music plays an important role in establishing the centrality of the family and its relationship to the nation. "The Sound of Music" unites the children and their father, while "Edelweiss" bonds parents and their children and, by extension, the Austrian people and their homeland. This powerful dynamic between home/homeland, family, and song assuaged fears that the very real fissures in 1960s America would ultimately tear it apart.

Like the musical rituals that occur year in and year out in these films, audiences return again and again to the sing-alongs at the Castro and the Hollywood Bowl. When Twentieth Century–Fox released *The Sound of Music* in 1965, one of the most striking aspects of its enormous box office success was that many audience members saw it multiple, even dozens of times.[19] Similarly, patrons make the fall sing-along event at the Hollywood Bowl an annual pilgrimage, dressing in costume, participating in the pre-show parade and competition, and, of course, singing along with the film. As one audience member said of her repeat attendance, "I go to the hills when my heart is lonely / I know I will hear what I've heard before. My heart will be blessed with the sound of music / And I'll sing once more!"[20] The ritualistic and cyclical qualities of attending the sing-along mirror the rituals of the film, in which Maria "goes to the hills" when her "heart is lonely." The return to these material places—the Hollywood Hills where the Bowl is located and the Austrian hillside of the film—brings rejuvenation.

One of the most popular instances of collectivity in *The Sound of Music* sing-along is the "Edelweiss" number performed by Captain Von Trapp, Maria, and the children toward the end of the film. In this scene, the Captain has allowed the family to perform at the annual Salzburg Folk Festival as a means of escaping the Nazi Party's order that he command the navy of the Third Reich. As the family sings "Edelweiss," a tune that the Captain describes as "a love song" to the people of Austria, the audience sings it back to them. This number begins on the stage, but the differences between performer and audience are soon eliminated.

The Captain prefaces the song by first alluding to his impending departure from the land he loves: "My fellow Austrians, I shall not be seeing you again perhaps for a very long time. I would like to sing for you now a love song." Dressed humbly and holding a guitar, he stands in front of his audience and sings this "love song" to his countrymen. Like the conflicts in most folk musicals, the separation from family and homeland is a cause for sorrow. Moreover, his is not a voluntary departure for a better life, but rather a journey that is forced upon him. As he begins the number, the film shows him in long shot on the stage with the audience in the foreground. In the typical pattern for show musicals, the film cuts between medium shots of the performer and his audience, including the Nazis who are waiting to take him away. Not surprisingly, they are not affected by the sentiment of the song.

When he arrives at the second verse, the Captain is overcome with emotion and cannot continue his performance. The camera then reveals Maria watching from the wings. When she hears the Captain falter, she leaves the children and walks to his side, picking up the song where he left off. The camera shows this movement in a pan across the stage. Once she is standing beside him, he regains his voice and the children join them. At this moment, what had been a solitary performance becomes a chorale. Sharing the song with his entire family, the Captain motions for his countrymen to sing along. The film then cuts to a long shot of the audience singing in unison, establishing the familiarity of the song among Austrians. A series of shots that eliminate the stage follows. Medium shots of different sections of the audience reveal ordinary Austrians raising their voices with the Von Trapps. The framing of this sequence levels the distance between stage and audience in order to foreground unity. The performance ceases to be a transaction between singer and listener. It begins as a form of entertainment, but the number transitions into a new social ordering. In such a society, music is not a commercial product but a mode of communal expression.

In the context of the film, what was a simple folk song also becomes a song of national identity in the face of a foreign threat. As all share in the number, it becomes one of protest and defiance. The song's message of love of country ("Edelweiss, edelweiss, bless my homeland forever") takes new meaning in the service of defending national sovereignty and freedom of expression against fascism.[21]

During the sing-along at the Bowl, audiences react to this number in less exuberant fashion than to the others. A solemnity among moviegoers results in an earnest rendition of "Edelweiss." As the Von Trapps sing to their friends in the audience, the film's audiences sing to the Von Trapps and the Austrians on the screen. Just as in the film, the barrier between performer and audience, screen space and audience space, breaks down. Collective expression of solidarity with the Von Trapp family and their homeland is at the foreground of this musical moment.

Sing-along audiences, however, mark this sequence in the film with their cell phones, those taboo objects of the movie theater. As many You-Tube videos demonstrate, audiences light up their cell phones and gently wave them through the air as they sing during this part of the film. Those who document the number with video cameras, tablet computers, or cell phones pan away from the screen in order to feature the galaxy of multi-colored lights produced by the devices.[22] In this space, an object of ever-ready, one-on-one communication is integrated into the experience of the sing-along. The communal act of lighting up one's cell phone creates camaraderie among thousands of people. But perhaps more importantly, it also elevates a form of technology that has the potential to be socially disruptive to an object of beauty and solemnity.

The sing-along can be interpreted as a return to the beginning of the cultural practice of moviegoing. Early film audiences regularly engaged with one another and with the screen in nickelodeons and the other early places of cinematic exhibition. As numerous scholars have shown, moviegoing in the first few decades of cinema was an interactive prac-tice through which group cohesion was reinforced. Audiences insisted on socializing with one another, bringing their disruptive children, and "talking back" to the screen to express a variety of emotional responses. Theater owners struggled against such behavior for the purposes of maintaining order and elevating moviegoing to a respectable middle-class pastime.[23]

As described in earlier chapters, marginalized groups in society experienced belonging in certain theater spaces that featured ethnic theater and movies made by and about those communities. Much like the relationship between Jewish theater audiences and Yiddish cinema, African American audiences and early black film, and Mexican immigrants and the *comedia ranchera*, the sing-along prioritizes identification and interactivity as central components of the moviegoing experience. Developed in the 1930s by these ethnic cinemas, the folk musical does not present entertainment to its audience, but rather formally and narratively functions to weave the audience into its world. In this way, it obscures its own mass-mediated and commercialized imperatives in order to serve the folk project. Temporarily alleviating the alienating experiences of social exclusion and cultural rupture with the past, the folk musical encourages spectatorship practices that privilege community over isolation through the shared medium of song and dance. The sing-along of the twenty-first century is the latest incarnation of this form of spectatorship. And it is one that has the dynamics of communal belonging at its core.

Although the early forms of interactive spectatorship were significant and widespread, they nevertheless met with a great deal of resistance from the industry, theater owners, and audiences who demanded orderliness and quiet. As new forms of exhibition were introduced, such as the drive-in theater, the midnight movie theater, and the VCR and home theater system, they brought with them possibilities for social engagement that was not condoned in the movie palace or multiplex.

And certainly, the cell phone has presented new challenges to theater owners who attempt to maintain the theatrical space as a quiet zone that allows the audience to become psychologically absorbed into a film. Most movie theater experiences involve a plea to the audience to sit quietly with cell phones turned off. Some of these pleas are made directly, others are more creative, but the message remains the same: do not engage in any behavior that might disturb the strangers around you.

The sing-along liberates movie spectators from these restrictions. Rather than limiting interactive, social activity, the format directly solicits it. The hosts of these events, like the opening act of a rock concert, work to get the crowd excited enough to overcome any inhibitions instilled by conventional moviegoing socialization. Eating, drinking, singing, dancing, and yelling at the screen are all essential components of the sing-along experience. Much like audiences of the early twentieth century, the sing-along audiences make the place of film exhibition theirs.

In their reviews of the experience on the Hollywood Bowl and Yelp websites, patrons of the sing-alongs consistently comment on how the joy of singing with others is one of the most rewarding features of these events.[24] Many express surprise at the lack of censure in the theater space: "It seems so wrong to do that in a movie theater but it was very welcomed here." One patron at *The Sound of Music* sing-along at the Castro wrote, "I did want to apologize to the gentlemen in front of me for my rather lousy voice and disproportionate enthusiasm, but they seemed unfazed. Once again . . . (damn Pollyanna gene), I found myself puddling up at this huge theater full of people uniting in silly and schmaltzy fun."[25] Another declared that she "embraced the chance to sing with others" the songs that were "ingrained" in her as a child.[26] Those who were more timid found that they could liberate themselves in this space. "I usually save my singing for the shower where no one else can hear me," reported one filmgoer, "but I could not help but belt out 'I am sixteen going on seventeen / i know that i'm naive . . .' right along with Liesel."[27]

One reason that moviegoing socialization can break down in this space is that the audience members constitute an imagined community of musical film lovers that has been convened for the event. They share knowledge of the songs and the film's narrative, to be sure, but they also are able to communicate their like-mindedness by dressing in costume and cheering for one another during the pre-film costume contest. The latter is far from a cutthroat competition that distinguishes some above others. At the Hollywood Bowl, for example, there are so many entries that it takes nearly several hours for all the individuals and groups to march across the stage as Marias, Von Trapp children, nuns, and more esoteric references, such as a "flibbertigibbet," curtains, and "ray, a drop of golden sun." As the contest draws to a close, it becomes clear that the point of this activity is not to select a winner but to celebrate the participation of this community. One entrant felt that she was "somehow part of an awesome yet ridiculous cult."[28] It is a folk community that regenerates itself as new generations of *The Sound of Music* fans take part in the event. Young and old, gay and straight, citizen and immigrant, and peoples of different ethnic backgrounds claim a place within the sing-along community. The integration happens, if for only a short while, both onscreen and off.

Making the theater space theirs, whether the more intimate space of the Castro Theatre or the large, open space of the Hollywood Bowl, audiences actively break down the barrier between themselves and the screen. Much of this interaction is scripted. For example, the sing-along host instructs the audience to cheer the first time the camera "finds" Maria on the hilltop, to "awwww" at Gretl, to hiss at the baroness, and to boo the Nazis. At the *Grease* sing-along, the audience is told to wave the pom-poms at the bonfire rally, "boo" Cha Cha (Sandy's rival), and whistle at the Pink Ladies. The audience more or less dutifully obliges.

Not surprisingly, however, audiences exert agency by diverging from the sanctioned activities of the event organizer. Premature "popping" of the poppers is a special point of contention and one that audiences like to use to heighten moments of sexual tension. Audiences particularly enjoy reading *The Sound of Music* in subversive ways and using the poppers to emphasize their alternative interpretations. As *The New Yorker* writer Anthony Lane noted in his review of the sing-along at the Prince Charles Cinema, "nothing can touch 'The Sound of Music' for sheer, blank indifference to the reproductive act." Unlike earlier, more spontaneous sing-alongs, such as *The Rocky Horror Picture Show*, *The Sound of Music* is "the most unwitting of cults" and "is blissfully up for grabs."[29] Audiences bring to the fore the underlying sexual meaning of the number "I Am Sixteen Going on Seventeen," in which Rolf sings to Liesl, "You need someone older and wiser / Telling you what to do / I am seventeen going on eighteen / I'll take care of you." Popping also occurs when the Captain and Rolf jointly hold a gun and stare into each other's eyes near the end of the film. In *Grease*, a decidedly less bashful film in its treatment of carnality, the poppers are meant for the moment when Sandy and Danny romantically reunite at the school fair, but audiences often prefer to use them when Rizzo and Kenickie prepare for sex in the back of his car. In each of these instances, audiences take action to make meaning that is satisfying to them and not necessarily to the event organizers.

The sing-alongs reveal the ways in which the musical—specifically, the folk musical—continues to have relevance in the twenty-first century. Although film studios and event organizers have a role in shaping this form of entertainment, ultimately the audiences claim it for their own purposes in the specific time and place in which they encounter it. Here we see a genre being given new life, not in the form of remakes, sequels, or even appreciative revivals, but in dynamic ways that connect the spaces of community and home on the screen to the place of exhibition. Far from the isolated and orderly experience of twenty-first-century moviegoing that is the norm, the sing-alongs privilege communal interaction and alternate readings of the films that are both subversive and rejuvenating, making home where the audience is.

Conclusion

Beyond the Rainbow

"A small town girl and a city boy meet on the Sunset Strip." So reads the tagline for the musical *Rock of Ages* (2012). The opening scene introduces us to the girl, Sherri Christian (Julianne Hough), sitting on a bus headed west. She casually sings along with the song "Sister Christian" on her headphones. Gradually, the bus driver and other passengers, including men, women, and children, join her: "Where you going / What you looking for. . . ." All express the sentiment of the song, the search for happiness and love. Like Dorothy in *The Wizard of Oz* (1939), Sherri eagerly anticipates a better life "beyond the rainbow."

Stepping off the bus and onto Sunset Boulevard, the traveler is excited and overwhelmed by the city's lights, noise, and commotion. Naïve and innocent, she trusts a stranger with her suitcase, only to have it stolen. Drew Boley (Diego Boneta), the "city boy," comes to her rescue, and their romance ensues.

Rock of Ages begins with an act of migration. Traveling between the country and the city, Sherri embodies the collision of two worlds. She has left her family behind in order to pursue her dreams of rock 'n' roll in the big city. Her trusting nature and wide-eyed optimism make her vulnerable to the hard-edged and sometimes hostile urban environment. She struggles to integrate into its patterns of life and establish new relationships. Her cultural adjustment process is eventually a successful one, made manifest by her romantic union with Drew and her triumphant performance onstage at the film's end.

Migration has been and continues to be relevant to American life. Contemporary debates question the processes by which immigrants should be allowed to enter and integrate into the country. The perception that the United States harbors aliens with bad intentions motivates the clamor for tighter border security. And fear of competition for the nation's dwindling resources hardens the anti-immigrant position of the conservative majority in states like Arizona. In all of these debates, the argument hinges on drawing distinct boundaries between "us" (Americans) and "them" (foreigners). Social belonging is granted or denied according to which side of the line one occupies.

Migration is often a necessity for those who undertake it. At best, it is an opportunity with liberating potential. At worst, it constitutes a rupture with all that is familiar and a reckoning with the unknown. The promise of social mobility is a seductive one posed by migration, but it is not always realized. When the host society erects barriers to social and cultural integration, the migrant must navigate a difficult path.

As the opening of *Rock of Ages* demonstrates, American forms of expressive culture treat migration as a shift in both spatial and temporal experience. The journey moves the individual from home to an unfamiliar place and from the past to the present. In musical film, migration is made more dramatic by situating the home in the country and the unfamiliar in the city. As the migrant undergoes her journey, she becomes further removed from her family collective in idyllic space and closer to the alienation of the modern world. This dynamic between such opposed spatio-temporal experiences continues to inform the structure of the American musical film.

Dreams of stardom more firmly ally *Rock of Ages* with the subgenre known as the show or backstage musical.[1] Although the film includes musical moments that express the feelings of individuals and collectives, its narrative turns on the characters' quest for success on the stage. Sherri could be easily compared to Ruby Keeler in *42nd Street* (1933) or Alice Faye in *Alexander's Ragtime Band* (1938) for the ways in which she transforms herself from an unknown into a star over the course of the film. Implied in this storyline, in Hollywood musicals of the past and present, is the transformation of the outsider into an insider and the realization of social mobility in American life.

Current popular culture owes much to the show musicals of Hollywood. In more ways than one, Gene Kelly's prediction that the variety shows on television would soon overtake the primacy of musical film has come true. Variety shows and musical competitions entertain audiences with numerous performances every week. Programs like *American Idol: The Search for a Superstar* (2002–), *The X Factor* (2004–), *So You Think You Can Dance* (2005–), and *Dancing with the Stars* (2005–) promise stardom and recording contracts for winning contestants. The comedy-drama *Glee* (2009–) offers the high school glee club as a refuge for the outsider teenager and features elaborate performances scripted to the talents of its cast. These programs preserve the narrative that Americans have the chance to achieve acceptance and social mobility via distinction on the musical stage.[2]

In particular, the competition shows give added meaning to the promise of stardom by drawing on another convention of the show musical: the backstage story. They explore the real lives of the contestants, interviewing them and their families on their personal backgrounds, dreams, and aspirations. As with the show musical, the backstage drama raises the stakes for the actual performance, rendering the ultimate success or failure all the more gripping.

These programs also structure performance sequences like the show musicals of old. They repeatedly cross-cut between the singer/dancer and his/her audience (including the judges). Such sequences, as in all show musicals, are self-referential. They demonstrate to the audience at home how the performer is faring, thus amplifying the drama of the final judgment.[3]

As we have seen from the popularity of sing-alongs for *The Sound of Music* (1965) and *Grease* (1978), the folk musical's privileging of the premigratory space, the space of home, has also been preserved in certain realms. Animation has played a significant role in sustaining and reviving the musical form and certainly warrants a more substantial treatment that it is possible to provide here. For my purposes, two contemporary examples, the film *South Park: Bigger, Longer + Uncut* (1999) and the television sitcom *Family Guy* (1999–), are cases in point. Both are the products of actors/musicians who have admitted to being deeply influenced by the musical during their childhoods. Matt Stone and Trey Parker open *South Park* with one of the signature features of the folk musical, the atmospheric chorale number, which celebrates place and community. Young Stan Marsh sings of the constancy of home as he walks from house to house to meet his friends: "Just another Sunday morning in my quiet mountain town." As in the folk musicals of the past, all characters in this space share in the song, including parents and children.

Family Guy, by Seth MacFarlane, also regularly portrays the members of its typical Rhode Island family singing as a form of self-expression. Often, these musical numbers are quotations from musical theater and film, such as the "Shipoopi" number in the "Patriot Games" episode of 2006. Having just scored a touchdown, Peter Griffin, the father, exclaims, "This calls for a victory tune!" He reenacts the number from *The Music Man* in the middle of the football field, soliciting the sung responses from the fans and cheerleaders. To his "shipoopi," they retort, "that girl is hard to get." Soon, everyone participates in the number, including football players, fans, band members, referees, and sports announcers. MacFarlane even goes so far as to faithfully re-create the number's original film choreography.

These quotations of the folk musical are not innocent. Their makers insert a healthy dose of irony and satire into their works. Aimed at an adult, mostly young male audience, these animated programs sustain the qualities of the folk musical only to subvert them. They call forth the comforting feelings of collectivity in numbers like "Mountain Town" and "Shipoopi" while simultaneously deconstructing the fantasy of social togetherness and moral decency. In the former, Stan Marsh casually steps over a homeless man while singing, "You see homeless people, but you just don't care." And in "Shipoopi," MacFarlane includes among the song's participants men embracing other men and sports fans who dance while relieving themselves at stadium urinals. These animated productions aim to deconstruct the notion of the musical as family-friendly entertainment.

This latest use of the folk musical is not surprising when one considers the many ways in which the generic pattern has been employed over time by multiple makers and within various modes of production. In the early years of sound, Warner Bros. explored the stark differences between the folk and the modern with *The Jazz Singer* (1927), a rarity in Hollywood for its explicit treatment of immigration and cultural adjustment. Embedded within this film are the two structural patterns that the musical film would develop in the twentieth century, the show and the folk. *The Jazz Singer* uses the show and the folk syntax to depict the different worlds that its main character occupies, the Old World immigrant home and the New World of the American stage. Occupying a racially liminal space, the immigrant Jew achieves social mobility via blackface and jazz performance, but only on the condition that he brings part of his Jewish self with him.

In the first Hollywood folk musicals, just two years after *The Jazz Singer*, MGM and Twentieth Century–Fox associated images of black life with an idyllic vision of the Old South. In their departure from the show musical format, the more dominant form at the time, the black-cast musicals of 1929 firmly associated racial Otherness with primitivism and musicality. Black folk, these films suggest, are musical creatures who draw their sustenance from the cotton fields and cabins of the South. As we understand from *Hallelujah!* (1929), when black folk migrate to the cities of the North, they are robbed of their folk spirit. In contrast to *The Jazz Singer*, mobility is not a possibility, a conclusion that contemporary black audiences and producers challenged.

Independent filmmakers such as Harry Gant, Clarence Brooks, and Sidney Goldin sought alternate depictions of the folk in films aimed at modern audiences of African Americans and Yiddish-speaking immigrant Jews. In *Georgia Rose* (1930), Gant and Brooks recast the folk to include the historical event of black migration out of the South. Somewhere between the country and the city, *Georgia Rose* conveys, can be found a happy existence for black folk that does not compromise the unity of the family and remains at a safe distance from southern racism. *Mayne Yiddishe Mame* (1930) similarly works to engage with the experience of Jewish immigration to New York by reinforcing the importance of filial piety for immigrant children. In both instances, the folk musical provides the narrative structure through which the effects of migration are mediated.

Operating within the burgeoning Mexican film industry, Fernando de Fuentes appropriated the folk for the purpose of redefining the values of the Mexican nation. It was the diasporic Mexican audience in the United States, however, that invested films like *Allá en el Rancho Grande* (1936) with special significance. To them, the film and its many imitators in the *comedia ranchera* genre ministered to the pains of leaving home. Its projections of a timeless, harmonious existence on the Mexican *rancho* offered solace in the face of change and social exclusion in the North. Mexican stars like Tito Guízar further developed the *comedia ranchera* to speak more directly to the experience of migrating to the United States.

It was not until the late 1930s and early 1940s that the studios truly embraced the folk musical syntax as an appropriate expression for white communities. As Arthur Freed asserted, the transformations wrought by modernity, including industrialization and urbanization, made mainstream audiences hungry for images of bucolic spaces ordered by stability rather than rattled change. Faced with an uncertain future during and after World War II, Freed and his collaborators positioned the folk musical as the quintessential expression of American values both at home and abroad. These values would become all the more pronounced by the early 1960s, when conservatives mobilized against what they perceived as moral and social decay. Audiences employed films like *The Music Man* (1962) and *The Sound of Music* in their cause for a clean and decent America devoid of sex, violence, and ethnic and racial strife.

Anticipated by *West Side Story* (1961), the folk musical of the 1970s returned to the experiences of ethnic and racialized peoples with varying degrees of success. With *Fiddler on the Roof* (1971), *The Wiz* (1978), and *Zoot Suit* (1981), filmmakers in Hollywood grappled with the place of specific cultural groups in the body politic of the post–civil rights era. Complicating the spaces of the folk musical, both city and country, with the admission of social oppression, *Fiddler on the Roof* and *Zoot Suit* are innovators of the form. In its focus on black self-realization, *The Wiz* unsuccessfully attempts to rewrite the folk musical's historical concern with belonging by inverting the source of the conflict to one that is internal rather than external.

The Wiz notwithstanding, the musical's project of convening and bolstering community has extended into the twenty-first century. In the singalong, we witness the embrace of older musical films like *Grease* and *The Sound of Music* by new generations and peoples of various backgrounds and orientations. Amplifying and extending the community-making project on the screen and into the audience space suggests the enduring relevance of collective expression in contemporary American life.

The folk musical has taken many forms over its history. It has moved from the independent margins to the Hollywood center. It has traveled from eastern Europe, Mexico, and the American South. And it has been wielded by ethnic and racialized groups as well as the white mainstream. The folk musical has also traveled across generations, spanning decades that have witnessed massive social upheaval and dramatic transformations in filmmaking techniques. Its construction of communities rooted in the land and stable in time has provided a means of expression for a diverse body of filmmakers and their audiences, for whom change was an inevitable fact of life. Ministering to the modern anxieties of people on the move, folk musicals have projected a vision of belonging for migrants in search of home.

NOTES

INTRODUCTION: THERE'S NO PLACE LIKE HOME

1. James Naremore, "Uptown Folk: Blackness and Entertainment in *Cabin in the Sky*," in *Vincente Minnelli: The Art of Entertainment*, ed. Joe McElhaney (Detroit: Wayne State University Press, 2009), 211.

2. M. M. Bakhtin, "Forms of Time and of the Chronotope in the Novel: Notes toward a Historical Poetics," in *The Dialogic Imagination: Four Essays by M. M. Bakhtin*, ed. Michael Holquist, trans. Caryl Emerson and Michael Holquist (Austin: University of Texas Press, 1981), 225.

3. In this important study, Altman identifies three subgenres within the musical film: the show musical, the folk musical, and the fairy tale musical. I disagree with his categorization of *The Wizard of Oz* as a fantasy musical, as I will explain in chapter 4. Rick Altman, *The American Film Musical* (Bloomington: Indiana University Press, 1987), 272–327.

4. Altman, *The American Film Musical*, 291–305.

5. For example, in making an argument about generic fluidity, Altman has documented how studio marketing departments often avoided generic nouns like "musical" in their publicity, preferring instead to use adjective-noun references to multiple genres, such as "western romance," in order to reach the broadest possible audience base. Rick Altman, "Reusable Packaging: Generic Products and the Recycling Process," in *Refiguring American Film Genres: History and Theory*, ed. Nick Browne (Berkeley: University of California Press, 1998), 7–9.

6. Arthur Freed quoted in Murray Schumach, "Hollywood Musicals, Producer Arthur Freed Sings Their Praises," *New York Times* (April 26, 1959). Bosley Crowther, "Ten Best of 1954," *New York Times* (December 26, 1954).

7. Here I am in agreement with Altman's argument for a "semantic/syntactic" approach to the study of film genre. Rick Altman, *Film/Genre* (London: British Film Institute, 1999), 16–26.

8. Thomas Schatz, *Hollywood Genres: Formulas, Filmmaking, and the Studio System* (Philadelphia: Temple University Press, 1981), 35.

9. Bakhtin, "Forms of Time and of the Chronotope in the Novel," 84.

10. Ibid., 206, 208; Raymond Williams, *The Country and the City* (1973; repr., London: Hogarth Press, 1985), 9.

11. Bakhtin, "Forms of Time and of the Chronotope in the Novel," 225.

12. In the order of publication, Robert Stam, *Subversive Pleasures: Bakhtin, Cultural Criticism, and Film* (Baltimore: Johns Hopkins University Press, 1989); Michael V. Montgomery, *Carnivals and Commonplaces: Bakhtin's Chronotope, Cultural Studies, and Film* (New York: Peter Lang, 1993); Vivian Sobchack, "Lounge Time: Postwar Crises and the Chronotope of Film Noir," in Browne, ed., *Refiguring American Film Genres*; and Paula J. Massood, *Black City Cinema: African American Urban Experiences in Film* (Philadelphia: Temple University Press, 2003).

13. Walter Benjamin, "The Work of Art in the Age of Mechanical Reproduction," in Benjamin, *Illuminations*, ed. Hannah Arendt, trans. Harry Zohn (New York: Schocken Books, 1968), 240. For the relationship between cinema and modernity, see Tom Gunning, "'Now You See It, Now You Don't': The Temporality of the Cinema of Attractions," *Velvet Light Trap* 32 (Fall 1993); Miriam Hansen, *Babel and Babylon: Spectatorship in American Silent Film* (Cambridge, MA: Harvard University Press, 1991); and Ben Singer, *Melodrama and Modernity: Early Sensational Cinema and Its Contexts* (New York: Columbia University Press, 2001).

14. Ella Shohat, "Ethnicities-in-Relation: Toward a Multicultural Reading of American Cinema," in *Unspeakable Images: Ethnicity and the American Cinema*, ed. Lester D. Friedman (Urbana: University of Illinois Press, 1991). For other discussions of ethnic displacement in Hollywood film, see Henry Jenkins, *What Made Pistachio Nuts? Early Sound Comedy and the Vaudeville Aesthetic* (New York: Columbia University Press, 1992); Mark Winokur, *American Laughter: Immigrants, Ethnicity, and the 1930s Hollywood Film Comedy* (New York: St. Martin's Press, 1996); and Charles Ramírez Berg, "The Margin as Center: The Multicultural Dynamics of John Ford's Westerns," in Ramírez Berg, *Latino Images in Film: Stereotypes, Subversion, Resistance* (Austin: University of Texas Press, 2002). For a discussion of whiteness as a racial category, see James R. Barrett and David Roediger, "Inbetween Peoples: Race, Nationality, and the 'New Immigrant' Working Class," *Journal of American Ethnic History* 16.3 (Spring 1997). Others who have studied the social and political racialization of Jewish immigrants include Matthew Frye Jacobson, *Whiteness of a Different Color: European Immigrants and the Alchemy of Race* (Cambridge, MA: Harvard University Press, 1998), and Karen Brodkin, *How Jews Became White Folks and What That Says about Race in America* (New Brunswick, NJ: Rutgers University Press, 1998). For discussions of other racialized groups' proximity to whiteness in American history, see Thomas A. Guglielmo, *White on Arrival: Italians, Race, Color, and Power in Chicago, 1890–1945* (New York: Oxford University Press, 2003), and Ian Haney López, *White by Law: The Legal Construction of Race* (New York: New York University Press, 1996).

15. Here again, Altman has provided important generic categorization in *The American Film Musical*, 200–271.

16. This discussion applies only to those show musicals in which a marginalized Other occupies both the narrative and the musical spaces of the film. As Sean Griffin has demonstrated, the stage/audience divide can also produce a cinematic segregation between the musical/stage space of racialized Others (such as the Nicholas Brothers and Carmen Miranda) and the narrative/audience space

of white characters. In such films, the romantic union of the white characters provides narrative resolution while the racialized, musical space remains separate as merely a form of presentational performance. Sean Griffin, "The Gang's All Here: Generic versus Racial Integration in the 1940s Musical," *Cinema Journal* 42.1 (Autumn 2002).

17. Krin Gabbard, *Jammin' at the Margins: Jazz and the American Cinema* (Chicago: University of Chicago Press, 1996).

18. Jane Feuer, "The Self-Reflective Musical and the Myth of Entertainment," in *Hollywood Musicals: The Film Reader*, ed. Steven Cohan (London, New York: Routledge, 2002), 36.

19. Arthur Knight, *Disintegrating the Musical: Black Performance and American Musical Film* (Durham, NC: Duke University Press, 2002); Eric Lott, *Love and Theft: Blackface Minstrelsy and the American Working Class* (New York: Oxford University Press, 1995); Andrea Most, *Making Americans: Jews and the Broadway Musical* (Cambridge, MA: Harvard University Press, 2004); Michael Rogin, *Blackface, White Noise: Jewish Immigrants and the Hollywood Melting Pot* (Berkeley: University of California Press, 1996).

20. Ramírez Berg, *Latino Images in Film.*

21. Martin Rubin, "Busby Berkeley and the Backstage Musical," in Cohan, ed., *Hollywood Musicals*, 53.

22. John Mueller, "Fred Astaire and the Integrated Musical," *Cinema Journal* 24.1 (Autumn 1984).

23. Altman, *The American Film Musical*, 19.

24. Robin D. G. Kelley, "Notes on Deconstructing 'The Folk,'" *American Historical Review* 97.5 (December 1992), 1402.

25. Lott, *Love and Theft*, 32.

26. Witness the cycle of *Dirty Dancing* films (1987, 2004) and their Othering of "Latin" styles of dance or Chris Tucker's role in "blacking up" the dance routine in *Silver Linings Playbook* (2012).

27. Altman, *The American Film Musical*, 287; Jane Feuer, *The Hollywood Musical* (Bloomington: Indiana University Press, 1982), 3.

28. Pauline Kael, *Kiss Kiss Bang Bang* (Boston: Little, Brown, 1968). As Lea Jacobs has demonstrated, the first decades of the twentieth century witnessed a general intellectual and artistic embrace of naturalism over sentimentality. Jacobs, *The Decline of Sentiment: American Film in the 1920s* (Berkeley: University of California Press, 2008).

29. Richard Dyer, *Only Entertainment* (London, New York: Routledge, 1992); Stuart Hall, "Notes on Deconstructing the Popular," in *People's History and Socialist Theory*, ed. Raphael Samuel (London, Boston: Routledge & Kegan Paul, 1981); Fredric Jameson, *Signatures of the Visible* (New York: Routledge, 1990).

30. Richard Dyer makes this argument regarding all musical films more generally in *Only Entertainment*. And Lawrence Levine explores the active relationship between audiences and escape into forms of popular culture in "The Folklore of Industrial Society: Popular Culture and Its Audiences," *American Historical Review* 97.5 (December 1992).

31. For sources on the interactivity of ethnic and racialized theater audiences, see Mary Carbine, "The Finest Outside the Loop: Motion Picture Exhibition in Chicago's Black Metropolis, 1905–1928," in *Silent Film*, ed. Richard Abel (New Brunswick, NJ: Rutgers University Press, 1996); Lizabeth Cohen, *Making a New Deal: Industrial Workers in Chicago, 1919–1939* (Cambridge: Cambridge University Press, 1990); Desirée J. Garcia, "Subversive Sounds: Ethnic Spectatorship and Boston's Nickelodeon Theatres, 1907–1914," *Film History* 19.3 (2007); Nicolás Kanellos, *A History of Hispanic Theatre in the United States: Origins to 1940* (Austin: University of Texas Press, 1990); Thomas Laurence Riis, *Just Before Jazz: Black Musical Theater in New York, 1890–1915* (Washington, DC: Smithsonian Institution Press, 1989); Nahma Sandrow, *Vagabond Stars: A World History of Yiddish Theater* (New York: Harper & Row, 1977); and Jacqueline Najuma Stewart, *Migrating to the Movies: Cinema and Black Urban Modernity* (Berkeley: University of California Press, 2005). For digressive models of spectatorship, also see Tom Gunning, "An Aesthetic of Astonishment: Early Film and the (In)credulous Spectator," *Art & Text* 34 (Spring 1989); Hansen, *Babel and Babylon*; and Barbara Klinger, "Digressions at the Cinema: Reception and Mass Culture," *Cinema Journal* 28.4 (Summer 1989).

32. Richard Bauman, "Differential Identity and the Social Base of Folklore," in Américo Paredes and Richard Bauman, eds., *Toward New Perspectives in Folklore* (Austin: Published for the American Folklore Society by the University of Texas Press, 1972), 39; Américo Paredes, *Folklore and Culture on the Texas-Mexican Border*, ed. Richard Bauman (Austin: Center for Mexican American Studies, University of Texas at Austin, 1993), 19.

1 THE *SHTETLS, SHUND,* AND SHOWS OF MUSICALS

1. *The Jazz Singer* pressbook, 16, *The Jazz Singer* subject file, New York Public Library for the Performing Arts, New York, New York (hereafter NYPL-PA).

2. Michael Rogin argues that blackface is a mask that at once hides and transforms the Jewish immigrant into an American. This "racial cross-dressing" can occur only because African Americans are absent onscreen. Michael Rogin, *Blackface, White Noise: Jewish Immigrants and the Hollywood Melting Pot* (Berkeley: University of California Press, 1996). Arthur Knight has provided an important alternative framework for analyzing blackface performance, especially in the numerous contexts in which African Americans themselves "blacked up" for the screen. Arthur Knight, *Disintegrating the Musical: Black Performance and American Musical Film* (Durham, NC: Duke University Press, 2002).

3. Rogin, *Blackface, White Noise*, 112. For a detailed discussion of the representation of jazz in cinema, see Krin Gabbard, *Jammin' at the Margins: Jazz and the American Cinema* (Chicago: University of Chicago Press, 1996), 17.

4. It is anachronistic to use the generic term "musical" in this instance, as it was not in contemporary use. I reference it here, however, in order to locate *The Jazz Singer* within the tradition of musical film that succeeded it.

5. MGM used this tagline in its promotion of *The Broadway Melody* (1929), released two years after *The Jazz Singer.*

6. See the film's pressbook and souvenir program, *The Jazz Singer* subject file, NYPL-PA.

7. Pressbook, *The Jazz Singer* subject file, NYPL-PA.

8. Rick Altman, *The American Film Musical* (Bloomington: Indiana University Press, 1987).

9. J. Hoberman, *Bridge of Light: Yiddish Film between Two Worlds* (New York: Museum of Modern Art/Schocken Books, 1991), 262.

10. Henry Ford, "The Jewish Aspect of the 'Movie' Problem—America's United Protest Against the Sex and Criminal Photoplay Has Gone Unheeded—Who and What Controls the Movies?" *Dearborn Independent* (February 12, 1921), 8–9.

11. For a discussion of the 1924 immigration act and "in-between peoples," see James R. Barrett and David Roediger, "Inbetween Peoples: Race, Nationality, and the 'New Immigrant' Working Class," *Journal of American Ethnic History* 16.3 (Spring 1997): 7. The process by which Jews achieved white racial status in the United States has been explored by Karen Brodkin, *How Jews Became White Folks and What That Says about Race in America* (New Brunswick, NJ: Rutgers University Press, 1998), and Matthew Frye Jacobson, *Whiteness of a Different Color: European Immigrants and the Alchemy of Race* (Cambridge, MA: Harvard University Press, 1998). For other histories of whiteness in the United States, see Thomas A. Guglielmo, *White on Arrival: Italians, Race, Color, and Power in Chicago, 1890–1945* (New York: Oxford University Press, 2003); Ian Haney López, *White by Law: The Legal Construction of Race* (New York: New York University Press, 1996); and David R. Roediger, *The Wages of Whiteness: Race and the Making of the American Working Class* (London, New York: Verso, 1991).

12. For the demographics of early cinema audiences, see Robert C. Allen, "Motion Picture Exhibition in Manhattan, 1906–1912: Beyond the Nickelodeon," *Cinema Journal* 18.2 (Spring 1979); Sabine Haenni, *The Immigrant Scene: Ethnic Amusements in New York, 1880–1920* (Minneapolis: University of Minnesota Press, 2008); Judith Mayne, "Immigrants and Spectators," *Wide Angle* 5.2 (1982); and Ben Singer, "Manhattan Nickelodeons: New Data on Audiences and Exhibitors," *Cinema Journal* 34.4 (Spring 1995).

13. Ford, "The Jewish Aspect of the 'Movie' Problem," 8–9.

14. In an early example of such attacks on the industry, New York City enforced the first censorship code upon producers in 1915. The court ruling on the passage of the code declared that, because the movie business was solely about profit making and therefore not "art," the moviemakers had no regard for audience morality and must be restrained. As historian Alison Parker states, this ruling undoubtedly reflected the stereotype of Jews as money-hungry materialists. Alison M. Parker, *Purifying America: Women, Cultural Reform, and Pro-Censorship Activism, 1873–1933* (Urbana: University of Illinois Press, 1997), 132, 142. On the 1915 code, see Robert Sklar, *Movie-Made America: A Cultural History of American Movies* (New York: Random House, 1975), 46.

15. Rogin, *Blackface, White Noise*, 66.

16. Scholarly arguments about the displacement of ethnicity onto formal struc-
tures in Hollywood film have been put forth by Ella Shohat, "Ethnicities-
in-Relation: Toward a Multicultural Reading of American Cinema," in
Unspeakable Images: Ethnicity and the American Cinema, ed. Lester Friedman
(Urbana: University of Illinois Press, 1991), and Mark Winokur, *American
Laughter: Immigrants, Ethnicity, and the 1930s Hollywood Film Comedy* (New
York: St. Martin's Press, 1996). Also, Neal Gabler has argued that the movie
moguls crafted the Hollywood studios as a place apart from mainstream
American society where they could recast their image as Americans rather
than immigrants. Gabler, *An Empire of Their Own: How the Jews Invented Holly-
wood* (New York: Doubleday, 1988).

17. Souvenir program, *The Jazz Singer* subject file, NYPL-PA.

18. Harry Warner, "The New Ambassadors of Good-Will—Mutual Understanding
Is Inherent in an Interchange of Pictures that Reach the Hearts and Minds of
People," *The American Hebrew* (March 15, 1929), 666.

19. *The Jazz Singer*, edited and with an introduction by Robert L. Carringer (Madison: University of Wisconsin Press for the Wisconsin Center for Film and Theater Research, 1979).

20. For accounts of these ghetto films, see Lisa Botshon, "Anzia Yezierska and the
Marketing of the Jewish Immigrant in 1920s Hollywood," in *Middlebrow Mod-
erns: Popular American Women Writers of the 1920s*, ed. Lisa Botshon and Meredith
Goldsmith (Boston: Northeastern University Press, 2003); Patricia Erens, *The Jew
in American Cinema* (Bloomington: Indiana University Press, 1984); and Lester D.
Friedman, *Hollywood's Image of the Jew* (New York: Ungar, 1982).

21. "'Shooting' Scenes on Orchard Street—The Teeming East Side Reproduced in
Warners Forthcoming Production of 'The Jazz Singer,'" *The American Hebrew*
(July 8, 1927), 341.

22. See Jacob A. Riis, *How the Other Half Lives: Studies Among the Tenements of New York*
(New York: C. Scribner's Sons, 1918).

23. "'Shooting' Scenes on Orchard Street," 341.

24. Eve Bernstein, "'The Jazz Singer'—And the Picture of the Future—Al Jolson in the
Title Role," *The American Hebrew* (September 23, 1927), 695.

25. *The Jazz Singer* pressbook, Warner Bros. Archives, School of Cinematic Arts, University of Southern California, Los Angeles (hereafter cited as WBA).

26. Jane Feuer, "The Self-Reflective Musical and the Myth of Entertainment," in
Hollywood Musicals: The Film Reader, ed. Steven Cohan (London, New York: Routledge, 2002), 38.

27. Linda Williams has pointed out the ways in which the sound and silent sections
of the film amplify the juxtaposed worlds of Jakie's black-inflected jazz and his
father's authority. See Linda Williams, *Playing the Race Card: Melodramas of Black
and White from Uncle Tom's Cabin to O. J. Simpson* (Princeton, NJ: Princeton University Press, 2001), 146–147.

28. *The American Hebrew* (October 14, 1927), 823.

29. Robert L. Carringer's interpretation is strongest in this regard, which Michael Rogin complicates with an analysis of the race-making processes at work in the film. Carringer, ed., *The Jazz Singer*, 46; Rogin, *Blackface, White Noise*, 13.

30. Here, I am in disagreement with Carringer's analysis that stresses Jakie's replacement of one world by another. Carringer, ed., *The Jazz Singer*, 46.

31. Hutchins Hapgood, *The Spirit of the Ghetto: Studies of the Jewish Quarter of New York* (1902; repr., New York: Funk & Wagnalls, 1965), 127. In his analysis of *The Jazz Singer*, J. Hoberman references a German-Jewish film, *The Ancient Law* (1923), which follows a Talmudic Jew who must choose between the "testament and the drama." Hoberman, *Bridge of Light*, 117–118. Nahma Sandrow describes Jewish audiences' emotional reactions in "Yiddish Theater and American Theater," in *From Hester Street to Hollywood: The Jewish-American Stage and Screen*, ed. Sarah Blacher Cohen (Bloomington: Indiana University Press, 1983), 24.

32. Eve Bernstein for *The Jewish Tribune*, "Al Jolson Re-lives His Own Life—America's Greatest Entertainer Reveals a Chapter of His Autobiography in His Moving Picture Role as 'The Jazz Singer,'" *The Jazz Singer* pressbook, *The Jazz Singer* subject file, NYPL-PA.

33. Franklin Gordon, "Jolson: Alchemist of the Emotions—Versatility of Leading American Comedian Reveals, Through Silver Screen, New Facets in the Art of One of the Most Dynamic Thespians," *The American Hebrew* (September 6, 1929), 422, 455.

34. Williams, *Playing the Race Card*, 136–138. The role that blackface played in Jolson's rise to fame and assimilation as an American has been studied in great detail. See Rogin, *Blackface, White Noise*; Knight, *Disintegrating the Musical*.

35. Mark Slobin, *Tenement Songs: The Popular Music of the Jewish Immigrants* (Urbana: University of Illinois Press, 1982), 59. In an important study, Irv Saposnik examines the ways in which the invocation of the Jewish mother in *The Jazz Singer* was also a means of referencing how parental roles were changing in America. Saposnik, "Jolson, *The Jazz Singer* and the Jewish Mother: or How My Yiddishe Momme Became My Mammy," *Judaism* 43 (Fall 1994): 432–442.

36. *The Jazz Singer* pressbook, *The Jazz Singer* subject file, NYPL-PA.

37. Richard Watts Jr., "'The Jazz Singer,' With Al Jolson, Opens at Warner," *New York Herald Tribune* (October 6, 1927).

38. Alexander Woollcott's review appeared in the *New York Evening Sun*. Both Woollcott's and Benchley's reviews are reprinted in *The Jazz Singer* souvenir program, *The Jazz Singer* subject file, NYPL-PA.

39. The Pale was the area in which the Russian government authorized Jews to settle. It spanned from the Baltic to the Black Sea.

40. Ben Cion Pinchuk, "Jewish Discourse and the *Shtetl*," *Jewish History* 15 (2001): 169–179; Ewa Morawska, "Changing Images of the Old Country in the Development of Ethnic Identity among East European Immigrants, 1880s–1930: A Comparison of Jewish and Slavic Representations," *YIVO Annual* 21 (1993). Michael Denning has shown how second-generation Jewish writers of the 1920s and 1930s expressed the condition of being "doubly apart," removed from the

culture of their immigrant parents as well as the American mainstream. Their works, he argues, are "ghetto pastorals" that reveal a "yoking of naturalism and the pastoral, the slum and the shepherd, the gangster and Christ in concrete, Cesspool and Lawd Today." Michael Denning, *The Cultural Front: The Laboring of American Culture in the Twentieth Century* (London, New York: Verso, 1997), 231.

41. Hoberman, *Bridge of Light*, 11. For Jewish immigrant adjustment patterns, see Nancy Foner, *From Ellis Island to JFK: New York's Two Great Waves of Immigration* (New Haven, CT: Yale University Press, 2000); Donna R. Gabaccia, *From the Other Side: Women, Gender, and Immigrant Life in the U.S., 1820–1990* (Bloomington: Indiana University Press, 1994); and Andrew R. Heinze, *Adapting to Abundance: Jewish Immigrants, Mass Consumption, and the Search for American Identity* (New York: Columbia University Press, 1990).

42. Some exceptions include Molly Picon's humorous portrayal of an Americanized Jewish girl who visits her relatives in Eastern Europe in *Ost und West* (East and West, 1923) and the musical comedy *Amerikaner Schadkhn* (American Matchmaker, 1940).

43. Hoberman, *Bridge of Light*, 5–9. An "allrightnik" was a Jewish immigrant who was successful in America and had adopted American slang (such as "alright"), dress, and behavior. See Heinze, *Adapting to Abundance*, 42.

44. *Mayne Yiddishe Mame* is an adaptation of Harry Kalmanowitz's play for the Yiddish theater. Hoberman, *Bridge of Light*, 158.

45. *The Jazz Singer* souvenir program, WBA. Michael Rogin discusses the ways in which the disjuncture between silent and sound sequences in the film are symbolic of white/black tensions, the rupture between immigrant father and American son, and the transition from silent to sound cinema. See Rogin, *Blackface, White Noise*, 81–84.

46. Joseph Cohen, "Yiddish Film and the American Immigrant Experience," in *When Joseph Met Molly: A Reader on Yiddish Film*, ed. Sylvia Paskin (Nottingham, UK: Five Leaves Publications, 1999), 11. J. Hoberman writes that Yiddish is "marked by the experience of dispersion and marginality" in *Bridge of Light*, 9.

47. Nahma Sandrow, "Yiddish Theater and American Theater," in *From Hester Street to Hollywood: The Jewish-American Stage and Screen*, ed. Sarah Blacher Cohen (Bloomington: Indiana University Press, 1983), 20, 23; Hoberman, *Bridge of Light*, 103.

48. Eric A. Goldman, *Visions, Images, and Dreams: Yiddish Film Past and Present* (Teaneck, NJ: Ergo Media, 1988), 56, 61. I base my analysis of the film on the script held at the Motion Picture Scripts Collection of the New York State Archives in Albany. The script details not only the dialogue but also the song lyrics and their integration into the narrative. Producer Joseph Seiden provided the English translation in order to submit the film to the state censoring body, the Motion Picture Division of New York. "My Yiddishe Mama" script translation, Motion Picture Scripts Collection, New York State Archives, Albany (hereafter NYSA).

49. "My Yiddishe Mama" script translation, NYSA.

50. Ibid.

51. In reality, this close relationship between Yiddish stage and screen would produce trouble for Judea Pictures. J. Hoberman has documented how the Hebrew Actors' Union took issue with Seiden's hiring of non-union actors for *Mayne Yiddishe Mame* and banned its members' participation in Yiddish films. Judea Pictures eventually worked out an agreement with the union, but not until production had been halted for several months. Hoberman, *Bridge of Light*, 157–158.

52. "My Yiddishe Mama" script translation, NYSA.

53. Slobin, *Tenement Songs*, 169.

54. "My Yiddishe Mama" script translation, NYSA.

55. I analyze the folk musicals *Hearts in Dixie* (1929) and *Hallelujah!* (1929) in chapter 2.

56. Seiden hoped to establish Yiddish talking pictures with *Mayne Yiddishe Mame*. He entered into a distribution deal with three theaters in Jewish-populated areas of New York City. The favorable response to the film in the Brighton Beach area of Brooklyn, the Lower East Side of Manhattan, and Prospect Avenue in the Bronx encouraged his efforts to continue with many more Yiddish features and shorts in the years to come. Goldman, *Visions, Images, and Dreams*, 57.

57. Subtitled and restored prints of these films have been created by the National Center for Jewish Film at Brandeis University, Waltham, MA.

58. There are a number of parallels between *Dem Khazns Zundl* and *The Jazz Singer*. While it is likely that Seiden and his audience were familiar with *The Jazz Singer*, scholars have not found any direct links between the production of the two films. For a comparison, see Eric A. Goldman, "*The Jazz Singer* and Its Reaction in the Yiddish Cinema," in Paskin, ed., *When Joseph Met Molly*.

59. Ford, "The Jewish Aspect of the 'Movie' Problem," 8–9.

2   THE MUSICALS OF BLACK FOLK: RACE CINEMA AND THE BLACK-CAST MUSICALS OF 1929

1. Text from the prologue comes from the *Hearts in Dixie* film script (February 26, 1929), Motion Picture Scripts Collection, New York State Archives, Albany (hereafter NYSA).

2. Paula J. Massood, *Black City Cinema: African American Urban Experiences in Film* (Philadelphia: Temple University Press, 2003).

3. Jacqueline Najuma Stewart, *Migrating to the Movies: Cinema and Black Urban Modernity* (Berkeley: University of California Press, 2005).

4. George P. Johnson, interview transcript by the UCLA Center for Oral History Research, 1970, 123. The Johnson Negro Film Collection, Department of Special Collections, Charles E. Young Research Library, University of California, Los Angeles.

5. Ibid., 153.

6. For a historical and critical analysis of race films, see Thomas Cripps, *Slow Fade to Black: The Negro in American Film 1900–1942* (New York: Oxford University Press, 1977); Jane M. Gaines, *Fire and Desire: Mixed-Race Movies in the Silent Era*

(Chicago: University of Chicago Press, 2001); and Ed Guerrero, *Framing Blackness: The African American Image in Film* (Philadelphia: Temple University Press, 1993).

7. For accounts of black moviegoing, see Alison Griffiths and James Latham, "Film and Ethnic Identity in Harlem, 1896–1915," in *American Movie Audiences: From the Turn of the Century to the Early Sound Era*, ed. Melvyn Stokes and Richard Maltby (London: British Film Institute, 1999); Charlene Regester, "From the Buzzard's Roost: Black Movie-going in Durham and Other North Carolina Cities during the Early Period of American Cinema," *Film History* 17 (2005): 113–124; Stewart, *Migrating to the Movies*; Dan Streible, "The Harlem Theater: Black Film Exhibition in Austin, Texas: 1920–1973," in *Moviegoing in America: A Sourcebook in the History of Film Exhibition*, ed. Gregory A. Waller (Malden, MA: Blackwell, 2002).

8. "A Partial list of white and Negro individuals and corporations organized to produce Negro films," Johnson Negro Film Collection, box 53, folder 32.

9. "Douglas Amusement Corporation," Johnson Negro Film Collection.

10. Johnson interview, 160.

11. Ibid., 132–134.

12. Ibid..

13. *California Eagle* (July 31, 1915).

14. Cripps, *Slow Fade to Black*, 77–78. Jane M. Gaines and Cedric J. Robinson are critical of these race films that emphasize the imperatives of bourgeois uplift over exposing the real sources of discrimination for black soldiers and civilians. Gaines, *Fire and Desire*; and Cedric J. Robinson, *Forgeries of Memory and Meaning: Blacks and the Regimes of Race in American Theater and Film before World War II* (Chapel Hill: University of North Carolina Press, 2007).

15. Gaines's study usefully foregrounds the interracial and mixed-race dynamics of these race films. Gaines, *Fire and Desire*.

16. Johnson interview, 73–77.

17. Robinson, *Forgeries of Memory*, 247.

18. To date, a print of this film has not been located. The film's script, upon which I base my analysis, is preserved in the Motion Picture Scripts Collection, NYSA. Promotional materials for the film, including some lobby cards and stills, can be found in the George P. Johnson Negro Film Collection.

19. See James R. Grossman, *Land of Hope: Chicago, Black Southerners, and the Great Migration* (Chicago: University of Chicago Press, 1989); and Carole Marks, *Farewell, We're Good and Gone: The Great Black Migration* (Bloomington: Indiana University Press, 1989).

20. Farah Jasmine Green, *Who Set You Flowin'? The African American Migration Narrative* (New York: Oxford University Press, 1995), 52–65. One can see this narrative at work in some race films of the era. Two examples are Micheaux's *Within Our Gates* (1919) and the Colored Players' *The Scar of Shame* (1927). Both films suggest ambivalence regarding the process of migration and its resulting effects on the black community.

21. "Movietone Boon to Our Actors," *Chicago Defender* (March 2, 1929), 7.

22. Ibid.

23. Eric Lott, *Love and Theft: Blackface Minstrelsy and the American Working Class* (New York: Oxford University Press, 1995), 32; Jon Cruz, *Culture on the Margins: The Black Spiritual and the Rise of American Cultural Interpretation* (Princeton, NJ: Princeton University Press, 1999), 4.

24. Salem Tutt Whitney, "Promoter Says Race Gets Little Return from Rush West to Movie Gold Coast," *Chicago Defender* (September 2, 1929), 7. Anna Everett provides an analysis of the essentialist arguments of black critics in response to black performance in Hollywood film. Anna Everett, *Returning the Gaze: A Genealogy of Black Film Criticism, 1909–1949* (Durham, NC: Duke University Press, 2001).

25. "Stepin Fetchit and Clarence Muse Score Heavily in Fox's Movietone 'Hearts in Dixie,'" *Chicago Defender* (July 13, 1929), 7.

26. Ibid., 7.

27. Eva Jessye, "'Hallelujah' Is Singing Rather than Talking Movie," *Afro American* (March 2, 1929), 9.

28. Cruz, *Culture on the Margins*, 32.

29. Everett, *Returning the Gaze*, 191.

30. "'Hearts of Dixie' Cast Entertained," *Chicago Defender* (March 23, 1929), 6; Alain Locke and Sterling A. Brown, "Folk Values in a New Medium," in *Black Films and Film-Makers: A Comprehensive Anthology from Stereotype to Superhero*, ed. Lindsay Patterson (New York: Dodd, Mead & Company, 1975), 25–26.

31. Locke and Brown, "Folk Values," 28–29.

32. Ibid., 27–29.

33. Clarence C. Muse, "Hearts of Dixie," *Chicago Defender* (February 9, 1929), 7.

34. Eva Jessye, "Ex-Afro Editor Directs Music of 'Hallelujah,'" *Afro-American* (March 2, 1929), 9.

35. Ibid.

36. Eva Jessye, "The Actors in 'Hallelujah' Didn't Get Enormous Salaries," *Afro-American* (July 5, 1930), 8; Jessye, "Ex-Afro Editor Directs Music of 'Hallelujah,'" 9.

37. Jessye, "The Actors in 'Hallelujah,'" 8.

38. Ibid.

39. Ibid.

40. Jessye, "Ex-Afro Editor Directs Music of 'Hallelujah,'" 9; Jessye, "The Truth about 'Hallelujah,'" *Afro-American* (July 12, 1930), 8.

41. Jessye, "The Truth about 'Hallelujah,'" 9.

42. Schiffman later became the vice president of Oscar Micheaux's film company.

43. The *Chicago Defender* reported an instance in which black actor and comedian Aubrey Lyles, of the team Miller and Lyles, resigned from the Actors and Performers Protective Association, which had decided in favor of the "Jim Crow plan." J. Winston Harrington, "Harlem Folks Claim Jim Crow Move in 'Hallelujah' Showing," *Chicago Defender* (August 24, 1929), 7.

44. James Gow, "Congressman DePriest Sees an Epoch of Race Progress in Premiere of 'Hallelujah' Film," *Chicago Defender* (August 31, 1929), 6–7.

45. Maurice Dancer, "South Wants to Bar Race from Movies," *Chicago Defender* (October 12, 1929), 6.

46. Ace, "Dixie's Attitude Toward 'Hallelujah' May Affect Future of Race in Films," *Chicago Defender* (January 11, 1930), 6.

47. In his cataloguing of race film companies, George P. Johnson referred to Aristo Films as an "all white firm," despite the collaboration of Brooks and other black actors. The terms on which Lincoln disbanded are not clear. Based on his description of Aristo Films and *Georgia Rose*, however, it is evident that Johnson took exception to the new company's efforts to associate with Lincoln: "In an effort to capitalize on the National [*sic*] reputation of the first film organization to produce high class Negro film dramas The Lincoln Motion Picture Co. back in 1916; the Camera [*sic*] man, the star and another actor of the Lincoln organization was used in addition to some of the advertising material and in a press notice under the heading 'NEW ALL RACE FILM' dated Los Angeles Calif [*sic*] Aug. 8 (ANP) states in part 'The Film [*sic*] is owned and controlled by the Lincoln Motion Picture Co.'" *Georgia Rose* file, Johnson Negro Film Collection, reel 1.

48. "'Georgia Rose,' Negro Film, Has Preview," *Afro-American* (July 26, 1930), 9.

49. The lobby card appears in the *Georgia Rose* file of the Johnson Negro Film Collection. For stills from the film, see "'Georgia Rose' Film Pioneers in Motion Picture Field," *Chicago Defender* (August 2, 1930), and "Capacity Crowd Expected at World Premiere of Great Talkie 'Georgia Rose,'" *California Eagle* (May 30, 1930).

50. *Georgia Rose* film script, NYSA.

51. "Gant Answers Critic Who Saw 'Georgia Rose,'" *Pittsburgh Courier* (August 18, 1930).

52. "Give Preview of 'Georgia Rose' at Regal," *Georgia Rose* file, Johnson Negro Film Collection, reel 1; "Gant Answers Critic."

53. "'Georgia Rose,' Negro Film, Has Preview."

54. The Lafayette Players changed hands over the 1920s and eventually settled at the Lincoln Theatre in Los Angeles in 1928. The broad experience of these actors also points to the ways in which race cinema built upon the tradition of black entertainment in musical and dramatic theater. The history of black musical theater has been explored by Thomas L. Riis, *Just Before Jazz: Black Musical Theater in New York, 1890–1915* (Washington, DC: Smithsonian Institution Press, 1989); and Paula Marie Seniors, *Beyond Lift Every Voice and Sing: The Culture of Uplift, Identity, and Politics in Black Musical Theater* (Columbus: Ohio State University Press, 2009).

55. "Capacity Crowd Expected."

56. Ibid. As Arthur Knight has demonstrated, blackface minstrelsy was a popular form of entertainment in black communities as well as white. See Arthur Knight, *Disintegrating the Musical: Black Performance and American Musical Film* (Durham, NC: Duke University Press, 2002).

57. "Clarence Brooks Goes on Road with Film," *Chicago Defender* (August 2, 1930); and "Movie Star Visits Windy City Theater," *Chicago Defender* (September 20, 1930).

58. "Give Preview of 'Georgia Rose' at Regal"; "Gant Answers Critic."

59. *Darktown Revue* is a case in point. The film is a series of performances set against a proscenium backdrop, flanked by classical columns and potted palms. The first performance is by the Heywood Choir, an elegant group adorned in

evening dress. Two minstrel comedy figures in blackface perform after them. The Heywood Choir sings again, only to be trailed by a preacher in blackface. As he performs, the choir remains on the stage. J. Ronald Green points out how members cast knowing glances at each other, highlighting the ridiculous and undignified nature of such forms of entertainment. In this way, Micheaux offers criticism within the context of the performance itself. Hollywood show musicals, by contrast, used shots of an audience inside of the film to signal the quality of the performance. Micheaux's revision of this formal convention is an efficient means of delivering his critique of caricature as entertainment. J. Ronald Green, *With a Crooked Stick—The Films of Oscar Micheaux* (Bloomington, Indianapolis: Indiana University Press, 2004), 110–111.

60. Green provides a deep analysis of the use of musical scoring in *The Exile* in order to highlight Micheaux's strategies for complicating the place of the city for black migrants. Green, *With a Crooked Stick*, 119–124.

61. *The Green Pastures* followed in 1936. Two black-cast musicals were produced in 1943, *Cabin in the Sky* and *Stormy Weather*.

62. Everett, *Returning the Gaze*, 186; Robinson, *Forgeries of Memory*, 365.

3   "NOT A MUSICAL IN ANY SENSE OF THE WORD": *ALLÁ EN EL RANCHO GRANDE* CROSSES THE BORDER

1. "Mexico Forges Ahead with Class 'A' Pictures," *Los Angeles Times* (January 1, 1938).

2. The film also brought Mexico its first international award, at the Venice Film Festival, where Gabriel Figueroa was honored for his photography.

3. Emilio Garcia Riera, *Historia documental del cine mexicano*, 18 vols. (Guadalajara, Jalisco, Mexico: Universidad de Guadalajara, 1992–1997), 1:238; Ana M. López, "A Cinema for the Continent," in *The Mexican Cinema Project*, ed. Chon A. Noriega and Steven Ricci (Los Angeles: UCLA Film and Television Archive, 1994), 8. The periodization of the "golden age" of Mexican film differs in the numerous critical accounts. Coinciding most closely with Carlos Monsivais's analysis, I consider the period to begin with the release of the nation's first international success, *Allá en el Rancho Grande*, in 1936 and to extend through the mid-1950s. For studies of the "golden age" in Spanish, see Jorge Ayala Blanco, *La aventura del cine mexicano* (Mexico: Ediciones Era, 1979); Aurelio de los Reyes, *Medio siglo de cine mexicano (1896–1947)* (Mexico, D.F.: Editorial Trillas, 1987); and Garcia Riera, *Historia documental del cine mexicano*. For studies in English, see John King, *Magical Reels: A History of Cinema in Latin America* (London: Verso, 1990); Carlos Monsivais, "Mexican Cinema: Of Myths and Demystifications," in *Mediating Two Worlds: Cinematic Encounters in the Americas*, ed. John King, Ana M. López, and Manuel Alvarado (London: British Film Institute, 1993), 139–146; Carl J. Mora, *Mexican Cinema: Reflections of a Society, 1896–1998* (Berkeley: University of California Press, 1982); Andrea Noble, *Mexican National Cinema* (London: Routledge, 2005); Paulo Antonio Paranaguá, ed., *Mexican Cinema*, trans. Ana M. López (London: British Film Institute, 1995); López, "A Cinema for the Continent"; Joanne Hershfield, *Mexican Cinema/Mexican Woman, 1940–1950* (Tucson: University of

Arizona Press, 1996); and Joanne Hershfield and David R. Maciel, eds., *Mexico's Cinema: A Century of Film and Filmmakers* (Wilmington, DE: Scholarly Resources, 1999).

4. King, *Magical Reels*, 46; Mora, *Mexican Cinema*, 47.

5. López, "A Cinema for the Continent," 9.

6. The term "ethnic Mexican" stems from David Gutierrez's study, *Walls and Mirrors: Mexican Americans, Mexican Immigrants, and the Politics of Ethnicity* (Berkeley: University of California Press, 1995), and refers to persons of Mexican descent, including Mexican Americans and Mexican immigrants, living in the United States. I use the term in order to communicate that *Allá en el Rancho Grande* found a receptive audience among Mexicans in the United States regardless of their nationality.

7. See Seth Fein, "From Collaboration to Containment: Hollywood and the International Political Economy of Mexican Cinema after the Second World War," in Hershfield and Maciel, eds., *Mexico's Cinema*, and Brian O'Neil, "The Demands of Authenticity: Addison Durland and Hollywood's Latin Images during World War II," in *Classic Hollywood, Classic Whiteness*, ed. Daniel Bernardi (Minneapolis: University of Minnesota Press, 2001).

8. George J. Sanchez, *Becoming Mexican American: Ethnicity, Culture, and Identity in Chicano Los Angeles, 1900–1945* (New York: Oxford University Press, 1993), 18.

9. Ibid., 19. For other accounts of Mexican life and labor in the United States, see Gabriela F. Arredondo, *Mexican Chicago: Race, Identity, and Nation, 1916–1939* (Urbana: University of Illinois Press, 2008); Matt Garcia, *A World of Its Own: Race, Labor, and Citrus in the Making of Greater Los Angeles, 1900–1970* (Chapel Hill: University of North Carolina Press, 2001); Gutierrez, *Walls and Mirrors*; Vicki Ruiz, *Cannery Women, Cannery Lives: Mexican Women, Unionization, and the California Food Processing Industry, 1930–1950* (Albuquerque: University of New Mexico Press, 1987); and Vicki Ruiz, *From Out of the Shadows: Mexican Women in Twentieth-Century America* (New York: Oxford University Press, 1998). On the Mexican Revolution, see Gilbert G. Gonzales and Raul A. Fernandez, eds., *A Century of Chicano History: Empire, Nations, and Migration* (New York: Routledge, 2003), and Alan Knight, *The Mexican Revolution* (New York: Cambridge University Press, 1986).

10. See Natalia Molina, *Fit to Be Citizens? Public Health and Race in Los Angeles, 1879–1939* (Berkeley: University of California Press, 2006).

11. Paul S. Taylor, *Mexican Labor in the United States*, vol. 2 (Berkeley: University of California Press, 1932; reprint, New York: Arno Press and the New York Times, 1970), 232.

12. For women, the images were just as constrained. Hollywood appropriated two female types, the "greaser girl of easy virtue" and the "cantina girl who falls for the Gringo," from the late nineteenth-century dime western and the western novel. See Rosa Linda Fregoso, *The Bronze Screen: Chicana and Chicano Film Culture* (Minneapolis: University of Minnesota Press, 1993); Charles Ramírez Berg, *Latino Images in Film: Stereotypes, Subversion, & Resistance* (Austin: University of Texas

Press, 2002); and Antonio Rios-Bustamente, "Latino Participation in the Hollywood Film Industry, 1911–1945," in *Chicanos and Film: Representation and Resistance*, ed. Chon A. Noriega (Minneapolis: University of Minnesota Press, 1992), 18–28. Also, see the documentary film *The Bronze Screen: 100 Years of the Latino Image in Hollywood* (Susan Racho, Nancy de Los Santos, 2002).

13. Noble, *Mexican National Cinema*.

14. Rios-Bustamente, "Latino Participation," 20–21.

15. For an analysis of *Martyrs of the Alamo*, see Richard Flores, *Remembering the Alamo: Memory, Modernity, and the Master Symbol* (Austin: University of Texas Press, 2002), and Rosa Linda Fregoso, *meXicana Encounters: The Making of Social Identities on the Borderlands* (Berkeley: University of California Press, 2003).

16. Ramirez Berg, *Latino Images in Film*.

17. For analyses of early twentieth-century Spanish-language theater in the United States, see Nicolás Kanellos, *A History of Hispanic Theatre in the United States: Origins to 1940* (Austin: University of Texas Press, 1990), and Tomás Ybarra-Frausto, "I Can Still Hear the Applause. La Farándula Chicana: Carpas y Tandas de Variedad," in *Hispanic Theatre in the United States*, ed. Nicolás Kanellos (Houston: Arte Publico Press, 1984).

18. N.T., "Showmen Leaders of the Pacific Coast," *Pacific Coast Showman* (September 16, 1938). For a history of the studios' foray into Spanish-language cinema, see Lisa Jarvinen, *The Rise of Spanish-Language Filmmaking: Out from Hollywood's Shadow, 1929–1939* (New Brunswick, NJ: Rutgers University Press, 2012).

19. N.T., "Showmen Leaders of the Pacific Coast"; "Spanish International Pictures" letterhead, March 10, 1938, Del Amo Estate Company Collection, Dominguez Hills Archives and Special Collections, California State University, Carson. In 1935, Fouce sold the Exchange to Ruben and Rafael Calderon, a father and son team operating out of El Paso. The newly named Azteca, Inc. would grow and, along with Clasa-Mohme, dominate the distribution of Mexican films in the United States through the 1960s.

20. Helen Delpar, *The Enormous Vogue of Things Mexican: Cultural Relations between the United States and Mexico, 1920–1935* (Tuscaloosa: University of Alabama Press, 1992), 7–10. In one example of this phenomenon, Hollywood's elite frequently traveled to the Padua Hills Theatre, a dinner theater in Claremont, where they watched Mexican plays while being served by Mexicans and Mexican Americans in traditional dress. Garcia, *A World of Its Own*.

21. Upon presidential decree, the Department of State began a "cultural affairs" division at the 1936 Inter-American Convention in Buenos Aires. Sumner Welles, *The Accomplishments of the Inter-American Conference for the Maintenance of Peace*, U.S. Department of State, Conference Series no. 26 (Washington, DC: GPO, 1937), 13. For a historical analysis of the Good Neighbor Policy, see Gerald K. Haines, "Under the Eagle's Wing: The Franklin Roosevelt Administration Forges an American Hemisphere," *Diplomatic History* 1 (1977): 373–388, and Steven R. Niblo, *War, Diplomacy, and Development: The United States and Mexico, 1938–1954* (Wilmington, DE: Scholarly Resources, 1995).

22. *Allá en el Rancho Grande*, Motion Picture Scripts Collection, New York State Archives, Albany (hereafter NYSA).

23. The figure of the *charro* in Mexican culture has its roots in nineteenth-century *costumbrista* literature, which celebrated local customs and settings. The *charro* became institutionalized in the twentieth century with the formation of the Federación Nacional de Charros (National Federation of *Charros*) in 1933. *Allá en el Rancho Grande* inaugurated the era of the singing *charro* on film. Olga Najéra-Ramírez, "Engendering Nationalism: Identity, Discourse, and the Mexican Charro," *Anthropological Quarterly* 67.1 (January 1994): 10, 14.

24. *Allá en el Rancho Grande*, NYSA.

25. See Yolanda Broyles-González, "*Ranchera* Music(s) and the Legendary Lydia Mendoza: Performing Social Location and Relations," in *Chicana Traditions: Continuity and Change*, ed. Norma E. Cantu and Olga Najéra-Ramírez (Urbana: University of Illinois Press, 2002), 183–206.

26. For the origins of the *huapango* and other forms of Mexican theater, see Kanellos, *A History of Hispanic Theatre in the United States*.

27. Hershfield and Maciel, eds., *Mexico's Cinema*, 15. The vast literature on the rise of Mexican nationalism and the significance of public murals includes Thomas Benjamin, *La Revolucion: Mexico's Great Rebellion as Myth, Memory, and History* (Austin: University of Texas Press, 2000), and Ricardo Pérez Montfort, *Estampas de nacionalismo popular mexicano: Ensayos sobre cultura popular y nacionalismo* (Mexico, D.F.: CIESAS, 1994).

28. Emilio Fernández would go on to become one of the most renowned directors of Mexican cinema. His films engaged with *indigenismo*, the interest in and glorification of indigenous cultures, and include *Flor Silvestre* (1943), *María Candelaria* (1944), and *La perla* (1947).

29. Grah., "*Allá en el Rancho Grande*—('There on the Great Ranch')—(With Songs)—(Mexican Made)," *Variety* (October 21, 1936), 17.

30. Edga., "*Allá en el Rancho Grande*—('There on the Great Ranch')—(With Songs)—(Mexican Made)," *Variety* (December 2, 1936), 38.

31. Ibid.

32. Mexican audiences did enjoy films that featured stage performances. Films that centered on women's experiences in modern, urban spaces like nightclubs were also released by the Mexican studios in the early 1930s. Mexico's first sound film, *Santa* (1932), and Arcady Boytler's *La mujer del puerto* (1933) are two early examples of the burgeoning *cabaretera* (cabaret) genre. See Noble, *Mexican National Cinema*.

33. *Cinema Reporter* (February 1, 1947).

34. Advertisement for *Allá en el Rancho Grande*, *La Opinión* (February 17, 1937), 4; "Hoy se Estreñará la Pelicula 'Allá en el Rancho Grande,'" *La Opinión* (February 18, 1937), 4. Translated by the author.

35. Fidel Murillo, "Una opinion sobre *Allá en el Rancho Grande*," *La Opinión* (February 14, 1937), 3. Translated by the author.

36. Najéra-Ramírez, "Engendering Nationalism," 2.

37. For an analysis of *música ranchera*, see Manuel Peña, *The Texas-Mexican Conjunto: History of a Working-Class Music* (Austin: University of Texas Press, 1985). The ways in which Mexican movie audiences of the 1930s created places of refuge are characteristic of border spaces in general. See José David Saldívar, *Border Matters: Remapping American Cultural Studies* (Berkeley: University of California Press, 1997).

38. *Cinema Reporter* (February 1, 1947).

39. Broyles-González, "*Ranchera* Music(s) and the Legendary Lydia Mendoza," 190.

40. *La Opinión* (February 21, 1937), 3.

41. "Most U.S. Companies Setting Plans for Features for Latin Countries," *Motion Picture Herald* (January 7, 1939).

42. De Fuentes also retained distribution rights in Mexico. Walter Gould to Harry D. Buckley, Office Rushgram, United Artists, December 1, 1936, Wisconsin Center for Film and Theater Research, Wisconsin Historical Society, Madison.

43. "Rotundo Exito De 'Allá en el Rancho Grande,'" *La Opinión* (February 21, 1937), 3. The conflation of virtual and live performance was an effect that the producers of Hollywood musicals strove to achieve through the use of direct address, framing, and the position of the audience both inside and outside of the film. See Rick Altman, *The American Film Musical* (Bloomington: Indiana University Press, 1987), and Jane Feuer, *The Hollywood Musical* (Bloomington: Indiana University Press, 1982).

44. Cheva Garcia, interviewed by the author, August 11, 2008.

45. Ibid.

46. José Davila Garcia, interviewed by the author, May 26, 2009.

47. Francisco Fouce Jr., interviewed by the author, April 17, 2006.

48. "Presentacion Personal Del Sr. Barcelata," *La Opinión* (February 28, 1937), 3.

49. J. Garcia interview.

50. Ibid.

51. Philip K. Scheuer, "Producers Turning to Latin Countries," *Los Angeles Times* (August 21, 1938), C3.

52. Rogelio Agrasánchez, *Mexican Movies in the United States: A History of the Films, Theaters, and Audiences, 1920–1960* (Jefferson, NC: McFarland, 2006), 54.

53. "*The Llano Kid*," 1939, Paramount Press Sheets, Margaret Herrick Library, Academy of Motion Picture Arts and Sciences, Beverly Hills, CA (hereafter MHL).

54. Douglas W. Churchill, "Hollywood's Formula for Diplomacy," *New York Times* (April 3, 1938).

55. Ibid. George Sanchez has conducted research on the U.S. Immigration Bureau's categorization of skin color of Mexican immigrants. See *Becoming Mexican American*, 30.

56. Altman, *The American Film Musical*.

57. Don Hartman and Frank Butler, "*Tropic Holiday* Script," August 12, 1937, Paramount Script Files, MHL.

58. Hartman and Butler, "*Tropic Holiday*," January 20, 1938, A-3, Paramount Script Files, MHL.

59. Hartman and Butler, "*Tropic Holiday* Script," August 12, 1937, Paramount Script Files, MHL.

60. Lamour's persona as an "exotic other" is self-consciously addressed in another Paramount film, *St. Louis Blues* (1939).

61. The "love and theft" of African American culture and the peculiar appeal of blackface minstrelsy in the nineteenth century is an example of this phenomenon. Similarly, the act of "going native" in the early twentieth century reflects paradoxical implications for the place of Native Americans in American culture. Americans felt nostalgic for the "vanishing Indian" and his closeness to nature at the same time that they facilitated his demise. See Shari M. Huhndorf, *Going Native: Indians in the American Cultural Imagination* (Ithaca, NY: Cornell University Press, 2001), and Eric Lott, *Love and Theft: Blackface Minstrelsy and the American Working Class* (New York: Oxford University Press, 1995).

62. Lott, *Love and Theft*, 32.

63. If not the first reference to Mexico as the "land of mañana," Harry L. Foster's travelogue, *A Gringo in Mañana-Land* (1924), certainly contributed to its widespread use. In the foreword, Foster explains, "The Spanish 'mañana'—literally, 'to-morrow'—is extremely popular south of the Rio Grande, where, in phrases suggesting postponement, it enables the inhabitant to solve many of life's most perplexing problems." Harry L. Foster, *A Gringo in Mañana-Land* (New York: Dodd, Mead and Co., 1924).

64. The film's initial title of "Mañana" is in keeping with this perception. After several scripts had been written, the title changed to "Ensenada," meaning "inlet" or "cove," which applied to the inlet of Tehuantepec. Hartman and Butler, "*Tropic Holiday* Script," August 25, 1937, Paramount Script Files, MHL.

65. Contracting with the California Fruit Growers' Exchange, the citrus marketing cooperative eventually renamed Sunkist, Paramount Studios devised a national advertising campaign for the release of *Tropic Holiday*. Studio publicists exploited the connections between oranges, the tropics, and nature that Sunkist had already established for its consumers. *Tropic Holiday* press booklet, Paramount Press Sheets, MHL.

66. Brian O'Neil, "Yankee Invasion of Mexico, or Mexican Invasion of Hollywood? Hollywood's Renewed Spanish-Language Production of 1938–1939," *Studies in Latin American Popular Culture* 17 (1998). The films that Guízar made with Faralla and Cobian include *Mis dos amores* (1938), *El trovador de la radio* (1938), *El otro soy yo* (1939), and *Cuando canta la ley* (1939). Each of these films engages with the theme of Mexican migration to varying degrees.

67. Philip K. Scheuer, "Producers Turning to Latin Countries: Foreign Business Sought in South America Through Spanish Studio Aides," *Los Angeles Times* (August 21, 1938), C3.

68. For a discussion of this debate, see O'Neil, "Yankee Invasion of Mexico."

69. Miguel de Zárraga, "The Spanish Films Made in Hollywood," *La Opinión* (July 3, 1938), 6. Translated by the author.

70. *Papa soltero*, NYSA. Ralph Freed, a frequent contributor to Spanish-language musical productions, must have drawn lessons from his brother Arthur Freed, who in 1939 would begin his musical producing career at MGM with *The Wizard of Oz*.

71. "Direction, Acting, Story Above Par," *Hollywood Reporter* (February 3, 1939).

72. *Papa soltero*, English translation of the script as provided by Paramount Studios to the New York State Censorship Board, October 28, 1939, NYSA.

73. Guízar contracted with E.F.A. studios of Argentina to make two films in which he would star. He became one of the ten shareholders of the company and also secured the right to full approval or rejection of scripts. Gabriel Navarro, "Ha Dicho Que No Filma Mas en Hollywood," *La Opinión* (August 27, 1939), 6.

74. See O'Neil, "Demands of Authenticity."

75. Some of Carmen Miranda's films for Twentieth Century–Fox Studios include *Down Argentine Way* (1940), *That Night in Rio* (1941), *Springtime in the Rockies* (1942), and *The Gang's All Here* (1943).

4 "OUR HOME TOWN": THE HOLLYWOOD FOLK MUSICAL

1. Arthur Freed quoted in Murray Schumach, "Hollywood Musicals, Producer Arthur Freed Sings Their Praises," *New York Times* (April 26, 1959).

2. Arthur Freed quoted in William R. Weaver, "Folk Lore and Folk Music Basic Freed Formula for Musicals," *Motion Picture Herald* (September 7, 1946), 33.

3. Rick Altman first identified and categorized this subgenre as the "folk musical" in *The American Film Musical* (Bloomington: Indiana University Press, 1987), 272–327.

4. Arthur Freed, "Making Musicals," *Films and Filming*, no. 16 (January 1956): 30.

5. Rick Altman has been critical of the way that film scholars have positioned integration as the "platonic ideal" for musicals. As he and others have documented, the integration of musical numbers was often paired with non-integrated ones, as in *Show Boat* (1936) and *High, Wide and Handsome* (1937). And as Sean Griffin has argued, musicals that ally more firmly with the tradition of vaudeville entertainment could offer minorities the chance to "'take over' the film, to momentarily reverse power relations, and place both the white lead characters and white audience members as outsiders." Rick Altman, *Film/Genre* (London: British Film Institute, 1999), 221; Sean Griffin, "The Gang's All Here: Generic versus Racial Integration in the 1940s Musical," *Cinema Journal* 42.1 (Autumn 2002): 22.

6. According to Aljean Harmetz, there was significant conflict over this number in the studio. Ceding to skepticism regarding the plausibility of Dorothy singing in a barnyard, Louis B. Mayer cut the song after the film's initial preview. The number was in and out of the film several times before being restored by Arthur Freed. Along with songwriters Harold Arlen and E. Y. Harburg, Freed understood the number to be significant because it provided the "dramatic point of the whole Kansas preface." Harmetz, *The Making of The Wizard of Oz* (New York: Hyperion, 1977), 82.

7. The "fairy tale musicals" constitute a third category of musical film that Altman identifies. Altman, *The American Film Musical*, 129–199.

8. John Mueller, "Fred Astaire and the Integrated Musical," *Cinema Journal* 24.1 (Autumn 1984).

9. This definition of the folk musical forces the elision of important works like *Show Boat*, the musical adaptation of Edna Ferber's 1926 novel. The 1927 Broadway production (and its Hollywood remakes of 1929, 1936, and 1951) is notable for its interracial cast, the integrated musical score, and the nostalgic setting. Nevertheless, this production revolves around romance rather than community collectivity, and its narrative takes place against the backdrop of a form of entertainment, which justifies many of the musical sequences. For an analysis of racial integration in *Show Boat*, see Linda Williams, *Playing the Race Card: Melodramas of Black and White from Uncle Tom to O. J. Simpson* (Princeton, NJ: Princeton University Press, 2001).

10. Benjamin Filene, *Romancing the Folk: Public Memory and American Roots Music* (Chapel Hill: University of North Carolina Press, 2000), 135; Pamela Grundy, "'We Always Tried to Be Good People': Respectability, Crazy Water Crystals, and Hillbilly Music on the Air, 1933–1935," *Journal of American History* 81.4 (March 1995).

11. Freed in Weaver, "Folk Lore and Folk Music," 33.

12. Guaranteeing that the studios would have the freedom to support the war with their pictures, the Roosevelt administration deferred the Justice Department's investigation of the studios for violations of the Sherman Anti-Trust Act. Revenues soared from $20 million in 1940 to $35 million in 1941 and skyrocketed to $60 million for the remainder of the war. Thomas Schatz, *Boom and Bust: American Cinema in the 1940s* (New York: Charles Scribner's Sons, 1997), 131, 139, 203.

13. Francis S. Harmon, "The Motion Picture and the World Community," address on the *Radio Forum* presentation, "The World of Sight and Sound." Broadcast nationally by NBC, July 31, 1943. For the transcript of this address, see Francis S. Harmon, *The Command Is Forward: Selections from Addresses on the Motion Picture Industry in War and Peace* (New York: North River Press, 1944), 34–36.

14. Ruth Vasey, *The World According to Hollywood, 1918–1939* (Madison: University of Wisconsin Press, 1997), 10, 44, 69.

15. As Steven Cohan has argued, the textual displacements that offered the possibility for multiple readings allowed the MGM musical, in particular, to offer a camp aesthetic that was at odds with the films' family-friendly orientation. Cohan, *Incongruous Entertainment: Camp, Cultural Value, and the MGM Musical* (Durham, NC: Duke University Press, 2005).

16. Elaine Tyler May, *Homeward Bound: American Families in the Cold War Era* (New York: Basic Books, 1988), 10–11.

17. Vivian Sobchak, "Lounge Time: Postwar Crises and the Chronotope of Film Noir," in *Refiguring American Film Genres: Theory and History*, ed. Nick Browne (Berkeley: University of California Press, 1998), 144.

18. Bob White, "'Music Is World Language,' Says Noted Film Genius," *Los Angeles Times* (June 2, 1946), PIII, 2.

19. The one exception is *Centennial Summer*, which includes as part of its cast African American railroad porters and a black minstrel who sings for the white patrons of a bar. Despite the historical setting of the film, the sequences in which these characters appear are anomalous and disjunctive to the narrative. The number "Cinderella Sue," performed by Avon Long and several children, disrupts and suspends the film's story while at the same time it privileges an instance of black performance and black faces.

20. Bosley Crowther, "Over the Rainbow—Some Thoughts on 'Escape' in Movies, Inspired by 'The Wizard of Oz,'" *New York Times* (May 1, 1949); Rimgaila Salys, *The Musical Comedy Films of Grigorii Aleksandrov: Laughing Matters* (Chicago: University of Chicago Press, 2009); Thomas Thompson, "Tuning U.S. Musicals to Overseas Box Office," *Life* (March 12, 1965), 55, 58.

21. Serafina Bathrick, "The Past as Future: Family and the American Home in *Meet Me in St. Louis*," *Minnesota Review* 6 (Spring 1976); Richard Dyer, *In the Space of a Song: The Uses of Song in Film* (Abingdon, UK, New York: Routledge, 2012); Gerald Kaufman, *Meet Me in St. Louis* (London: British Film Institute, 1994); James Naremore, *The Films of Vincente Minnelli* (Cambridge: Cambridge University Press, 1993).

22. As Gerald Kaufman has found, screenwriters Fred Finklehoffe and Irving Brecher desired to create a "unity of place" by basing most of the action in and around the Smith home. Toward this aim, they eliminated planned scenes at Princeton University, the Smiths' grandparents' home in Wisconsin, and Mr. Smith's office. Kaufman, *Meet Me in St. Louis*, 12.

23. Letter from Arthur Freed to William A. Orr, n.d., "The Harvey Girls," Arthur Freed Collection, box 55, folder 1, Cinematic Arts Library, University of Southern California, Los Angeles (hereafter USC-CAL).

24. Jack Moffitt, "Donen Direction, Cumming Prod'n Make Hilarious Pic," *Hollywood Reporter* (June 1, 1954); Lowell F. Redelings, "'7 Brides for 7 Brothers': MGM Musical Picture Imaginative, Exciting," *Hollywood Citizen-News* (September 18, 1954); "'The Sobbin' Women' by Stephen Vincent Benet," M-G-M Collection, USC-CAL.

25. Jane Feuer, *The Hollywood Musical* (Bloomington: Indiana University Press, 1982), 5.

26. Studio executive Darryl F. Zanuck advised that the "Ubangi Village" scene "be dropped completely" in a script conference on November 29, 1945. "First Draft Continuity Script, May 8, 1944," Twentieth Century-Fox Collection, USC-CAL.

27. Hobe., "*Summer Holiday* (Color-Musical)," *Variety* (March 3, 1948), 8.

28. "The Sobbin' Women" script, September 16, 1953, box 11, Frances Goodrich and Albert Hackett Papers, 1927–1961, Wisconsin Center for Film and Theater Research, Wisconsin Historical Society, Madison.

29. Here I am in disagreement with Salman Rushdie, who argues that *The Wizard of Oz* is "unarguably a film about the joys of going away. . . ." Rushdie, *The Wizard of Oz* (London: British Film Institute, 1992), 23.

30. Prologue for *The Harvey Girls*, Arthur Freed Collection, USC-CAL.

31. Gerald Kaufman reveals how Sally Benson's original story contains only three pages devoted to the prospect of moving to New York. Kaufman, *Meet Me in St. Louis*, 12.

See also Hugh Fordin, *The World of Entertainment! Hollywood's Greatest Musicals* (New York: Doubleday, 1975), 91.

32. "Have Yourself a Merry Little Christmas," lyrics by Martin and Blane not used in the film, in Kaufman, *Meet Me in St. Louis*, 9.

33. The darkest of the sentiments in this new version ("until then, we'll have to muddle through somehow") has since been rewritten by Martin as "hang a shining star upon the highest bough." Ibid.

34. Abel., "*Meet Me in St. Louis* (Technicolor; Songs)," *Variety* (November 1, 1944), 10.

35. "Rouben Mamoulian Discusses Arthur Freed," October 29, 1971, RYL 1687, Recorded Sound Division, Library of Congress, Washington, DC.

36. "State Fair," Twentieth Century-Fox pressbook, USC-CAL.

37. Ibid.

38. Crowther, "Over the Rainbow"; "Old Friends Return," *New York Times* (April 10, 1949).

5 "TAHITI, ROME, AND MASON CITY, IOWA": MUSICAL MIGRANTS IN THE POSTWAR ERA

1. Lela Simone transcript, oral history with Rudy Behlmer, conducted by telephone between October 1990 and January 1991, 80, 178. Margaret Herrick Library, Academy of Motion Picture Arts and Sciences, Beverly Hills, CA (hereafter MHL).

2. Harry Clein, "Is There a Future for the Hollywood Musical?" *Entertainment World* (March 6, 1970).

3. Kevin Thomas, "Gene Kelly Singing the Blues Over State of U.S. Musicals," *Los Angeles Times* (August 30, 1966).

4. Murray Schumach, "Score on a Hollywood Music Man," *New York Times* (February 16, 1964).

5. John Cutts, "Bye Bye Musicals," *Films and Filming*, no. 110 (November 1963): 42–45.

6. For example, *West Side Story* (Robert Wise, 1961) grossed $31 million at the box office at home and abroad. Thomas Thompson, "Tuning U.S. Musicals to Overseas Box Office," *Life* (March 12, 1965), 55, 58.

7. This box office figure includes receipts in Canada as well as the United States. A. H. Weiler, "'Sound of Music' Adieu," *New York Times* (July 15, 1969).

8. "Moody Critic Aside, 'Sound of Music' Might Be Out-Blowing Top 'Wind,'" *Variety* (January 19, 1966).

9. Tom Gray, "Musicals Making a Big Comeback," *Motion Picture Herald* (September 25, 1968).

10. Will Tusher, "Cy Feuer Sees Big Rewards in Mid-Budget Musical Films," *Hollywood Reporter* (April 6, 1972).

11. Arguments about the musical film's sustained popularity in the 1960s have been put forth by Steve Neale, "'Last Good Time We Ever Had?' Revising the Hollywood Renaissance," in *Contemporary American Cinema*, ed. Linda Ruth Williams and Michael Hammond (Maidenhead, UK: Open University Press, 2006), 91; and Brett Farmer, "The Singing Sixties: Rethinking the Julie Andrews

Roadshow Musical," in *The Sound of Musicals*, ed. Steven Cohan (London: British Film Institute, 2010), 117.

12. Lisa McGirr, *Suburban Warriors: The Origins of the New American Right* (Princeton, NJ: Princeton University Press, 2001), 66–67.

13. Bosley Crowther, "A Fanciful Music Man," *New York Times* (September 20, 1962). In her article that compares the nearly concurrent release of *West Side Story* and *The Music Man*, Carol J. Oja also interprets Harold Hill as a symbol of the immigrant Other. Oja, "*West Side Story* and *The Music Man*: Whiteness, Immigration, and Race in the US during the Late 1950s," *Studies in Musical Theatre* 3.1 (August 2009).

14. For a fascinating analysis of *The Music Man* and its relationship to the histories of American salesmen, librarians, and consumers, see Harriet Malinowitz, "Textual Trouble in River City: Literacy, Rhetoric, and Consumerism in *The Music Man*," *College English* 62.1 (September 1999).

15. And indeed, many of these items are obsolete today and require multiple "Music Man definitions" in books and on websites. One such website is http://www.doggedresearch.com/wilson/glossary.htm.

16. "The Current Cinema—Sweet Corn," *The New Yorker* (September 8, 1962).

17. Karen Halttunen, *Confidence Men and Painted Women: A Study of Middle-Class Culture in America 1830–1870* (New Haven, CT: Yale University Press, 1982).

18. Harold's claim that his hometown is Gary, Indiana, proves to be a lie.

19. Marion Hargrove, *The Music Man* story treatment, January 13, 1960, 5–6, *The Music Man* Collection, Warner Bros. Archives, School of Cinematic Arts, University of Southern California, Los Angeles (hereafter WB Archives).

20. *The Music Man* story draft, January 14, 1960, 42, WB Archives.

21. John C. Waugh, "Three Musicals in Three Cinematic Styles," *Christian Science Monitor* (April 26, 1961).

22. *The Music Man* story, original playscript, September 23, 1957, WB Archives.

23. *The Music Man* story treatment, November 3, 1960, by Marion Hargrove, WB Archives.

24. *The Music Man* story, original playscript, September 23, 1957, WB Archives.

25. Meredith Willson, *But He Doesn't Know the Territory: The Making of Meredith Willson's The Music Man* (Minneapolis: University of Minnesota Press, 2009), 43–44.

26. Ibid., 3–44. Jane Feuer provides a useful discussion of recent musical films that attempt to rationalize or legitimize musical numbers in "The International Art Musical: Defining and Periodising the Post-1980s Musical," in Cohan, ed., *The Sound of Musicals*.

27. Willson, *But He Doesn't Know the Territory*, 43–44.

28. Here, the film demonstrates its "dual-focus narrative," a formal structure that Rick Altman has identified as being central to the organization and function of many Hollywood musicals. Altman, *The American Film Musical* (Bloomington: Indiana University Press, 1987).

29. Disney Studios produced a number of live-action, family-friendly films in the 1950s and early 1960s, many of which were based on children's stories:

Treasure Island (1950), *Old Yeller* (1957), *Swiss Family Robinson* (1960), and *The Parent Trap* (1961).

30. For studies of small-town exhibition, see Kathryn H. Fuller, *At the Picture Show: Small-Town Audiences and the Creation of Movie Fan Culture* (Washington, DC: Smithsonian Institution Press, 1996); Henry Jenkins III, "'Shall We Make It for New York or for Distribution?': Eddie Cantor, *Whoopee*, and Regional Resistance to the Talkies," *Cinema Journal* 29.3 (Spring 1990). Ruth Vasey provides important documentation on the relationship between the MPPDA and small-town exhibitors in *The World According to Hollywood, 1918–1939* (Madison: University of Wisconsin Press, 1997).

31. Report from R. E. Heffner to Charles Boasberg, November 22, 1961, WB Archives.

32. Jenkins, "Shall We Make It for New York."

33. W. Kumins to Charles Boasberg, November 30, 1961, WB Archives.

34. Ibid.

35. Ibid.

36. Ibid.

37. See Shelley Stamp, *Movie-Struck Girls: Women and Motion Picture Culture after the Nickelodeon* (Princeton, NJ: Princeton University Press, 2000).

38. As one writer for the *Hollywood Reporter* observed, "The crews of workers on 'Music Man' made it look like the good old days when livewire studios and home offices had planters traveling nationally as a regular routine." Don Carle Gillette, "Trade Views," *Hollywood Reporter* (June 25, 1962); *The Music Man* pressbook, WB Archives.

39. Meredith Willson to Jack Warner, June 19, 1962, Jack Warner Files, WB Archives.

40. "Marlon Brando: How He Wasted $6 Million by Sulking on the Set," *Saturday Evening Post* (June 16, 1962).

41. Jack L. Warner, "Tahiti, Rome, and Mason City, Iowa," reprinted in *The Music Man* pressbook, WB Archives.

42. Ibid.

43. Due to the restrictions placed on this archival material by Warner Bros. Inc., I can only paraphrase these letters here. Nevertheless, the exuberant and heartfelt wording used by many of the authors is difficult to capture without using direct quotations. Researchers can read the letters in the "Jack Warner files" of the *The Music Man* collection in the WB Archives.

44. Letter from Pete Smith to Jack Warner, June 19, 1962, WB Archives.

45. Letter from P. H. Hartzell to Jack Warner, June 20, 1962, and letter from Frank Cooper, Frank Cooper Associates Agency, Inc., Artists' Manager, to Jack Warner, June 20, 1962, WB Archives.

46. Letter from Shirley Elaine Sandhoff, Saginaw, MI, to Jack Warner, August 12, 1962; letter from Robert Leonard, Schenectady, NY, to Jack Warner, August 14, 1962; letter from Robert S. Nordyke, Indianapolis, IN, to Jack Warner, 1962, WB Archives. Maria Gyarmathy, Los Angeles, CA, to Morton DaCosta, September 15, 1963, Morton DaCosta Papers, box 5, folder 3, Billy Rose Theatre Division, New York Public Library for the Performing Arts, New York, NY.

47. "Too Many Trombones," *Time* (July 20, 1962); Tube, "Film Review—*The Music Man*," *Variety* (April 12, 1962); Morton DaCosta, "Movies Remain Basic Entertainment," *Hollywood Reporter* (1962), Morton DaCosta Papers, box 10, folder 31.

48. See David Bordwell, Kristin Thompson, and Janet Staiger, *The Classical Hollywood Cinema: Film Style and Mode of Production to 1960* (New York: Columbia University Press, 1985).

49. Richard Dyer, *Only Entertainment* (London, New York: Routledge, 1992), 46.

50. Gyarmathy to DaCosta, Morton DaCosta Papers.

51. Linda Meyer, Hayward, CA, to Jack Warner, n.d., WB Archives.

52. "Bell Ringer Award Given to Warners' 'Music Man,'" May 15, 1962, *The Music Man* general file, MHL.

53. Ben Shlyen, *Boxoffice Magazine*, to J. Warner, September 21, 1962, WB Archives.

54. "New York Sound Track," *Variety* (May 2, 1962).

55. *The Sound of Music* would be surpassed by *The Godfather* in 1972.

56. Dyer, *Only Entertainment*, 54.

57. Joan Barthel, "Biggest Money-Making Movie of All Time—How Come?" *New York Times Magazine* (November 20, 1966).

58. Robert Wise, "Why 'Sound of Music' Sounds Differently," *Los Angeles Times* Calendar (January 24, 1965).

59. "Bob Wise Will Curb Schmaltz—'Sound of Music' Needs a Spare Visualization—Omit Yodel—Trapp Kids a Camera-Eye Problem," *Variety* (February 5, 1964).

60. Kael's review appeared in the April 1966 issue of *McCall's*.

61. Barthel, "Biggest Money-Making Movie of All Time."

62. Vernon Scott, "A Progress Report—'Sound of Music' a Staggering Smash," *Variety* (September 29, 1965); "Moody Critic Aside, 'Sound of Music' Might Be Out-Blowing Top 'Wind,'" *Variety* (January 19, 1966).

63. Barthel, "Biggest Money-Making Movie of All Time."

64. Ibid.

65. Scott, "A Progress Report."

66. Velma West Sykes, "'The Sound of Music' (20th-Fox) Wins April Blue Ribbon Award," *Boxoffice* (April 1965).

67. The body included Brigham Young University, the church newspaper, *The Deseret-News*, the church magazine, *Improvement Era*, and KSL television and radio. "In Second Year—'Sound of Music' High in Acclaim for Artistry," *Citizen-News* (April 26, 1966); "Film Project Launched," *Los Angeles Times* (March 25, 1966).

68. "Japanese 'Music' Fan Takes Care of Orphans," *Film Daily* (August 20, 1965).

69. "'Music' Tops 'El Cid' as Mexico's Long-Run," *Variety* (July 13, 1966).

70. John Kafka, "Munich (Hitler's Hotbed) Slashes 20th's 'Music,' Eliminating Nazis as Heavies," *Variety* (June 1, 1966); "Wise Hits 'High-Handed' 20th Staffer Who Slashed Nazi Footage from 'Music,'" *Variety Daily* (June 2, 1966).

71. *The Sound of Music* subject file, MHL.

6 "EASE ON DOWN THE ROAD":
FOLK MUSICALS OF THE ETHNIC REVIVAL

1. Bosley Crowther, "Showing the Flag: Mr. Murrow's Request for a 'Healthy Image' in Films Is Routine," *New York Times* (December 10, 1961).

2. Michael H. Cardozo, "Readers' Views of Movie Matters," *New York Times* (December 3, 1961).

3. *South Pacific* (1958) also included a topical narrative treatment of racism in American society. See Andrea Most, *Making Americans: Jews and the Broadway Musical* (Cambridge, MA: Harvard University Press, 2004), and Sean Griffin, "Bloody Mary Is the Girl I Love: US White Liberalism vs. Pacific Islander Subjectivity in *South Pacific*," in *The Sound of Musicals*, ed. Steven Cohan (London: British Film Institute, 2010).

4. Herman Gray, *Watching Race: Television and the Struggle for Blackness* (Minneapolis: University of Minnesota Press, 2004), 16–17.

5. David A. Hollinger, *Postethnic America: Beyond Multiculturalism* (New York: Basic Books, 2000), 98–99.

6. Ibid.

7. Thomas Schatz, "The New Hollywood," in *Film Theory Goes to the Movies*, ed. Jim Collins, Hilary Radner, and Ava Preacher Collins (New York: Routledge, 1993), 8–9.

8. Norman Jewison to Hal Ashby, 1970, Hal Ashby Papers, box 85, folder 928, Margaret Herrick Library, Academy of Motion Picture Arts and Sciences, Beverly Hills, CA (hereafter Ashby Papers, MHL).

9. Matthew Frye Jacobson, *Roots Too: White Ethnic Revival in Post–Civil Rights America* (Cambridge, MA: Harvard University Press, 2006), 19.

10. The influence of *Fiddler on the Roof* extended into the 1980s with the remake of *The Jazz Singer* (1980) and Barbra Streisand's *Yentl* (1983).

11. Norman Jewison to Hal Ashby, 1970, box 85, folder 928, Ashby Papers, MHL.

12. Vincent Canby, "Screen: 'Fiddler' on a Grand Scale," *New York Times* (November 4, 1971).

13. David V. Picker, "To the Editor: Favors Fiddler," *New York Times* (November 14, 1971).

14. Denton Stein, "To the Editor: 'Elitist,'" *New York Times* (December 26, 1971).

15. John Vitale, "To the Editor," *New York Times* (January 9, 1972).

16. Norman Jewison to Hal Ashby, 1970, box 85, folder 928, Ashby Papers, MHL.

17. Ken Frieden, "A Century in the Life of Sholom Aleichem's Tevye," in *When Joseph Met Molly: A Reader on Yiddish Film*, ed. Sylvia Paskin (Nottingham, UK: Five Leaves Publications, 1999), 261.

18. Norman Jewison to Hal Ashby, 1970, box 85, folder 928, Ashby Papers, MHL.

19. Paula J. Massood, *Black City Cinema: African American Urban Experiences in Film* (Philadelphia: Temple University Press, 2003), 83.

20. Richard Dyer, *In the Space of a Song: The Uses of Song in Film* (Abingdon, UK, New York: Routledge, 2012), 158.

21. Warren N. Lieberfarb, "Correspondence, Oct. 1975–July 1976," Ken Harper Papers, box 14, series 3, Billie Rose Theatre Division, New York Public Library for the Performing Arts, New York, NY (hereafter Harper Papers, NYPL-PA).

22. Booklet, box II, folder 17, Harper Papers, NYPL-PA.

23. Diane Weathers, "Fantasy in Black Theater: A New Kind of Freedom," *Encore American & Worldwide News* (April 21, 1975); Mary Ellen Butler, "Mr. Wiz Ken Harper Had a Special Dream," *Washington Star* (June 18, 1978).

24. Everett Evans, "Producer Nurtures 'Wiz,'" *Houston Chronicle* (January 10, 1979).

25. Weathers, "Fantasy in Black Theater."

26. Quoted in ibid.

27. Warren N. Lieberfarb, "Correspondence, Oct. 1975–July 1976," Harper Papers, NYPL-PA.

28. Dan Yakir, "Wiz Kid," *Film Comment* 14.6 (November/December 1978): 49–54.

29. George Lipsitz, *American Studies in a Moment of Danger* (Minneapolis: University of Minnesota Press, 2001), 199–200.

30. Michael Omi and Howard Winant, *Racial Formation in the United States: From the 1960s to the 1990s*, 2nd ed. (New York: Routledge, 1994), 129.

31. Nat Freedland, "Motown Expands Film & Broadway Plans," *Billboard* (December 15, 1973).

32. Joel Dreyfuss, "Motown's $10 Million Gamble," *Black Enterprise* (July 1981).

33. Warren N. Lieberfarb, "Correspondence, Oct. 1975–July 1976," Harper Papers, NYPL-PA.

34. *The Wiz* souvenir book, Harper Papers, NYPL-PA.

35. Ibid. Even though the great migration out of the South had effectively reoriented African Americans to city life in the North and West, migration continued to be a reality. For example, James Gregory has documented how African Americans experienced out-migration from the South and return migration to the burgeoning Sun Belt throughout the 1970s. Between 1975 and 1980, some 210,800 African Americans migrated back to the South due to the economic developments in that area. Gregory, *The Southern Diaspora: How the Great Migrations of Black and White Southerners Transformed America* (Chapel Hill: University of North Carolina Press, 2005), 40.

36. Paula J. Massood shows how the depiction of African American mobility increased in the 1970s with blaxploitation films such as *Cotton Comes to Harlem* (1970), *Sweet Sweetback's Baadasssss Song* (1971), and *Super Fly* (1972). Typically, however, these films emphasize "localized movement" by depicting characters moving around the city. *The Wiz* was in keeping with this trend. Massood, *Black City Cinema*, 115.

37. Yakir, "Wiz Kid," 49–54.

38. Gray, *Watching Race*, 19.

39. Haile Gerima quoted in Massood, *Black City Cinema*, 114.

40. It should be noted that one of the few references to discrimination, however indirect, occurs in the repeated "off-duty" cab joke in the film. Specific to black New Yorkers, the joke held that taxicabs would automatically flash "off duty" when African Americans tried to hail them. Even Lumet, however, insisted that few audience members would understand this reference.

41. Dyer, *In the Space of a Song*, 154.

42. Given Ross's own separation from The Supremes in order to pursue a solo career in 1970, it is difficult not to read this theme in *The Wiz* as a self-reflexive reference.

43. Charles Schreger, "Trade Wisdom Shaping Re 'Wiz' Biz," *Variety* (November 1, 1978).

44. Frank Segers, "Universal's Gamble: Will 'The Wiz' Ease on Down the Road to Box-Office Ahs?" *Variety* (October 12, 1978).

45. Ibid.

46. Steven Ginsberg, "Chi Study on White 'Crossover,'" *Variety* (November 1, 1978).

47. Ibid. In the end, *The Wiz* grossed more than any other "black picture" to date, including *Shaft, Sounder,* and *Lady Sings the Blues.*

48. Luis Valdez, seminar for the American Film Institute, May 13, 1987, El Teatro Campesino Archives, CEMA 5, Department of Special Collections, Davidson Library, University of California, Santa Barbara (hereafter El Teatro Campesino Archives).

49. Ibid.

50. Ibid.

51. Luis Valdez in Carl Heyward, "El Teatro Campesino: Getting after the Truth about America," *High Performance* (October 1985), El Teatro Campesino Archives.

52. Yolanda Broyles-González, *El Teatro Campesino: Theater in the Chicano Movement* (Austin: University of Texas Press, 1994), 171; Yvonne Yarbro-Bejarano and Tomás Ybarra-Frausto, "Un analisis critic de *Zoot Suit* de Luis Valdez," unpublished ms., El Teatro Campesino Archives; Rosa Linda Fregoso, "*Zoot Suit*: The 'Return to the Beginning,'" in *Mediating Two Worlds: Cinematic Encounters in the Americas*, ed. John King, Ana M. López, and Manuel Alvarado (London: British Film Institute, 1993); Rosa Linda Fregoso, *The Bronze Screen: Chicana and Chicano Film Culture* (Minneapolis: University of Minnesota Press, 1993).

53. Fregoso, *Bronze Screen*, 26.

54. Broyles-Gonzales, *El Teatro Campesino*, 211.

55. In the 1970s and early 1980s, studio personnel, marketers, and distributors most frequently used the term "Hispanic" to describe the domestic market of Spanish speakers as well as the international markets in Latin America.

56. Tomás Martinez, "How Advertisers Promote Racism," *Civil Rights Digest* (Fall 1969). For an account of Chicano resistance to the Frito Bandito campaign, see Chon A. Noriega, *Shot in America: Television, the State, and the Rise of Chicano Cinema* (Minneapolis: University of Minnesota Press, 2000).

57. Lawrence Christon, "Zoot Suit on Film: A Tailor Made Transition," *Los Angeles Times* (March 3, 1981).

58. Charles Schreger, "Screen Adaptation of 'Zoot Suit' Aimed at Country's Latino Audience," *Los Angeles Times*, reprinted in the *Arizona Republic* (July 4, 1980).

59. "World Premiere: Zoot Suit," *Plaza de la Raza* 1.3 (September 1981), El Teatro Campesino Archives.

60. Jane Feuer, "The Self-Reflective Musical and the Myth of Entertainment," in *Hollywood Musicals: The Film Reader*, ed. Steven Cohan (London, New York: Routledge, 2002).

61. Kenneth Brecher in "World Premiere: Zoot Suit," *Plaza de la Raza* 1.3 (September 1981), El Teatro Campesino Archives.

62. See Matt Garcia, *A World of Its Own: Race, Labor, and Citrus in the Making of Greater Los Angeles 1900–1970* (Chapel Hill: University of North Carolina Press, 2001), and Luis Alvarez, *The Power of the Zoot: Youth Culture and Resistance during World War II* (Berkeley: University of California Press, 2008).

63. Luis Valdez cited *Our Town* as being an influence on *Zoot Suit* in a talk given at the Tanner Symposium, Utah State University, April 2–4, 2008.

64. Christine List has described how El Pachuco is an outgrowth of Valdez's interest in myth and archetype, two cultural forms that dominate modes of cinematic storytelling. Christine List, *Chicano Images: Refiguring Ethnicity in Mainstream Film* (New York: Garland Publishing, 1996), 62. See also Dieter Herms, "Luis Valdez, Chicano Dramatist: An Introduction and an Interview," in *Essays on Contemporary American Drama*, ed. Hedwig Bock and Albert Wertheim (Munich: M. Heuber, 1981), 266.

65. Herms, "Luis Valdez," 154.

66. Ibid., 155.

67. Tomas Benitel, "Facing the Issues Beyond 'Zoot Suit': An Interview with Playwright Luis Valdez," *New World* 3 (1978): 36, El Teatro Campesino Archives.

68. Luis Reyes, "The Hispanic Movie Market," *Caminos* (November 1982); Horlick Levin Hodges, Inc., "Positioning *Zoot Suit*," March 6, 1981, El Teatro Campesino Archives.

69. Michael Maza, "'Zoot Suit' to Dress Up Screen—If It Opens," *Arizona Republic* (October 25, 1981).

70. Bill Jones, "Not Even Camelback Inn Daunts," *Phoenix Gazette* (October 28, 1981).

7 HOME IS WHERE THE AUDIENCE IS: THE SING-ALONG

1. Jane Feuer, "The International Art Musical: Defining and Periodising Post-1980s Musicals," in *The Sound of Musicals*, ed. Steven Cohan (London: British Film Institute, 2010), 55, 62.

2. For an analysis of genres as ritual, see Thomas Schatz, *Hollywood Genres: Formulas, Filmmaking, and the Studio System* (Philadelphia: Temple University Press, 1981).

3. John Skipper, "Sing Along to 'The Music Man' at Interactive Movie Showing," *Globe Gazette* (January 23, 2012).

4. Ryan Torok, "'Fiddler on the Roof' Christmas Eve Sing-Along Draws Nearly 250 People," *JewishJournal.com* (December 25, 2010), http://www.jewishjournal.com/ bloggish/item/fiddler_on_the_roof_christmas_eve_sing-along_draws_nearly _250_people/; Kenneth Turan, "'Fiddler on the Roof' Singalong: Kenneth Turan's Film Pick," *Los Angeles Times* (December 22, 2011), http://latimesblogs .latimes.com/movies/2011/12/fiddler-on-the-roof-christmas-eve-sing-along -kenneth-turans-film-pick-of-the-week.html.

5. Des Patridge, "The Stalls Are Alive: What's the World Coming to When a Singalong 'Sound of Music' Becomes the Feel-Good Hit of the Year," *Courier Mail* (Queensland, Australia) (July 7, 2001), M12.

6. The Prince Charles has since added other sing-along events, including *Grease* and *Moulin Rouge.* Christopher Bowen, "Caught in a Von Trapp: 'Sing-A-Long Sound of Music' Lets Fans Role-Play as a Few of Their Favorite Things," *San Francisco Gate* (February 11, 2001).

7. Susan King, "The 'Sound' of Celebration: The Hollywood Bowl Audience Will Be Able to 'Climb Ev'ry Mountain' along with the Film," *Los Angeles Times* (June 28, 2001).

8. Rick Altman refers to this structure as the "dual-focus narrative" of musical film. Rick Altman, *The American Film Musical* (Bloomington: Indiana University Press, 1987).

9. Anthony Lane, "The Maria Problem: Going Wild for 'The Sound of Music'—With Subtitles," *The New Yorker* (February 14, 2000).

10. J. P. Telotte, "Beyond All Reason: The Nature of the Cult," in *The Cult Film Experience: Beyond All Reason*, ed. J. P. Telotte (Austin: University of Texas Press, 1991), 6, 8.

11. Umberto Eco, "*Casablanca*: Cult Movies and Intertextual Collage," *SubStance* 47 (1985): 3, 5.

12. Telotte, "Beyond All Reason," 14–15.

13. M. M. Bakhtin, "Forms of Time and of the Chronotope in the Novel: Notes toward a Historical Poetics," in *The Dialogic Imagination: Four Essays by M. M. Bakhtin*, ed. Michael Holquist, trans. Caryl Emerson and Michael Holquist (Austin: University of Texas Press, 1981), 54.

14. Here again we see how, as Jane Feuer has theorized, musical numbers have the ability to reaffirm the place of musical entertainment (and musical films) in the audience's lives. Feuer, "The Self-Reflective Musical and the Myth of Entertainment," in *Hollywood Musicals: The Film Reader*, ed. Steven Cohan (London, New York: Routledge, 2002).

15. Michael Ryan and Douglas Kellner, *Camera Politica: The Politics and Ideology of Contemporary Hollywood Film* (Bloomington: Indiana University Press, 1988), 76–77.

16. Fredric Jameson, *Signatures of the Visible* (New York: Routledge, 1990), 224.

17. Films of the 1970s and 1980s, before and after *Grease*'s release, similarly used the 1950s high school in order to structure space and time in ways that would be relevant for their audiences. *The Last Picture Show* (1971), *American Graffiti* (1973), and *Racing with the Moon* (1984) presented nostalgic images of lost innocence and fraying friendships in the context of the transitional moment of a group's high school years.

18. As a musical of the ethnic revival, *Grease* shows the interethnic student body as a matter of course rather than as a subject to be explored by the narrative. Similarly, in the school dance sequence, we see evidence of racial integration among the student body with the placement of several African American couples on the dance floor. Matthew Frye Jacobson has analyzed *Grease* in the context of the ethnic revival, a period in which white ethnics, the descendants of immigrants, celebrated their ethnicity in the post–civil rights era. Jacobson,

Roots Too: White Ethnic Revival in Post–Civil Rights America (Cambridge, MA: Harvard University Press, 2006).

19. See chapter 5 for an account of 1960s audiences and repeat attendance for *The Sound of Music.*

20. JayChan H., Beverly Hills, CA, July 6, 2007, http://www.yelp.com/biz/hollywood-bowl-hollywood?q=jaychan (accessed March 9, 2013).

21. "Edelweiss" is a song written by Oscar Hammerstein II and Richard Rogers for the original production of *The Sound of Music* in 1959. They used the symbol of the small white flower that is native to Austria in order to communicate the Captain's connection to his country.

22. See, for example, the posting on September 23, 2012, by "kizofdragon," "Edelweiss—Sing–a-long Sound of Music," http://youtu.be/OZ6vAWmBGkg (accessed March 9, 2013).

23. Mary Carbine has found that African American moviegoers not only resisted segregation by supporting black-owned and -operated movie theaters, but also found ways of mitigating and transforming the films made by white producers through musical accompaniment and vocal interaction with the movie screen. Movie theaters could be places for the assertion of "consciousness" and "social difference" in addition to the consumption of mainstream entertainment. Carbine, "'The Finest Outside the Loop': Motion Picture Exhibition in Chicago's Black Metropolis, 1905–1928," in *Silent Film*, ed. Richard Abel (New Brunswick, NJ: Rutgers University Press, 1996), 235. For other studies on ethnic film spectatorship, see Lizabeth Cohen, *Making a New Deal: Industrial Workers in Chicago, 1919–1939* (Cambridge: Cambridge University Press, 1990); Desirée J. Garcia, "Subversive Sounds: Ethnic Spectatorship and Boston's Nickelodeon Theatres, 1907–1914," *Film History* 19.3 (2007); Russell Merritt, "Nickelodeon Theatres, 1905–1914: Building an Audience for the Movies," in *The American Film Industry*, ed. Tino Balio (Madison: University of Wisconsin Press, 1976); Charlene Regester, "From the Buzzard's Roost: Black Movie-going in Durham and Other North Carolina Cities during the Early Period of American Cinema," *Film History* 17 (2005); and Vicki Ruiz, "'Star Struck': Acculturation, Adolescence, and the Mexican American Woman, 1920–1950," in *Building with Our Hands: New Directions in Chicana Studies*, ed. Adela de la Torre and Beatríz M. Pesquera (Berkeley: University of California Press, 1993).

24. In his most recent work, Richard Dyer has explored the neurological effects of singing both alone and with others. See *In the Space of a Song: The Uses of Song in Film* (Abingdon, UK, New York: Routledge, 2012).

25. K., Berkeley, CA, November 28, 2009, http://www.yelp.com/biz/hollywood-bowl-hollywood?q=sound+of+music+sing+along (accessed August 1, 2012).

26. Janet H., San Francisco, CA, January 11, 2009, http://www.yelp.com/biz/hollywood-bowl-hollywood?q=sound+of+music+sing+along (accessed August 1, 2012).

27. Fancypants X., San Francisco, CA, July 20, 2009, http://www.yelp.com/biz/hollywood-bowl-hollywood?q=sound+of+music+sing+along (accessed August 1, 2012).

28. Nikki M., San Francisco, CA, March 4, 2009, http://www.yelp.com/biz/hollywood
-bowl-hollywood?q=sound+of+music+sing+along (accessed August 1, 2012).

29. Lane, "The Maria Problem."

CONCLUSION: BEYOND THE RAINBOW

1. Rick Altman, *The American Musical Film* (Bloomington: Indiana University Press, 1987).

2. Kevin Thomas, "Gene Kelly Singing the Blues over State of U.S. Musicals," *Los Angeles Times* (August 30, 1966).

3. Jane Feuer, "The Self-Reflective Musical and the Myth of Entertainment," in *Hollywood Musicals: The Film Reader*, ed. Steven Cohan (London, New York: Routledge, 2002).

BIBLIOGRAPHY

Agrasánchez, Rogelio. *Mexican Movies in the United States: A History of the Films, Theaters, and Audiences, 1920–1960*. Jefferson, NC: McFarland, 2006.

Allen, Robert C. "Motion Picture Exhibition in Manhattan, 1906–1912: Beyond the Nickelodeon." *Cinema Journal* 18.2 (Spring 1979): 2–15.

Altman, Rick. *The American Film Musical*. Bloomington: Indiana University Press, 1987.

———. *Film/Genre*. London: British Film Institute, 1999.

———. "Reusable Packaging: Generic Products and the Recycling Process." In *Refiguring American Film Genres: History and Theory*, edited by Nick Browne, 1–41. Berkeley: University of California Press, 1998.

Alvarez, Luis. *The Power of the Zoot: Youth Culture and Resistance during World War II*. Berkeley: University of California Press, 2008.

Arredondo, Gabriela F. *Mexican Chicago: Race, Identity, and Nation, 1916–1939*. Urbana: University of Illinois Press, 2008.

Bakhtin, M. M. *The Dialogic Imagination: Four Essays by M. M. Bakhtin*. Edited by Michael Holquist, translated by Caryl Emerson and Michael Holquist. Austin: University of Texas Press, 1981.

Barrett, James R., and David Roediger. "Inbetween Peoples: Race, Nationality, and the 'New Immigrant' Working Class." *Journal of American Ethnic History* 16.3 (Spring 1997): 3–44.

Bathrick, Serafina. "The Past as Future: Family and the American Home in *Meet Me in St. Louis*." *Minnesota Review* 6 (Spring 1976): 132–139.

Bauman, Richard. "Differential Identity and the Social Base of Folklore." In *Toward New Perspectives in Folklore*, edited by Américo Paredes and Richard Bauman, 31–41. Austin: Published for the American Folklore Society by the University of Texas Press, 1972.

Benjamin, Thomas. *La Revolucion: Mexico's Great Rebellion as Myth, Memory, and History*. Austin: University of Texas Press, 2000.

Benjamin, Walter. "The Work of Art in the Age of Mechanical Reproduction." In Walter Benjamin, *Illuminations*, edited by Hannah Arendt, translated by Harry Zohn. New York: Schocken Books, 1968.

Blanco, Jorge Ayala. *La aventura del cine mexicano*. Mexico: Ediciones Era, 1979.

Bordwell, David, Kristin Thompson, and Janet Staiger. *The Classical Hollywood Cinema: Film Style and Mode of Production to 1960*. New York: Columbia University Press, 1985.

Botshon, Lisa. "Anzia Yezierska and the Marketing of the Jewish Immigrant in 1920s Hollywood." In *Middlebrow Moderns: Popular American Women Writers of the 1920s*, edited by Lisa Botshon and Meredith Goldsmith, 203–226. Boston: Northeastern University Press, 2003.

Brodkin, Karen. *How Jews Became White Folks and What That Says about Race in America*. New Brunswick, NJ: Rutgers University Press, 1998.

Broyles-González, Yolanda. "Ranchera Music(s) and the Legendary Lydia Mendoza: Performing Social Location and Relations." In *Chicana Traditions: Continuity and Change*, edited by Norma E. Cantu and Olga Najéra-Ramírez, 183–206. Urbana: University of Illinois Press, 2002.

———. *El Teatro Campesino: Theater in the Chicano Movement*. Austin: University of Texas Press, 1994.

Carbine, Mary. "The Finest Outside the Loop: Motion Picture Exhibition in Chicago's Black Metropolis, 1905–1928." In *Silent Film*, edited by Richard Abel, 234–262. New Brunswick, NJ: Rutgers University Press, 1996.

Carringer, Robert L., ed. *The Jazz Singer*. Madison: University of Wisconsin Press for the Wisconsin Center for Film and Theater Research, 1979.

Cohan, Steven. *Incongruous Entertainment: Camp, Cultural Value, and the MGM Musical*. Durham, NC: Duke University Press, 2005.

Cohen, Joseph. "Yiddish Film and the American Immigrant Experience." In *When Joseph Met Molly: A Reader on Yiddish Film*, edited by Sylvia Paskin, 10–37. Nottingham, UK: Five Leaves Publications, 1999.

Cohen, Lizabeth. *Making a New Deal: Industrial Workers in Chicago, 1919–1939*. Cambridge: Cambridge University Press, 1990.

Cripps, Thomas. *Slow Fade to Black: The Negro in American Film, 1900–1942*. New York: Oxford University Press, 1977.

Cruz, Jon. *Culture on the Margins: The Black Spiritual and the Rise of American Cultural Interpretation*. Princeton, NJ: Princeton University Press, 1999.

Delpar, Helen. *The Enormous Vogue of Things Mexican: Cultural Relations between the United States and Mexico, 1920–1935*. Tuscaloosa: University of Alabama Press, 1992.

Denning, Michael. *The Cultural Front: The Laboring of American Culture in the Twentieth Century*. London, New York: Verso, 1997.

Dyer, Richard. *In the Space of a Song: The Uses of Song in Film*. Abingdon, UK, New York: Routledge, 2012.

———. *Only Entertainment*. London, New York: Routledge, 1992.

Eco, Umberto. "*Casablanca*: Cult Movies and Intertextual Collage." *SubStance* 47 (1985): 3–12.

Erens, Patricia. *The Jew in American Cinema*. Bloomington: Indiana University Press, 1984.

Everett, Anna. *Returning the Gaze: A Genealogy of Black Film Criticism, 1909–1949*. Durham, NC: Duke University Press, 2001.

Farmer, Brett. "The Singing Sixties: Rethinking the Julie Andrews Roadshow Musical." In *The Sound of Musicals*, edited by Steven Cohan, 114–127. London: British Film Institute, 2010.

Fein, Seth. "From Collaboration to Containment: Hollywood and the International Political Economy of Mexican Cinema after the Second World War." In *Mexico's Cinema: A Century of Film and Filmmakers*, edited by Joanne Hershfield and David R. Maciel, 123–164. Wilmington, DE: Scholarly Resources, 1996.

Feuer, Jane. *The Hollywood Musical*. Bloomington: Indiana University Press, 1982.

———. "The International Art Musical: Defining and Periodising the Post-1980s Musical." In *The Sound of Musicals*, edited by Steven Cohan, 54–63. London: British Film Institute, 2010.

———. "The Self-Reflective Musical and the Myth of Entertainment." In *Hollywood Musicals: The Film Reader*, edited by Steven Cohan, 31–40. London, New York: Routledge, 2002.

Filene, Benjamin. *Romancing the Folk: Public Memory and American Roots Music*. Chapel Hill: University of North Carolina Press, 2000.

Flores, Richard. *Remembering the Alamo: Memory, Modernity, and the Master Symbol*. Austin: University of Texas Press, 2002.

Foner, Nancy. *From Ellis Island to JFK: New York's Two Great Waves of Immigration*. New Haven, CT: Yale University Press, 2000.

Fordin, Hugh. *The World of Entertainment! Hollywood's Greatest Musicals*. New York: Doubleday, 1975.

Fregoso, Rosa Linda. *The Bronze Screen: Chicana and Chicano Film Culture*. Minneapolis: University of Minnesota Press, 1993.

———. *meXicana Encounters: The Making of Social Identities on the Borderlands*. Berkeley: University of California Press, 2003.

———. "*Zoot Suit*: The 'Return to the Beginning.'" In *Mediating Two Worlds: Cinematic Encounters in the Americas*, edited by John King, Ana M. López, and Manuel Alvarado, 269–278. London: British Film Institute, 1993.

Frieden, Ken. "A Century in the Life of Sholom Aleichem's Tevye." In *When Joseph Met Molly: A Reader on Yiddish Film*, edited by Sylvia Paskin, 255–272. Nottingham, UK: Five Leaves Publications, 1999.

Friedman, Lester D. *Hollywood's Image of the Jew*. New York: Ungar, 1982.

Fuller, Kathryn H. *At the Picture Show: Small-Town Audiences and the Creation of Movie Fan Culture*. Washington, DC: Smithsonian Institution Press, 1996.

Gabaccia, Donna R. *From the Other Side: Women, Gender, and Immigrant Life in the U.S., 1820–1990*. Bloomington: Indiana University Press, 1994.

Gabbard, Krin. *Jammin' at the Margins: Jazz and the American Cinema*. Chicago: University of Chicago Press, 1996.

Gabler, Neal. *An Empire of Their Own: How the Jews Invented Hollywood*. New York: Doubleday, 1988.

Gaines, Jane M. *Fire and Desire: Mixed-Race Movies in the Silent Era*. Chicago: University of Chicago Press, 2001.

Garcia, Desirée J. "Subversive Sounds: Ethnic Spectatorship and Boston's Nickelodeon Theatres, 1907–1914." *Film History* 19.3 (2007): 213–227.

Garcia, Matt. *A World of Its Own: Race, Labor, and Citrus in the Making of Greater Los Angeles, 1900–1970*. Chapel Hill: University of North Carolina Press, 2001.

Garcia Riera, Emilio. *Historia documental del cine mexicano.* 18 vols. Guadalajara, Jalisco, Mexico: Universidad de Guadalajara, 1992–1997.

Goldman, Eric A. "*The Jazz Singer* and Its Reaction in the Yiddish Cinema." In *When Joseph Met Molly: A Reader on Yiddish Film,* edited by Sylvia Paskin, 39–48. Nottingham, UK: Five Leaves Publications, 1999.

———. *Visions, Images, and Dreams: Yiddish Film Past and Present.* Teaneck, NJ: Ergo Media, 1988.

Gonzales, Gilbert G., and Raul A. Fernandez, eds. *A Century of Chicano History: Empire, Nations, and Migration.* New York: Routledge, 2003.

Gray, Herman. *Watching Race: Television and the Struggle for Blackness.* Minneapolis: University of Minnesota Press, 2004.

Green, Farah Jasmine. *Who Set You Flowin'? The African American Migration Narrative.* New York: Oxford University Press, 1995.

Green, J. Ronald. *With a Crooked Stick—The Films of Oscar Micheaux.* Bloomington, Indianapolis: Indiana University Press, 2004.

Gregory, James. *The Southern Diaspora: How the Great Migrations of Black and White Southerners Transformed America.* Chapel Hill: University of North Carolina Press, 2005.

Griffin, Sean. "Bloody Mary Is the Girl I Love: US White Liberalism vs. Pacific Islander Subjectivity in *South Pacific.*" In *The Sound of Musicals,* edited by Steven Cohan, 104–113. London: British Film Institute, 2010.

———. "The Gang's All Here: Generic versus Racial Integration in the 1940s Musical." *Cinema Journal* 42.1 (Autumn, 2002): 21–45.

Griffiths, Alison, and James Latham. "Film and Ethnic Identity in Harlem, 1896–1915." In *American Movie Audiences: From the Turn of the Century to the Early Sound Era,* edited by Melvyn Stokes and Richard Maltby, 46–63. London: British Film Institute, 1999.

Grossman, James R. *Land of Hope: Chicago, Black Southerners, and the Great Migration.* Chicago: University of Chicago Press, 1989.

Grundy, Pamela. "'We Always Tried to be Good People': Respectability, Crazy Water Crystals, and Hillbilly Music on the Air, 1933–1935." *Journal of American History* 81.4 (March 1995): 1591–1620.

Guerrero, Ed. *Framing Blackness: The African American Image in Film.* Philadelphia: Temple University Press, 1993.

Guglielmo, Thomas A. *White on Arrival: Italians, Race, Color, and Power in Chicago, 1890–1945.* New York: Oxford University Press, 2003.

Gunning, Tom. "An Aesthetic of Astonishment: Early Film and the (In)credulous Spectator." *Art & Text* 34 (Spring 1989): 31–45.

———. "'Now You See It, Now You Don't': The Temporality of the Cinema of Attractions." *Velvet Light Trap* 32 (Fall 1993): 3–12.

Gutierrez, David. *Walls and Mirrors: Mexican Americans, Mexican Immigrants, and the Politics of Ethnicity.* Berkeley: University of California Press, 1995.

Haenni, Sabine. *The Immigrant Scene: Ethnic Amusements in New York, 1880–1920.* Minneapolis: University of Minnesota Press, 2008.

Haines, Gerald K. "Under the Eagle's Wing: The Franklin Roosevelt Administration Forges an American Hemisphere." *Diplomatic History* 1 (1977): 373–388.

Hall, Stuart. "Notes on Deconstructing the Popular." In *People's History and Socialist Theory*, edited by Raphael Samuel, 227–239. London, Boston: Routledge & Kegan Paul, 1981.

Halttunen, Karen. *Confidence Men and Painted Women: A Study of Middle-Class Culture in America 1830–1870*. New Haven: Yale University Press, 1982.

Haney López, Ian. *White by Law: The Legal Construction of Race*. New York: New York University Press, 1996.

Hansen, Miriam. *Babel and Babylon: Spectatorship in American Silent Film*. Cambridge, MA: Harvard University Press, 1991.

Hapgood, Hutchins. *The Spirit of the Ghetto: Studies of the Jewish Quarter of New York*. 1902. Reprint, New York: Funk & Wagnalls, 1965.

Heinze, Andrew R. *Adapting to Abundance: Jewish Immigrants, Mass Consumption, and the Search for American Identity*. New York: Columbia University Press, 1990.

Herms, Dieter. "Luis Valdez, Chicano Dramatist: An Introduction and an Interview." In *Essays on Contemporary American Drama*, edited by Hedwig Bock and Albert Wertheim, 257–278. Munich: M. Hueber, 1981.

Hershfield, Joanne. *Mexican Cinema/Mexican Woman, 1940–1950*. Tucson: University of Arizona Press, 1996.

Hershfield, Joanne, and David R. Maciel, eds. *Mexico's Cinema: A Century of Film and Filmmakers*. Wilmington, DE: Scholarly Resources, 1999.

Hoberman, J. *Bridge of Light: Yiddish Film between Two Worlds*. New York: Museum of Modern Art/Schocken Books, 1991.

Hollinger, David A. *Postethnic America: Beyond Multiculturalism*. New York: Basic Books, 2000.

Huhndorf, Shari M. *Going Native: Indians in the American Cultural Imagination*. Ithaca, NY: Cornell University Press, 2001.

Jacobs, Lea. *The Decline of Sentiment: American Film in the 1920s*. Berkeley: University of California Press, 2008.

Jacobson, Matthew Frye. *Roots Too: White Ethnic Revival in Post–Civil Rights America*. Cambridge, MA: Harvard University Press, 2006.

———. *Whiteness of a Different Color: European Immigrants and the Alchemy of Race*. Cambridge, MA: Harvard University Press, 1998.

Jameson, Fredric. *Signatures of the Visible*. New York: Routledge, 1990.

Jarvinen, Lisa. *The Rise of Spanish-Language Filmmaking: Out from Hollywood's Shadow, 1929–1939*. New Brunswick, NJ: Rutgers University Press, 2012.

Jenkins, Henry. *What Made Pistachio Nuts? Early Sound Comedy and the Vaudeville Aesthetic*. New York: Columbia University Press, 1992.

Kanellos, Nicolás. *A History of Hispanic Theatre in the United States: Origins to 1940*. Austin: University of Texas Press, 1990.

Kaufman, Gerald. *Meet Me in St. Louis*. London: British Film Institute, 1994.

Kelley, Robin D. G. "Notes on Deconstructing 'The Folk.'" *American Historical Review* 97.5 (December 1992): 1400–1408.

King, John. *Magical Reels: A History of Cinema in Latin America*. London: Verso, 1990.

Kisch, John, and Edward Mapp. *A Separate Cinema: Fifty Years of Black-Cast Posters*. New York: Farrar, Straus, and Giroux, 1992.

Klinger, Barbara. "Digressions at the Cinema: Reception and Mass Culture." *Cinema Journal* 28.4 (Summer 1989): 3–19.

Knight, Alan. *The Mexican Revolution.* New York: Cambridge University Press, 1986.

Knight, Arthur. *Disintegrating the Musical: Black Performance and American Musical Film.* Durham, NC: Duke University Press, 2002.

Levine, Lawrence. "The Folklore of Industrial Society: Popular Culture and Its Audiences." *American Historical Review* 97.5 (December 1992): 1369–1399.

Lipsitz, George. *American Studies in a Moment of Danger.* Minneapolis: University of Minnesota Press, 2001.

Locke, Alain, and Sterling A. Brown. "Folk Values in a New Medium." In *Black Films and Film-Makers: A Comprehensive Anthology from Stereotype to Superhero,* edited by Lindsay Patterson, 25–29. New York: Dodd, Mead & Company, 1975.

López, Ana M. "A Cinema for the Continent." In *The Mexican Cinema Project,* edited by Chon A. Noriega and Steven Ricci, 7–12. Los Angeles: UCLA Film and Television Archive, 1994.

Lott, Eric. *Love and Theft: Blackface Minstrelsy and the American Working Class.* New York: Oxford University Press, 1995.

Malinowitz, Harriet. "Textual Trouble in River City: Literacy, Rhetoric, and Consumerism in *The Music Man.*" *College English* 62.1 (Sept. 1999): 58–82.

Marks, Carole. *Farewell, We're Good and Gone: The Great Black Migration.* Bloomington: Indiana University Press, 1989.

Massood, Paula J. *Black City Cinema: African American Urban Experiences in Film.* Philadelphia: Temple University Press, 2003.

May, Elaine Tyler. *Homeward Bound: American Families in the Cold War Era.* New York: Basic Books, 1988.

Mayne, Judith. "Immigrants and Spectators." *Wide Angle* 5:2 (1982): 32–40.

McGirr, Lisa. *Suburban Warriors: The Origins of the New American Right.* Princeton, NJ: Princeton University Press, 2001.

Molina, Natalia. *Fit to Be Citizens? Public Health and Race in Los Angeles, 1879–1939.* Berkeley: University of California Press, 2006.

Monsivais, Carlos. "Mexican Cinema: Of Myths and Demystifications." In *Mediating Two Worlds: Cinematic Encounters in the Americas,* edited by John King, Ana M. López, and Manuel Alvarado, 139–146. London: British Film Institute, 1993.

Montgomery, Michael V. *Carnivals and Commonplaces: Bakhtin's Chronotope, Cultural Studies, and Film.* New York: Peter Lang, 1993.

Mora, Carl J. *Mexican Cinema: Reflections of a Society, 1896–1998.* Berkeley: University of California Press, 1982.

Morawska, Ewa. "Changing Images of the Old Country in the Development of Ethnic Identity among East European Immigrants, 1880s–1930: A Comparison of Jewish and Slavic Representations." *YIVO Annual* 21 (1993): 273–341.

Most, Andrea. *Making Americans: Jews and the Broadway Musical.* Cambridge, MA: Harvard University Press, 2004.

Mueller, John. "Fred Astaire and the Integrated Musical." *Cinema Journal* 24.1 (Autumn 1984): 28–40.

Najéra-Ramírez, Olga. "Engendering Nationalism: Identity, Discourse, and the Mexican Charro." *Anthropological Quarterly* 67.1 (January 1994): 1–14.

Naremore, James. *The Films of Vincente Minnelli*. Cambridge: Cambridge University Press, 1993.

———. "Uptown Folk: Blackness and Entertainment in *Cabin in the Sky*." In *Vincente Minnelli: The Art of Entertainment*, edited by Joe McElhaney, 205–228. Detroit: Wayne State University Press, 2009.

Neale, Steve. "'The Last Good Time We Ever Had?': Revising the Hollywood Renaissance." In *Contemporary American Cinema*, edited by Linda Ruth Williams and Michael Hammond, 90–108. Maidenhead, UK: Open University Press, 2006.

Niblo, Steven R. *War, Diplomacy, and Development: The United States and Mexico, 1938–1954*. Wilmington, DE: Scholarly Resources, 1995.

Noble, Andrea. *Mexican National Cinema*. London: Routledge, 2005.

Noriega, Chon A. *Shot in America: Television, the State, and the Rise of Chicano Cinema*. Minneapolis: University of Minnesota Press, 2000.

Oja, Carol J. "*West Side Story* and *The Music Man*: Whiteness, Immigration, and Race in the US during the Late 1950s." *Studies in Musical Theatre* 3.1 (August 2009): 13–30.

O'Neil, Brian. "The Demands of Authenticity: Addison Durland and Hollywood's Latin Images during World War II." In *Classic Hollywood, Classic Whiteness*, edited by Daniel Bernardi, 359–385. Minneapolis: University of Minnesota Press, 2001.

———. "Yankee Invasion of Mexico, or Mexican Invasion of Hollywood? Hollywood's Renewed Spanish-Language Production of 1938–1939." *Studies in Latin American Popular Culture* 17 (1998): 79–105.

Paranaguá, Paulo Antonio, ed. *Mexican Cinema*. Translated by Ana M. López. London: British Film Institute, 1995.

Paredes, Américo. *Folklore and Culture on the Texas-Mexican Border*. Edited by Richard Bauman. Austin: Center for Mexican American Studies, University of Texas at Austin, 1993.

Parker, Alison M. *Purifying America: Women, Cultural Reform, and Pro-Censorship Activism, 1873–1933*. Urbana: University of Illinois Press, 1997.

Peña, Manuel. *The Texas-Mexican Conjunto: History of a Working-Class Music*. Austin: University of Texas Press, 1985.

Pérez Montfort, Ricardo. *Estampas de nacionalismo popular mexicano: Ensayos sobre cultura popular y nacionalismo*. Mexico, D.F.: CIESAS, 1994.

Pinchuk, Ben Cion. "Jewish Discourse and the Shtetl." *Jewish History* 15 (2001): 169–179.

Ramírez Berg, Charles. *Latino Images in Film: Stereotypes, Subversion, & Resistance*. Austin: University of Texas Press, 2002.

Regester, Charlene. "From the Buzzard's Roost: Black Movie-going in Durham and Other North Carolina Cities during the Early Period of American Cinema." *Film History* 17 (2005): 113–124.

Reyes, Aurelio de los. *Medio siglo de cine mexicano (1896–1947)*. Mexico, D.F.: Editorial Trillas, 1987.

Riis, Jacob A. *How the Other Half Lives: Studies among the Tenements of New York*. New York: C. Scribner's Sons, 1918.

Riis, Thomas L. *Just Before Jazz: Black Musical Theater in New York, 1890–1915.* Washington, DC: Smithsonian Institution Press, 1989.

Ríos-Bustamente, Antonio. "Latino Participation in the Hollywood Film Industry, 1911–1945." In *Chicanos and Film: Representation and Resistance*, edited by Chon A. Noriega, 18–28. Minneapolis: University of Minnesota Press, 1992.

Robinson, Cedric J. *Forgeries of Memory and Meaning: Blacks and the Regimes of Race in American Theater and Film before World War II.* Chapel Hill: University of North Carolina Press, 2007.

Roediger, David R. *The Wages of Whiteness: Race and the Making of the American Working Class.* London, New York: Verso, 1991.

Rogin, Michael. *Blackface, White Noise: Jewish Immigrants and the Hollywood Melting Pot.* Berkeley: University of California Press, 1996.

Rubin, Martin. "Busby Berkeley and the Backstage Musical." In *Hollywood Musicals: The Film Reader*, edited by Steven Cohan, 53–61. London, New York: Routledge, 2002.

Ruiz, Vicki. *Cannery Women, Cannery Lives: Mexican Women, Unionization, and the California Food Processing Industry, 1930–1950.* Albuquerque: University of New Mexico Press, 1987.

———. *From Out of the Shadows: Mexican Women in Twentieth-Century America.* New York: Oxford University Press, 1998.

Ryan, Michael, and Douglas Kellner. *Camera Politica: The Politics and Ideology of Contemporary Hollywood Film.* Bloomington: Indiana University Press, 1988.

Saldívar, José David. *Border Matters: Remapping American Cultural Studies.* Berkeley: University of California Press, 1997.

Salys, Rimgaila. *The Musical Comedy Films of Grigorii Aleksandrov: Laughing Matters.* Chicago: University of Chicago Press, 2009.

Sanchez, George J. *Becoming Mexican American: Ethnicity, Culture, and Identity in Chicano Los Angeles, 1900–1945.* New York: Oxford University Press, 1993.

Sandrow, Nahma. *Vagabond Stars: A World History of Yiddish Theater.* New York: Harper & Row, 1977.

———. "Yiddish Theater and American Theater." In *From Hester Street to Hollywood: The Jewish-American Stage and Screen*, edited by Sarah Blacher Cohen, 18–28. Bloomington: Indiana University Press, 1983.

Saposnik, Irv. "Jolson, *The Jazz Singer* and the Jewish Mother: or How My Yiddishe Momme Became My Mammy." *Judaism* (Fall 1994): 432–442.

Schatz, Thomas. *Boom and Bust: The American Cinema in the 1940s.* New York: Charles Scribner's Sons, 1997.

———. *Hollywood Genres: Formulas, Filmmaking, and the Studio System.* Philadelphia: Temple University Press, 1981.

———. "The New Hollywood." In *Film Theory Goes to the Movies*, edited by Jim Collins, Hilary Radner, and Ava Preacher Collins, 8–36. New York: Routledge, 1993.

Seniors, Paula Marie. *Beyond Lift Every Voice and Sing: The Culture of Uplift, Identity, and Politics in Black Musical Theater.* Columbus: Ohio State University Press, 2009.

Shohat, Ella. "Ethnicities-in-Relation: Toward a Multicultural Reading of American Cinema." In *Unspeakable Images: Ethnicity and the American Cinema*, edited by Lester D. Friedman, 215–250. Urbana: University of Illinois Press, 1991.

Singer, Ben. "Manhattan Nickelodeons: New Data on Audiences and Exhibitors." *Cinema Journal* 34.3 (Spring 1995): 5–35.

———. *Melodrama and Modernity: Early Sensational Cinema and Its Contexts.* New York: Columbia University Press, 2001.

Sklar, Robert. *Movie-Made America: A Cultural History of American Movies.* New York: Random House, 1975.

Slobin, Mark. *Tenement Songs: The Popular Music of the Jewish Immigrants.* Urbana: University of Illinois Press, 1982.

Sobchack, Vivian. "Lounge Time: Postwar Crises and the Chronotope of Film Noir." In *Refiguring American Film Genres: History and Theory*, edited by Nick Browne, 129–170. Berkeley: University of California Press, 1998.

Stam, Robert. *Subversive Pleasures: Bakhtin, Cultural Criticism, and Film.* Baltimore: Johns Hopkins University Press, 1989.

Stamp, Shelley. *Movie-Struck Girls: Women and Motion Picture Culture after the Nickelodeon.* Princeton, NJ: Princeton University Press, 2000.

Stewart, Jacqueline Najuma. *Migrating to the Movies: Cinema and Black Urban Modernity.* Berkeley: University of California Press, 2005.

Streible, Dan. "The Harlem Theater: Black Film Exhibition in Austin, Texas: 1920–1973." In *Moviegoing in America: A Sourcebook in the History of Film Exhibition*, edited by Gregory A. Waller, 268–278. Malden, MA: Blackwell, 2002.

Taylor, Paul S. *Mexican Labor in the United States.* Vols. 1–2. Berkeley: University of California Press, 1928–1932. Reprint, New York: Arno Press and the New York Times, 1970.

Telotte, J. P. "Beyond All Reason: The Nature of the Cult." In *The Cult Film Experience: Beyond All Reason*, edited by J. P. Telotte, 5–17. Austin: University of Texas Press, 1991.

Vasey, Ruth. *The World According to Hollywood, 1918–1939.* Madison: University of Wisconsin Press, 1997.

Williams, Linda. *Playing the Race Card: Melodramas of Black and White from Uncle Tom's Cabin to O. J. Simpson.* Princeton, NJ: Princeton University Press, 2001.

Williams, Raymond. *The Country and the City.* 1973. Reprint, London: Hogarth Press, 1985.

Winokur, Mark. *American Laughter: Immigrants, Ethnicity, and the 1930s Hollywood Film Comedy.* New York: St. Martin's Press, 1996.

Ybarra-Frausto, Tomás. "I Can Still Hear the Applause. La Farándula Chicana: Carpas y Tandas de Variedad." In *Hispanic Theatre in the United States*, edited by Nicolás Kanellos, 45–61. Houston: Arte Publico Press, 1984.

INDEX

42nd Street (1933), 203

Abie's Irish Rose (1928), 24
actors, African American. *See* African Americans: actors
Actors and Performers Protective Association, 219n43
advertisements, 81, 141; racial stereotypes in, 173
African American culture, 130, 226n61
African Americans: in audiences, 161, 239n23; beliefs about, 52–53, 60; in blackface, 212n2; actors, 48–49, 58–62, 67, 229n19; in films, 51, 60, 161, 212n2; "progress," 63; rights, 167. *See also* black: actors; black: audiences; Great Migration
Aleichem, Sholom, 158
Alexander's Ragtime Band (1938), 94, 203
Allá en el Rancho Grande (1936), 72–74, 77–84, 87, 111, 206; advertisements, 81, 84; awards, 221n2; dance sequence, 79; distribution, 82, 225n42; lobby card, 78; as model, 86; music, 80, 84; musical numbers, 77–80; premiere, 82; publicity, 82; reviews, 80; song: "Canción mixteca," 78; song: "Rancho Grande," 78; structure, 80
Allen, Robert C., 213n12
Altman, Rick, 4, 11, 20, 209n3, 209n7, 225n43, 227nn3,5, 238nn7,8
Alvarez, Luis, 238n8
American: essentialism, 105; identity, 9, 10; immigrant past, 160, 176; life, in movies, 137–138, 152–153, 180; values, onscreen, 104–106, 122, 128, 207
American Graffiti (1973), 238n17
The American Hebrew [magazine], 23, 25, 26, 29, 32
Americanism, depiction in films, 105
Amerikaner Schadkhn (1940), 216n42
amusement parks, 128
The Ancient Law (1923), 215n31
animated musicals, 204–205
antimodernism, 156

Anything Goes (1956), 125
Aquarius Theatre, Hollywood, 174
Aristo Films, 63, 67, 71, 220n47
Arizona Republic [newspaper], 182
Arlen, Harold, 227n6
Arredondo, Gabriela F., 222n9
Ashby, Hal, 156
Astaire, Fred, star persona, 101
atmospheric chorales. *See* chorales in folk musicals
audiences, 22, 76, 79–84, 127–144, 155, 165, 171, 213n12; as community, 191–194; demographics, 139, 213n12; diegetic, in films, 9, 27, 174–177, 196, 220–221n59; ethnic, 82, 239n23; for family films, 149–151; feedback from, 197–200; for films, 137, 153; for folk musicals, 122; Hispanic, 173–174; inclusion of, 159, 225n43; international, 150; interracial, 166, 183; mainstream, 161–162; multiethnic, 33, 35, 170–171, 175–176; in musical numbers, 177; participation, 144, 185–201; performing, 196–198; queer, 191; for race films, 66; racialized, 212n31; sing-along, 185–201. *See also* black: audiences; Mexican: audiences; Spanish-speaking audiences
awards, 144, 149. *See also by name of award*
Ayala Blanco, Jorge, 221n3
Azteca, Inc., 223n19

Bakhtin, M. M., 2, 6, 192
Baltimore Afro-American [newspaper], 60, 66
Barcelata, Lorenzo, 84
Barrett, James R., 8, 22, 210n14
Bathrick, Serafina, 229n21
Baum, L. Frank, *The Wonderful Wizard of OZ*, 164
Bauman, Richard, 14
Benchley, Robert, 33
Benét, Stephen Vincent, "The Sobbin' Women" [short story], 110
Benjamin, Thomas, 224n27
Benjamin, Walter, 7

ABOUT THE AUTHOR

DESIRÉE J. GARCIA is an assistant professor in the Program in Film and Media Studies at Arizona State University.